DEAD TIDE

JANE MARKS

IC Publishing
Cape Cod

COPYRIGHT

PUBLISHED BY IC PUBLISHING, CAPE COD a
division of Invention City, Inc.
www.icpublish.com
Copyright © 2022 by Jane Marks
All rights reserved.

ISBN: 979-8-9861973-2-6 (trade pback)
ISBN: 979-8-9861973-1-9 (trade ebook-kindle)

For Annette Marks
who shared her love of books with me.

Nana, this one's for you.

ACKNOWLEDGMENTS

I am so grateful for the community of family and friends who helped me complete *DEAD TIDE*. First, a big thank you to my dad who never got tired of listening to me brainstorm this story and kept a fire under my butt to execute. This couldn't have been possible without his dedication and belief. Thank you to my mom for being the first reader and for inspiring me to move forward. Thanks to my friends and family who took time out of law school, 80-hour work weeks and scheduling non-profit galas to read drafts and give me honest feedback: Kaylee Wallace, Jeanne Marks, Rob Goldberg, Julia Stribula, Jo Ann Colker-Arison, Mackenzie Hunt, Suzanne Young Hunt, Noa Yoder, Boris Marks, Jessica Taylor, Margie Wallace, Debi Burkholder and Nick Griffiths. I really appreciate the time each of you spent and the feedback you provided. All of you have contributed to making *DEAD TIDE* the best version of itself.

Another thank you to Chuck Carmen, President of the Epilepsy Association, for spending hours on the phone with me as I researched this book. Thank you to Emma Karlson, Annika Ericsson, Adam Redfern, Whitney Knowlton-Wardle, Meimi McDonagh, Lydia Hauser, Grace Givens, Sofia Horan, Mali Rivera, Emma Stearns and Nicole Stribula for letting me bounce ideas off of you for days on end.

I am incredibly lucky to have all these people and countless others in my life who supported me and this project. Thank you all!

1

Memorial Day weekend always brought the Kane family to Cape August. Summering in this town for the past twenty years, everyone who shared the last name used the same house: aunts, uncles, second cousins . . .

This year wasn't any different. On the Friday before the holiday, the house was overflowing with Kanes. Too full for Jamie Kane's taste. It was downright chaotic, but not in a fun way with beer pong and skinny dipping. Instead, it was fraught with useless arguments about pizza toppings or what room grandma would stay in.

A text finally saved Jamie from the madness. It was from one of his summer friends. Alton Something. He could never remember his last name. It didn't matter. He went by 'Alt' anyway.

Jamie looked down at his phone.

Alt: Bro! Bonfire at the Spit.

Jamie couldn't get out the door fast enough. He wouldn't be gone for long. An hour or two tops.

He didn't bother leaving a note.

Within twenty minutes, Jamie was sitting next to a roaring fire nursing his fifth lukewarm beer.

"*Now* it's summer," he sighed, leaning back, and stretching into the cool sand. He wiggled his Sperry-free toes closer to the fire. Behind him, rolling waves sizzled up the beach.

"You're tellin' me," Alt said, before whacking Jamie's leg. "Yo, Kane. You got eyes on ya."

Jamie looked up. Sure enough, one of the girls from across the dancing flames was looking at him. She was pretty. At least, pretty enough. Thick hair. Big eyes. Pink lips.

Kane shot her a dashing smile. He knew he was handsome, but more importantly, he had already lost his virginity and had the swagger to prove it.

"I think her name's Nina," Alt yelled in what was supposed to be a whisper.

Giggling to her friend, Nina crawled around the fire toward them.

"Gina, actually," she corrected, tucking a stray strand of hair behind her ear. "Can I sit with you?"

"Looks like you already are," Jamie said with a shrug. He had to play it cool.

Gina giggled, settling deeper into the sand. "Are you local?"

Kane made a noncommittal grunt. "Does it matter?"

"Probably not," Gina admitted with a smirk. She looked away from the group toward where the fire's light struggled to penetrate. "Then again, locals are much better swimmers than tourists."

"Is that a challenge?" Jamie asked his speech just a little slurred.

"Only if you accept," the girl giggled, leaping up and skipping away from the group. She smiled over her shoulder at Jamie.

"I'll catch ya later, Alt," Jamie said before stumbling up. "Don't wait up."

"Don't get her pregnant!" Alt called, laughing as he slurped at his beer.

Jamie grinned, then ran after Gina.

"Come on, you," she said, grabbing his hand and dragging him down the beach. Jamie tried not to trip.

"Where are we going?" he asked.

"To the water!" she cried, running ahead, and leading them far from the group. Jamie could just make out her form as she began to shed her clothes. Her discarded shirt hit Jamie square in the face, still warm.

He couldn't believe his luck.

"Hold on," he said, trying to follow and take off his pale-green polo at the same time. It got stuck over his head and he fell face-first into the sand. He wiggled onto his knees. "I'm coming!"

"Better hurry up," she called, her voice carrying sweetly through the salty air.

"Mmhmm," Jamie chuckled to himself, fumbling with his belt.

Distantly, Gina ran barefoot and naked toward the water, laughing as the waves nipped tenderly at her toes. She paused for only a moment, before running straight in. She gasped as the cool water slid over her body, grinning to herself. Come fall, she would be going to Rice University, but until then she had an entire summer to celebrate on the Cape. Her entire life lay ahead of her.

If only she knew what lay waiting and watching in the shadows that night. Lurking, just beyond those waves she had crashed through. If she had, she might not have squealed with glee as a stray strand of seaweed brushed against her leg. She might not have spun around carelessly, sending seawater high into the night sky.

She might not have forgotten about the boy that was supposed to be joining her . . . If she had known.

But as she swam out to a yellow bobbing buoy, Jamie Kane lay at the water's edge. His eyes were open but unseeing as his blood dyed the wet sand a deep, dark red.

2

Black eyes watched the body. It was still, save for the slight heaving motion with each crashing wave. The water made the dead boy's chest rise and fall almost like he was still breathing.

Almost.

"Chief Ramos?" A voice called from a distance, making the dark eyes flash up and watch a stout figure approach.

"Glenn," Ramos greeted, giving a nod.

"You got here fast," Glenn noted, hobbling next to him. He cursed under his breath as he rubbed his bad knee. Arthritis.

"I was doing a little night fishing nearby," Ramos said, shoving his calloused hands deep into his worn blue jeans. "With the moon bright and all."

"Any luck?" Glenn asked.

Ramos shrugged noncommittally, looking back at the body. "Was he alive when you found him?"

"Nah," Glenn said, clearing his throat gruffly. "I was walkin' the mutt around the point when I heard that girl screamin'. Set o' lungs on her, lemme tell ya."

"Where is she now?" Ramos asked.

"I had the missus bring her inside. Make her a cup of tea or somethin'," Glenn muttered. He ran a hand over his balding head.

"Seemed like the thing to do. 'Specially after all her friends scattered. Left their fire goin' and everythin'."

The two men stood side by side. Ramos had about a foot over Glenn, casting a moonlit shadow that almost reached the corpse's fingertips. Glenn shifted uncomfortably. Even with thirty years of gutting and cleaning fish, he couldn't help but feel a little squeamish looking at the body. Fish blood was something he could tolerate. This, on the other hand . . .

He turned away first.

"This look the same as that girl?" Glenn asked.

"Pretty similar," Ramos said, staring. Unable to tear his gaze away from the boy.

Another wave crashed, tilting Jamie Kane's head back on the beach. The water opened his gaping neck slightly wider, the red wound stretching on the moon-bathed beach. Just like the first.

3

ELLE

Thirteen missed calls from Zoey and my mailbox was full. I winced, feeling guilty that I hadn't called her back right away. Some best friend I was. Luckily, I knew she'd understand. My job was really kicking my butt these days. I loved having to travel for stories, but spending two weeks without a place to charge my phone while I was interviewing Rhode Island's first "totally off the grid man," wasn't exactly glamourous. My throat was still burning from his homemade moonshine, not that it stopped me from drinking it. It helped me sleep in the worn-out hammock he loaned me.

Waiting for the pump to finish putting just enough gas in my car to get me home, I scanned through the other unread text messages on my phone. There were a lot. Mostly from Zoey. She must've resorted to texting when calling wasn't working. Zoey was my best friend growing up on Cape August and we still talked almost every day. She moved back to the Cape to pursue her dream of opening an art gallery. It was only her second summer with the gallery.

Zoey: WTF! YOU'RE A JOURNALIST! PICK UP YOUR PHONE!

I winced again. She was probably freaking out about the upcoming summer. She was having problems getting the paintings she wanted for the gallery, and with summer descending on Cape August, being low on merchandise wasn't an option.

I kept scrolling.

Zoey: HAVE YOU EVEN SEEN THE NEWS?!

The gas pump clunked as I took my fingers off the lever and pulled up my news app. It was a little hard to see through the shattered screen. I should've gotten it fixed ages ago, but I was making do.

I froze when I read what I almost wished the shattered screen could block out.

On the island where I grew up there had been two murders within the last two weeks. The most recent was a boy I didn't recognize, but the first—

"Holy shit," I gasped, bringing the screen so close to my face my nose almost touched it.

I looked at the picture of the girl and didn't need the headline to tell me her name. I used to babysit her growing up. We'd go get stale bread from the mom-and-pop bakery on the corner before heading to the beach to feed the seagulls. I'd drop her off at the bookstore her dad owned down on Main Street, where he'd give me a copy of the newest "must-read" for free if it got damaged in shipping.

I spent my childhood watching Molly Edgars grow up, and now she was dead.

* * *

The sand was cold and damp under my feet as I stumbled along the dark beach. I squinted ahead, trying to see through the inky night. The air was cool, but not cold enough to justify the goosebumps covering my body. Something felt wrong. Off-kilter.

No sooner had I formed the thought than I heard a bloodcurdling scream. It was a woman's scream. No. A girl's. I ran toward it, my movements clumsy and sluggish in the sand.

"Hello?" I called. I tried to run but couldn't. It felt like I was moving in slow motion. Staggering. It was getting even darker. Something solid sent me sprawling across the sand. I landed hard and scrambled frantically to regain my footing. I squinted at the ground, my eyes straining to identify the thing I had tripped over. Except it wasn't a thing. It was a person. A girl. She lay on the ground in an awkward position, resting on her knees with her head down. Light-brown, shoulder-length hair hung limply from her head. It would have looked like she was praying if her body hadn't been so rigid. Her face was pressed into the sand so hard that I wondered how she was able to breathe.

"Miss . . ." I started, reaching out a trembling hand toward her. She screamed again, the sand muffling her cries. They sounded pained. Strangled. Horrified.

"What's wrong? Are you hurt?" I tried to touch her, but my hand felt blocked as if there was an invisible wall keeping me away. I forced my hand harder against it, desperate to break through. If I could reach her, everything would be all right. If I could just reach her. She screamed again, louder this time, her voice cracking under the effort. Her hands dug into the sand, smashing it between her frail fingers. I lunged, trying in vain to bridge the distance. I found myself screaming too. Screaming at the invisible barricade holding me back. Screaming at whatever force was causing this girl such agony. Screaming at my own uselessness.

The girl's shrieks grew deafening, stifling the sound of my own. It was a sound of such despair that it sucked the breath from my lungs. I looked away from her, screwing my eyes shut and clamping my hands over my ears in a desperate attempt for relief. An awful gasping seeped into the wail until it sounded like the girl was being ripped apart. It was guttural. Primal. I felt compelled to look at her again, despite a voice in the back of my head begging me not to. I tried to fight the compulsion, somehow knowing that what I would see would be the thing of nightmares. But the urge was too great. It was as if something was forcing my head up and pulling my eyelids apart to see . . .

I woke up with a gasp as the girl's scream morphed into the blaring of a smoke alarm.

"What the . . ." I muttered, bringing the heel of my palms up to rub the sleep from my eyes.

"Sorry!" A deep male voice called into the living room from the kitchen. "I was smoking the bacon and I got a little carried away." Eric crossed the room with long, quick strides to open the window. He was tall with a strong jaw, and thick, black hair. He used his large hands to scoop smoke out of the room. It felt like an eternity before the alarm finally stopped.

"Sorry, Elle," Eric apologized again sheepishly. "Oh God, you were asleep . . ." He sat on the corner of the couch next to me.

"It's ok," I assured him with a smile. "It wasn't exactly relaxing."

"Were you dreaming about it again?" Eric asked, stroking a few loose hairs from my face.

"Yeah. I just can't believe it," I muttered.

"It happened where you grew up," Eric reasoned. "Besides, you knew her."

"I haven't seen her in years," I clarified.

"Yeah, but it's a small town. Everybody knows everybody, right?"

I nodded. That couldn't be more true. Cape August had a population of less than two thousand, so everyone's lives were intertwined. With only one bridge connecting it to the mainland, the community was tight-knit and fiercely protective of one another. It felt like the safest place in the world . . . which was why the events of the past week were so shocking. I still couldn't wrap my head around it. Fifteen-year-old Molly Edgars was the daughter of Nelson and Charlotte Edgars. Charlotte had died of cancer when Molly was two, leaving Nelson to raise their daughter alone. While many of the neighbors offered to pitch in, Nelson was a man's man, wanting to do it on his own, not wanting to accept handouts or 'pity parties' as he put it. As it turned out, Nelson seemed to do all right by himself, and Molly had always seemed happy. The two had been very close. I could only imagine what he was feeling right now. A week had passed since Molly had been found dead on the beach with her throat slashed.

"Were you able to reach your parents?" Eric asked. My parents, as luck would have it, were visiting cousins in Greece. Cell service was limited at best, especially in the places my dad had decided to book.

"No. And I don't really want to put this in an email," I sighed. My parents didn't know the Edgars well, but still.

"Is there anything you need?" Eric asked.

"No. I'm ok," I reassured him. "I just wish they knew what happened." Granted, no one seemed to know. It was completely mystifying why someone would have wanted to hurt the girl. She was shy, sweet, and totally unassuming. Mayor Sully kept repeating that it was a 'totally isolated incident,' but he had his priorities. With the summer season around the corner, he wanted to make sure that people would still come to Cape August for their vacation.

"Isn't your ex a police officer there?" Eric asked carefully.

"Yeah . . ." I confirmed, nervously tugging on my fingers.

"Well, you could call him and see what's going on," Eric offered with a shrug. He got up to head back to the kitchen. "Wine?"

"I mean . . . I could, but he probably wouldn't tell me much," I said, forcing myself off the couch to follow him. I grabbed two wine glasses, all the while watching Eric's expression.

"You could try," he said, his face genuine. "It's obviously eating away at you." He was right about that. I was absolutely obsessing over it.

"Zoey probably told me everything anyone knows at this point," I said with a dry laugh.

"That's probably true," Eric chuckled. "She'd probably camp out at the police station herself if you asked." I smiled at Eric before remembering the last conversation with my old friend on my drive home last night. Zoey had told me how the entire town seemed to be in a state of shock, and that shop owners were 'freaking out.' It was entirely understandable. The timing couldn't have been worse. Cape August survived on tourism, so the fact that this had happened a week before Memorial Day was, as Zoey so fatefully put it, a 'death sentence for small-business owners.'

Eric poured two healthy-sized glasses of wine, handing me the slightly bigger one. If that wasn't love I didn't know what was.

"Thank you," I breathed, "for being so patient. I must be driving you crazy with this."

"You always drive me crazy," he said, pressing a quick but tender kiss on my lips. "And you're going to keep driving me crazy." The man smiled down at the engagement ring on my finger. Eric and I had been dating for three years, and it was just as easy now as it had been in the beginning. So, when he had knelt down on one knee next to the pretzel shack where we had our first date, with a ring masterfully intertwined between the folds of the baked bread, I had, of course, said yes. Everyone who knew us said that we were meant for each other. We had even been told that we even looked alike . . . which was a stretch. He was a giant of six-foot-three and built like an ox, while I barely reached five-foot-four and was a wisp of a person despite the large quantities of pasta I shoveled into my body. Even though we both had Greek heritage, my dad's Italian blood made my olive-tinted skin lighter than Eric's and added a woodsy tone to my dark hair. We both had gray eyes, but there was something that seemed different about them. A different shade.

"What are you making anyway?" I asked as he poured oil into a pan.

"Fresh linguine in a white wine and garlic sauce with house-smoked bacon," he said with a smile.

"Can I do anything to help?"

"Nope," he said, pretending to be stern. "You just got back. The only thing I want you to do is sip that." He directed his eyes toward the wine glass in my hand.

"That's a tall order," I teased, taking a long swig. So much better than the paint-thinner-esque moonshine.

"I know you can handle it," he said with a wink as he took the freshly made pasta dough out of the fridge. I leaned back against the counter as Eric worked, watching his hands pound and sculpt the dough.

"Want to watch a movie tonight? It might take your mind off everything," Eric suggested. "Maybe The Sound of Music?"

I couldn't help but grin at the offer. That musical oozed happiness. I nodded enthusiastically, despite the fact that all I really wanted to do was scan every news outlet for scraps of information about Molly. I needed to let it go. Obsessing over it would get me nowhere. But that didn't stop my mind from wandering. I tried to focus on Eric's chatter over dinner, forcing a smile and offering vague, lukewarm responses. Even the movie couldn't distract me from the thoughts swirling in my head. The worry. The fear. The burning curiosity.

* * *

News outlets were still having an absolute field day after Jamie Kane was found dead with his throat slashed. With the clear connection to Molly's murder, reporters were quick to claim that a savage killer was on the loose on Cape August. One newscaster called this the 'new Ted Bundy,' while another made a reference to this being the 'human version of *Jaws*' . . . which one had to admit was mildly clever.

All the while, Cape August officials plastered calm expressions on their faces, assuring the public that everything was under control. Mayor Sully, with his flawless hair and crisply ironed button-down, claimed that it was a fluke. Something that would be worked out well before the summer season really took off.

"Cape August is perfectly safe," he announced to the camera, waving to the beach behind him. "And ready for the best summer yet!"

It became clear that most of the locals shared his sentiment. As I watched the morning news, I saw shop owners being interviewed one by one, and they all said something eerily similar. It was hard to blame them. The ice cream stores, surf shops, knick-knack stores . . . They all needed visitors to keep their livelihoods afloat.

I paced the floor in front of the TV. I thought about all the people I knew on Cape August. Were they in danger? Would they be able to pay their bills if this summer turned out to be a bust?

My phone buzzed. It was Zoey.

"Did you see?" she started to ask before I could get the phone fully to my ear. "It's getting worse!"

"Yeah," I said. "Are you okay?"

"Honestly? I'm totally flipped," she said, her voice rising a couple of octaves. "Fearing for our lives is bad enough, but what if they close the beaches for the summer? Do you know how many people won't be able to afford their mortgages? The entire town will go under."

I grimaced. "What's Sully telling the locals?"

"He keeps saying to proceed like we normally would," she said. "Which everyone is pretty much doing. They don't want to scare away the tourists, so they'd rather pretend like everything is fine. Which is fifty shades of fucked! But, like, what choice do we have?"

"How's the gallery handling it?" I asked carefully.

"Ugh," she groaned. "It's so bad, dude. We need this summer to break even for the year. Otherwise, we're gonna have to sell the place."

I winced sympathetically. Zoey had put everything she had into that gallery.

I resumed my pacing as soon as we hung up. One thing was perfectly clear. I had to go back to Cape August. I looked at the clock. I had over an hour before I was due at work. If I started now, maybe I could work up a fresh story pitch for my boss. Something that would give me a reason to go back.

To go home.

I grabbed my laptop (the thing almost flew out of my sweaty palms) and started looking at the kinds of stories that were being written, but more importantly, the ones that weren't. Rushing out the door an hour later, I ran out of the apartment so fast that I forgot my shoes. I only realized when my bare feet touched the pavement. Good thing I kept an extra pair in my car.

I sped the entire way there, making it through the doors of the magazine headquarters in record time. A quick look at his desk told me that Tony wasn't in yet.

Tony was the head editor, and he was . . . interesting. There was something about him that was just a tad greasy. Even so, he was good at acting as the catalyst for talented photographers and writers, while expertly keeping the magazine afloat.

It was another half hour before he walked in, wearing a blindingly white suit, purple tie, and alligator boots. "Good morning, ladies and gents," he crowed, his boots squeaking as he walked to his desk in the center of the room. He once had a private office but found it 'constricting.'

I forced myself to give the man a full sixty seconds to settle before approaching his desk.

"Hey, Tony. Could I talk to you about a pitch when you have a second?"

"For you, Elle, I have many seconds," Tony grinned suggestively. I repressed a shiver and pressed on.

"I want to write a story about what's happening on Cape August," I said.

Tony let out an undignified snort. "Why does that not surprise me?"

"I've already worked up some angles that haven't been covered yet."

"Ahh," Tony mused. "Your Spidey senses are tingling then?"

"Erm . . . yes," I agreed carefully. "I think this is something readers would be really interested in."

"And this has nothing to do with the fact that you just want to know what's going on back home?" Tony asked, twirling his fingers above his upper lip. He used to have a mustache, but his wife had made him shave it off when she saw a bug crawl out of it one night. Now, he just fiddled with an imaginary one.

"Well, of course, I want to know what's going on," I admitted. "But so should you. I mean, the piece practically writes itself. It's basically . . ." I grimaced when I saw no choice, ". . . *Jaws* come to life."

"*Oh* . . ." Tony breathed loudly at the title. "Now that could be something." He started humming a theme song to something I only half-recognized. I knew better than to talk during his 'creative process.'

"It could be a pretty interesting story . . . but you would need to know what was going on with the investigation itself . . ." He raised his bushy eyebrows. "How would you manage that? I would want new information. Not just regurgitated shit from the papers."

"I'd figure it out," I said. I could always call up a certain ex-boyfriend, but I didn't want to go there unless I absolutely had to.

"I'm not paying you to just go and 'figure it out,'" Tony said bluntly.

Fine. I guess I'll go there.

"Well, it just so happens that I have a friend who works as a police officer in town," I said. I wondered how Andrew might cringe if he heard me refer to him as nothing more than a 'friend.'

"Why didn't you lead with that?" Tony leaped up from his chair. There was a bloodthirsty glint in his eyes that made me want to take a step back. "You know how hard it is getting the cops to spill! This is great! You should leave first thing tomorrow. I want an update every few days. And I want you to keep the creative juices flowing while you're there. There might be other stories we can milk out of this."

I cringed at his wolfish expression and escaped back to my desk.

Tony let me leave early to go home and pack. The entire drive back, I dreaded the call I knew I had to make now. Before I knew it, I was fumbling with my keys and tripping into my apartment. A meow came from the living room and Watkins ran to greet me.

"Hey, buddy," I cooed, scratching the orange tabby under the chin. With a sigh, I plopped myself onto the couch and threw a worn-out blanket over my legs. Watkins leaped onto my lap, butting his head into my chest. I was thankful for the moral support as I dug my phone out of my pocket and opened the contact list. Right away I was staring at the name I needed. Why did his name have to be at the beginning of the alphabet?

I looked at Watkins imploringly.

"How much would it take for you to do this for me?" I asked him. He purred, looking up at me with his bright green eyes. "A million dollars? You drive a hard bargain, but you got yourself a deal." The tabby rubbed his chin against my fingers.

Without overthinking it a second longer, I pressed my thumb to the name. It only took two rings before he picked up.

"Hello?" I heard the familiar male voice on the other end of the line and smiled.

"Hey, Andrew," I said. "I hope I'm not interrupting." *What a stupid thing to say? He's investigating a double homicide. Of course, you're interrupting!*

I mentally facepalmed.

"No, no. You're good." I heard him say. "What's up? It's been forever."

"Yeah. I know," I laughed nervously. I hadn't seen him in at least a year and a half. Eric had started coming home with me, and I really didn't see the benefit of that *specific* introduction.

Not to mention the diamond that was now weighing down my ring finger.

"How are you?" I asked, trying to keep my voice casual. I could still hear a telltale squeak.

"I'm all right," Andrew said. "I mean . . . you probably heard what happened."

"Erm . . . yeah . . ." I admitted. "Are you okay?"

"I'm fine. I just want to catch whoever did this," he grumbled, sounding tired. "Anyway, how are you?"

"I'm fine," I said, guilt beginning to fester as I stared down at my engagement ring. "I'm actually coming to Cape August tomorrow."

"Woah. Really? Because of the case?" Andrew asked. "But you aren't working as a news journalist anymore. Unless you switched back?"

"No, I work for a magazine that wants me to do a story about all of this," I said. "I wanted to focus more on how a small-town deals with this kind of thing. I would love to see how you guys are going about solving it."

With all my cards on the table, I felt oddly excited.

"Oh," Andrew said, clearly surprised. "Well, swing by the station. It's a little chaotic around here as you can imagine, but I'm sure the guys would love to see you."

"Really?" I almost shouted, scaring Watkins off my lap. He gave me an angry glare as he skulked to the far corner of the room. "That would be awesome! Thank you!"

I heard Andrew chuckle in my ear. "Well, duh," he said, and I could almost hear the smile behind the last word. He always made fun of me for saying 'duh' in response to . . . well everything. I used to argue that the word should be in the dictionary. "Come by whenever you're settled. I'll be here."

Hanging up the phone, I grinned at Watkins.

"This might be totally fine!" I beamed. "What's the worst that could happen?"

4

ROSLYN

The faucet dripped slowly as if the liquid congealing at the top was a substance thicker than water. I tried to focus on it. To use it as a distraction from the shudder that threatened to force me back onto my knees. My teeth clenched as I attempted to distance myself from my body. To force it all away. The shakiness. The nausea. My fingers clutched the metal basin I hunched over. Fighting the tremble of my hands.

"Get it together," I growled at myself. I had a meeting with the Boston Police Chief in a matter of minutes. Next to me, Jasper whined, nuzzling his black snout into my leg. It was a sweet gesture, but I didn't have the time or the mind space to appreciate it.

I forced a breath through my nose. Another minute, then I had to go. There was no choice. A harsher wave of nausea threatened to derail my resolve.

Behind me, I heard a light knock on the bathroom door.

Fuck me.

"Roslyn?" a man's voice called. It was soft. Delicate. I sighed, allowing myself to feel some relief. It was Oliver, the communications liaison for the FBI team. Out of everyone, he was the least invasive about my personal life. He wouldn't have intruded at all except that he was supposed to be joining the meeting. The meeting that was in . . . I pulled out my phone . . . Fuck. Five minutes.

Which meant I was already late.

"Are you okay?" the man squeaked through the door of the one-person bathroom.

I swallowed thickly. "Yes. I'm fine," I croaked, trying to sound like I meant it. The pause on the other side of the door told me I wasn't convincing.

"I can try to reschedule," he started. "Or I can—"

"No," I said. "I'll be right out."

"Okay," Oliver said. He knew better than to fight with his boss. The muffled sound of footsteps was just audible as he shuffled away. I turned my attention to my reflection in the mirror. The woman staring back at me was too pale. Too lifeless. But she would have to do.

I straightened my posture, taking a step away from the sink as I rolled my shoulders back and adjusted the collar of my shirt. I slid the mask of professionalism over my features, locking away the weakness of moments ago, and pushed back the wisps of blonde hair that had come loose from the hair clip. The layers in my hair were proving more trouble than they were worth.

Satisfied enough, I walked out of the bathroom, whistling at Jasper to follow. He lengthened his gait to match my stride. I held my head high, forcing away the remnants of weariness as I approached the conference room. I had to lock away the woman from ten minutes ago. The woman who had been lying helplessly on the bathroom floor.

I held back an internal snarl.

No. That woman couldn't exist in the presence of anyone else, even if I couldn't escape her within the confines of my own reality these days.

5

ELLE

"Promise me you'll be careful," Eric said as he lifted the last bag into the back of my 1962 Volvo Amazon. My brother, Stevie, had found the car right before it was about to be sold for scrap. He had somehow found a way to re-engineer the entire engine to salvage it and gave it to me as a going-away present when I went off to college.

"Of course," I agreed offhandedly.

"I mean it," Eric pressed, his voice as serious as I had ever heard it. "Keep the sleuthing to areas where people can see you." He gave me an 'or-else-you're-grounded' look.

"I'll be fine," I assured him, grabbing Watkins' travel carrier. Eric would be out of town for a week, and it just seemed to make more sense for me to take the little guy with me. The cat meowed in protest as I put him on the floor of the passenger's side.

"I just don't want you to push your luck," Eric warned. "Remember what happened in Oklahoma?"

I cringed at the memory. I had been writing about underground cult-like communities and had accidentally attended an initiation ceremony . . . They were surprisingly understanding when I said I couldn't be branded with their logo on my left butt cheek.

After a few more assurances and a quick kiss goodbye, I was on the road. The drive was quick; under two hours. Watkins yowled until he was lulled to sleep by the vibrating of the engine.

I found the spare key to my parents' house wedged in a crack in the bright-blue mailbox. That had been my dad's brilliant idea. I still remember that look of pride stretched over his face when he had discovered such a 'prime' location.

Grabbing Watkins' carrier, I entered my childhood home. It was modestly sized, with caramel-colored wood floors, egg-shell walls, and huge windows. It still smelled the same – the slight aroma of lavender and lemon, with a hint of salt. Released, Watkins skulked from his box and gave a sleepy sniff at the house while I set up his litterbox in the laundry room.

I lugged my bags upstairs to my old room, now the guest room. Despite the evolution of the space, it still contained much of my old decor. In the corner, the oversized bookshelf held original Nancy Drew books. On one wall hung my antique picture of Agatha Christie, while on the wall adjacent to that was a framed *Boston Globe* newspaper with the signature of *Spotlight*'s own Marty Baron.

I plopped my bags at the base of the bed before walking over to the window. The room was the smallest in the house, but I never noticed. Growing up, I was too much of a people person to spend much (or any) time alone here. I was always with friends or bugging my brothers to go on an adventure.

I was the youngest of three kids and the only girl. Dan, the eldest, now owned an outdoor-equipment store in Colorado, while Stevie was a software engineer for a gaming company right outside of San Francisco. Dan and Stevie were nothing alike. Dan was tanned, muscular, rugged-looking, and always had some sort of facial hair. Stevie was thin, paler – because he hated being outside – and always cleanly shaven. There was also the fact that Dan was the most social human I had ever met, while Stevie was much more introverted. But that probably had something to do with his autism.

My parents had realized Stevie was different early on, and he was diagnosed in second grade. There were times when he wouldn't be able to understand social situations or moments when he would say something inappropriate.

But to me, that was always just how Stevie was.

Smiling, I glanced toward his old room. My dad had since made it his office but kept my brother's decor: on the far wall hung old car gears, designs of gigabyte mechanisms, and a drawing I had made for him when I was five years old. Stevie wasn't very sentimental, but the asymmetrical, crayon puppy had apparently made the cut.

After an hour of unpacking and settling in, I headed to the police station. I drummed my fingers along the steering wheel as I drove. My eyes zeroed in on my engagement ring as if it had its own personal spotlight.

Maybe you should just take it off. Just for the first time you see Andrew. There's no harm in that, right?

After a moment's consideration, I shook my head. That just had 'terrible idea' written all over it. Like a bad omen or something.

Still, I had to admit it was rather tempting.

I fidgeted all the way to the police station, unable to sit still. I was still tugging and adjusting the collar of my shirt as I walked up to the precinct doors. I wasn't even at the base of the stairs when I heard someone yell.

"Elle!"

An excited Andrew leaped out of his police cruiser and rushed toward me. Before I could say anything, he wrapped his arms around my waist and swung me into the air.

Suddenly, I couldn't keep the smile from my face. "Hello to you too!"

Andrew's energy was contagious. He hadn't changed at all in the last year. He was tall, with brown hair that he always kept short. He was in great shape, with a broad chest and thickly muscled arms. He had played football in high school, and still looked the part of the classically good-looking quarterback.

He flashed a brilliant smile. "How was the drive?"

"Watkins yelled at me for half of it," I laughed, feeling the tension in my shoulders relax.

"Of course, he did," he chuckled. "Are you staying at your parents'?"

"Yeah, but they're still in Greece."

"Oh . . . I knew that actually," Andrew admitted, looking sheepish. "I asked around when they weren't home."

"How did you know they weren't home?" I asked.

"I went over to make sure they were okay. Ya know, after everything. I hope that's all right." Andrew looked nervous and rubbed the back of his neck.

"Oh, yeah!" I said quickly. "Thank you." That was Andrew. The guy you dumped, and he still goes and checks on your parents.

We'd dated for the last two years of high school, and then all through college. It was only when I got my first writing job in South Carolina that we had had to make a change. Or at least, I had felt like we had to . . . It had seemed like the only option at the time. He was still going to be here and I was going to be hours away. Sure, we had done long distance in college, but I couldn't do it forever. It seemed ironic that only a couple of years later I was just two hours away in Providence. But, to his credit, Andrew never brought up that particular point. After the break-up, we had stayed friends, even if I had taken a step back since Eric joined the picture.

But being here with him made it feel like nothing had changed. In a good way.

"Of course," Andrew said with a warm smile. "Well, wanna head in?"

He led the way toward the station.

"Where were you coming from anyway?" I asked Andrew as we walked up the last few steps.

"Blocking off the second crime scene area *again*," he sighed. "Some kids on the beach must've gotten drunk and broke the tape."

Andrew held the door open for me as we headed into the station. It was an old building that had accumulated an odd assortment of modern architecture to keep from falling to the ground over the years.

"Well, look who it is," a dry, low voice cracked as soon as we stepped inside. I turned to see Phil Gregory. He had been a cop there since I was little and was just as gruff and crusty as I remembered. His greasy hair had grayed some and he sat in a wrinkled uniform. He swung his chair around to face us, man-spreading his legs all the while.

"Miss Elle Wolfe, in the flesh. Ya look just as beautiful now as when ya left this godforsaken town."

"Hey, Phil," I said, forcing a smile.

"How's life as a big-shot lady writer?" Phil asked, leaning back as he stuck a cigarette between his teeth.

"Great," I said, fighting the urge to crinkle my nose as he blew a big puff of smoke in my direction.

"Come on, Phil," Andrew sighed as he eyed the cigarette. "You gotta take that outside."

"Since when?"

"Since this station became a smoke-free zone nine months ago."

"Cops should be allowed to light a goddamn cig if they want to," Phil muttered but got up from his seat. Andrew, as lieutenant of the station, outranked him.

"He hasn't changed a bit," I said to Andrew once Phil was outside. "Just as charming."

"He means well," Andrew offered. Somehow I wasn't sure that was always true.

"Elle! No way, man!" A younger voice cried. I turned to see a large guy with thick hair. It took me a second to recognize him with the haircut.

"Hey, Jay," I said, beaming. The tank of a man dwarfed me in a crushing embrace. Jay was a few years younger than me and used to live around the corner from my family. I babysat him and his sister once upon a time.

"What's up? What's going on?" Jay asked excitedly, a toothy grin stretched across his broad face. It was nothing short of miraculous that even with everything going on, he had such an upbeat aura.

"Oh, you know, life," I said, looking him over. "What about you? I swear you get taller every time I see you."

"Ha! Rounder maybe!" Jay laughed. "Makes me buoyant for surfing, so what do I care?" He laughed again.

"Your hair," I started, raising an eyebrow at the notably shorter length. Even as a kid, Jay had insisted on keeping his hair long. Now the curls were cut above the ears.

"I know." Jay grimaced. "Station rules."

From behind him, a small, raven-haired boyish head peeked around the corner. Benjie shouted my name, haphazardly rushing to see me. He was easily the least coordinated person I had ever met but in the most lovable way possible. He was Jay's age but looked like he could still be in high school.

As we all caught up, there was a tense undertone to the pleasantries. Behind the smiles, there was stress and worry. I tried to keep the moment light, avoiding why I was back. I could assume they already knew . . .

As we talked, a gray-haired man came out of the back office. Chief Antonio Ramos had been head of the station for the last twenty-five years.

"Elle Wolfe. I was wondering when we'd be seeing you again," he rumbled, his voice just as deep as I remembered. "I wish you were able to visit at a happier time."

His acknowledgment of the unspoken situation brought a gravity to the room.

"Me too," I said quietly. I paused, considering my words. "But it's actually why I'm here." I swallowed hard. I needed to be completely transparent. The last thing they needed was for me to get in the way while I was trying to sniff out a story. "I know this is difficult and that there's a lot of pressure on all of you, especially with some of the rumors being thrown around. I want to help. I want to cover the story from your perspective: the perspective of those who grew up here, went to school here, have children here. You all know this place. I want to share your point of view."

Silence fell over the entire room, the expressions on everyone's faces showing varying forms of shock. Some of them nodded once the words soaked in. Some looked unsure as they glanced at Ramos for his input. The chief scratched his cheek in thought.

"I only want to help," I repeated.

"I'm assuming she already pitched this to you?" Ramos asked Andrew.

"More or less," Andrew admitted. "Elle will do a good job. We all know we can trust her." He smiled encouragingly at me, while a murmur of agreement swept around the room.

"Besides," Andrew continued, directing his words at Ramos. "It would be good to have someone telling the truth about what's going on, as opposed to spinning it like most of the media. It might help the town bounce back once all of this is over."

Ramos studied me before a smile stretched his face. "Well, boys," he began. "It looks like we are going to get some help in the PR department."

Jay whooped, slapping me so hard on the shoulder it almost sent me flying.

6

ELLE

I spent the day in the station learning everything known about the case, which wasn't much. There hadn't been any DNA left on either of the bodies; not under their fingernails, not in their mouths, or their more . . . intimate areas. The ocean had likely washed away anything that would have been there.

The parents of the victims hadn't been very helpful either. Nelson Edgars was so distraught after Molly's death that even getting him into the station was a struggle. He was practically catatonic, but no one could blame him. He had lost his only real family. I mean, his brother hadn't even come to the funeral. And with his wife gone, he was completely alone. Apparently, he spent most nights in the bookstore he owned on Main Street.

Jamie Kane's folks hadn't been any better. The entire extended family had crammed into the small station, yelling over one another and demanding answers. With fifteen of them, it was almost a riot. One particularly aggravated aunt had thrown a complete fit, chucking a paperweight across the room . . . It explained the dent in the wall by Phil's desk . . . at eye level.

To make matters worse, there were still no obvious suspects.

According to Andrew, the most likely scenario was that someone from out of town was responsible. It would explain why the killings had started so suddenly, and why they coincided with the beginning of the summer season.

"This is a vacation destination for people all over the world. I bet our guy joined the masses," Andrew reasoned. "Or maybe the tourists drew him here. More options to choose from."

I shivered at the thought. He made it sound like choosing cereal at the grocery store.

Despite the confidence Andrew portrayed with the theory, I couldn't help but feel like he was grasping at straws. At least from where I sat, I didn't see anything to suggest that it was a tourist over a local. But I didn't dare voice that opinion. It wouldn't have been helpful, and it was hardly my area of expertise.

Then again, it wasn't exactly their expertise either. The Cape August cops, or Station Boys as they were called, were in over their heads. For as long as the town had existed, the most exciting thing for a Cape August police officer was the occasional traffic violation or firework debacle. Now, in a matter of weeks, two people had been murdered.

I sat in the office for hours, and before I knew it, the church down the street struck seven. Slowly, officers began filing out of the station to get some much-needed rest.

"Want to grab some dinner?" Andrew offered as he got up and cracked his back.

I nodded as I flexed my fingers.

"Is that dive bar in town still as good as it used to be?" I asked, rubbing the back of my wrist in an attempt to work out the knot that had formed. For some reason, Andrew suddenly seemed very interested in watching me stretching my hands. Odd . . . His eyes were fastened to one spot in particular . . .

I looked down and suddenly lost my appetite. In the dim station, my engagement ring seemed to glow, reflecting every light beam the room had to offer.

Fuck. I totally forgot.

I looked back at Andrew to say something, but he had looked away, suddenly engrossed in tidying his desk.

"Yeah," he said before I had the chance to speak. "Want to do that?"

"Umm . . . Sure," I said lamely, wondering if I should acknowledge what he had just come to realize.

He must be okay enough, right? I thought to myself. *He's still willing to get dinner with me. That had to be a good sign. Right? Right?!*

It was a short drive from the station to the restaurant, but it felt like eight hours of torture. Andrew made useless small talk, something I knew he hated, only proving to me that he didn't want to discuss the accidental reveal. That was fine by me. Maybe we could just ignore it and move on. Who knows, maybe he would forget?

It was late enough that we didn't have to wait for a table. Inside the restaurant, antique license plates lined the dark wood walls. Candles flickered on red-checkered tablecloths, and the smell of beer wafted through the air.

We were seated by Nancy, the waitress who never smiled, but knew my order even though I didn't even live here anymore. Before I knew it, I was cradling a bacon-swiss burger in one hand, while trying to keep the other under the table and out of view.

"You don't need to hide it," Andrew said. "I'm a big boy. I can handle it."

I gulped the bite I had taken, the half-chewed burger sliding painfully down my throat. I had half a mind to grab my plate and make a run for it.

"Sorry," I mumbled.

I knew I should have taken the ring off. Stupid. Stupid. Stupid!

"It's okay. It was bound to happen eventually," Andrew said with a shrug. "Who's the guy?"

"Someone I met at work," I said casually. I didn't bore him with the details. Who cares that Eric and I met when I interviewed him for a tech story that I barely understood? Something about a high-powered battery something-or-other. I even wrote the story and I couldn't remember.

"How long have you two been dating?" Andrew asked. He was trying to sound neutral but I could hear the tightness in his voice.

"A couple of years."

Andrew gave me a smile that didn't reach his eyes. "Congrats."

"Thanks," I said.

I hate this friggin' ring, I growled internally.

"What about you?" I asked, desperate for some relief in the conversation. "Seeing anyone?"

Andrew shrugged. "No one serious."

I nodded, unsure how to continue. This was unbearably uncomfortable, but I wasn't sure how to fix it.

"Is that why you haven't been around?" Andrew asked before I could think of something. I opened my mouth to deny it, but I saw the small knowing smile on his lips. He knew.

"Kinda," I admitted. "I didn't want to ruin anything. We were doing so well at . . . you know . . . being friends."

To my surprise, Andrew's smile grew.

"I'm not that fragile," he said. "Besides, my life would be too boring not having you to deal with. Even if it's just once in a while."

I laughed, feeling the tension melt away. The rest of the night was easy as Andrew and I caught up. Apparently, he had taken up surfing again, although he still got his ass kicked by Jay. They had even tried to teach Benjie, which had gone worse than anyone could have anticipated.

"He was underwater for a solid minute," Andrew grimaced, recounting a particular wipeout. "Couldn't find him anywhere."

"Oh my god," I whispered.

"Jay pulled him out. Poor guy spat up water for twenty minutes."

He asked me about my life in Rhode Island and I told him about working as a magazine writer, my friends, my life, although I still avoided mentioning Eric. Even if Andrew said he was okay with the whole engagement thing, I didn't need to rub his nose in it.

By the end of the night, I felt like the entire situation had gone as smoothly as possible. As I drove past my house, I looked at the front door longingly. I was exhausted, but I had promised to see Zoey for a drink. She lived with her boyfriend Travis a couple of streets over, so it was easy enough to swing by. Glancing at the car clock, I swore to myself that I wouldn't stay longer than an hour. I knew it was an empty promise. Time with Zoey always had a way of getting away from me.

After pulling into her driveway, I hadn't even turned off the engine before Zoey was sprinting toward me. Wrenching open my car door herself, she threw herself into my lap to crush me in a hug.

"It's about friggin' time!" she cried.

"I missed you too," I gasped through her clutches. Despite being small, Zoey was surprisingly strong. When she finally released her hold, she led me into the house where the tall and lanky Travis was waiting.

"Look who it is," he said, pushing his square glasses up the bridge of his long nose.

"I've decided to bless you all with my presence," I said dramatically, giving a little curtsy.

Before long, I was on their tan, plush couch with a dangerously full glass of red wine. We chatted, tiptoeing around the reason why I was there. That was mostly Travis' doing. Zoey clearly wanted to talk about it, but every time she tried, Travis would steer the conversation in another direction. I wasn't surprised. He hated dark topics even when it was hypothetical. Crime shows made him nauseous.

"How's Prince Charming?" Zoey asked, trying to wiggle her eyebrows at me. It wasn't a skill she possessed, so it just looked like she was scrunching and un-scrunching her forehead.

I rolled my eyes. "Eric's fine."

She leaned forward, eyes gleaming. "How's the sex life?"

"Z!" Travis yelped, looking at her incredulously. I wasn't sure why he was always so surprised. They had been together for almost four years. He should know what she was like by now.

"Well, I still have one," I chuckled.

"That's a good start. Engagements can often be the kiss of death for erections," she said solemnly. "It's like the appendage is trying to rebel against monogamy."

Travis' mouth hung open, struggling for words.

I grinned at her. "Well, Eric continues to *rise* to the occasion."

She let out a whoop. "I'm sure he does!" she hooted. "At least, the most important part of him! Damn. I always hoped he had an amazing—"

"Okay." Travis cut her off, jumping up from the couch. "I think that's my cue. I'm going to bed." He shot a strict glance at Zoey. "Ladies, try and keep it clean."

"You know I don't have that kind of restraint," she sighed. He chuckled, leaning down to plant a kiss on her forehead.

"So I've come to realize," he murmured. He turned back to me. "I'm sure you'll be over all the time, so I shouldn't say goodbye, right?"

"Right." I nodded. He knew the deal. When I was in town, Zoey tried to have me around as much as possible to maximize our time.

Once he had disappeared into their room, Zoey skooched closer to me, eyes laser-focused. "Spill. How was seeing Andrew?"

I took a long swig of wine and shrugged. "Fine," I said. "Everything seemed normal enough."

Zoey grabbed my left hand. "Did he see the giant boulder on your finger?"

Ugh. Don't remind me of that.

"Yeah . . . " I started.

"Oof," Zoey hissed through her teeth. "How was that?"

"Honestly, it was totally fine," I said again. I subconsciously twisted the ring around my finger. It seemed tighter than normal.

"Uh-huh," Zoey said, sounding completely unconvinced.

"No, really," I argued. "He was totally supportive, and understanding, and—"

"And full of shit." Zoey cut me off. "You guys dated for, like, a billion years. No way is he actually okay with it."

"First of all, it was only six years—"

"Which is a billion years."

"And second of all," I continued, "he's moved on."

"No, he hasn't."

"How would you know?" I argued. "It's not like you guys are friends."

"True . . . He's never been able to appreciate the artistic mind." Zoey shrugged. "But it's a small town, so I know that he hasn't been on a date since you ended it."

I looked at her, blinking blankly.

"Exactly."

"Well, maybe he just hasn't found the right person," I said slowly.

"Because he's still hung up on you."

"No," I corrected. "I would have noticed that today."

"I doubt it. You want to think he's fine, so that's what you would see," Zoey reasoned.

I shook my head. I could feel a headache forming behind my eyes. Maybe it was the wine.

"Honestly, it doesn't really even matter," I sighed, knocking back the rest of the contents in my glass. "It's not like there's anything I can do about it. Besides, everyone has bigger problems at the moment."

"Good point." Zoey's expression turned grave. "What did he say about all of that?"

I sighed before starting in, explaining only what Zoey would be allowed to know and skimming over the details. I knew that the specifics were confidential, but I had a pretty good sense of what I was allowed to share.

She kept silent while I explained, something that was altogether out of character for her. She couldn't help herself most of the time. But with this . . . it was different.

"Fuck," Zoey breathed, sinking farther into the couch when I had finished. "But they have suspects, right?" Hope tinted her words.

"I can't talk about all that," I said, trying to keep my tone neutral. I knew on so many levels that I couldn't answer her. Zoey knew me so well, I was worried that she might be able to hear the answer in my inflection alone.

"Yeah . . . Okay," Zoey huffed. I sighed internally in relief. It wasn't just the investigation I was protecting, but Zoey too. How would she feel if she knew the truth? If she knew how little the cops knew? I didn't want to put that burden on her . . . I barely wanted to know it myself.

7

On a beach further up the Cape August coast, a figure paced along the sand. He was gangly, with reddish-brown hair that constantly threatened to fall into his eyes. He grumbled to himself as he re-read the Post-It in his hand.

"It's not you, it's me," he announced to the waves, then paused, before adding: "Well, no, it's not really *me* . . . It's . . . Umm . . . Just the situation?" Felix waited a beat, looking at the ocean as if hoping it would respond.

He shook his head. Sarah would slap him for sure if he said that. She hated clichés.

Felix took out the crayon he had stolen from his little sister's backpack. *Barf Green*, she called it. It was her least favorite (for obvious reasons), so he figured he'd have it back before she realized it was missing. Felix crossed out his messy handwriting on the yellow sticky note. Thinking hard, he wrote a new line, nodding with such conviction that it sent his overgrown hair into his eyes.

He cleared his throat, looking out to his watery audience. "The sex was great but remember that one time—" he cut himself off, swallowing the rest. "Nope. I can't say that one out loud."

He crossed through the line with extra crayon before blowing out a breath.

This shouldn't be that hard.

He exhaled loudly, shaking out his arms and looking out at the ocean again.

Focused. Ready.

"I just think we should break up," he blurted out. He let the air absorb his words, watching the waves break on the sand with a resounding *splat.*

"Ugh!" Felix huffed, slapping his hand across his face. "I'm so fucked."

He had tried to break up with Sarah at least four times, but each and every time something came up. It was too close to Valentine's Day; she had just gotten rejected from Northwestern; her cat had been diagnosed with schizophrenia (he was pretty sure she just pulled that one out of her ass . . .)

This time, he was going to make sure nothing stood in his way. He was going to kill this relationship if it was the last thing he did.

He glared at the ocean defiantly.

"I don't even *like* you," he said, before envisioning Sarah's fist coming straight for his nose. And she knew it was his best feature!

Felix growled, pacing the beach again. The sand crunched as he stomped.

He had debated doing this over text, but that was a known douche move. The kind of douche move that would follow him into his senior year of high school if he wasn't careful.

He would never get laid again.

As he continued to brainstorm, his fingers began to tug subconsciously at the woven bracelet on his wrist. Sarah had bought it on her Aspen trip because 'it made her think of him.' He had no idea why. He didn't ski, never wore jewelry, and had never been to Aspen. He hated the thing. The leather itched and it was a size too small. Sometimes he thought it might draw blood, it was so tight. And yet the fear of Sarah catching him without it kept it fastened on his wrist at all times.

He yanked on it as he inched closer to the water. He inhaled the salty spray, ignoring another buzz from his phone. He should have been back at the cottage rental at least twenty minutes ago. His tiny slice of vacation was over. Back to the life of driving a golf cart for some old guy smelling of prunes and dandruff shampoo.

8

He was twenty minutes late. Malorie Walker clicked her tongue. She wanted to be on the road by nine to beat the traffic.

"Kimmy, did your brother say which beach he was going to?" Malorie asked, looking at the pig-tailed girl coloring on the blue rug that boasted an obnoxiously white anchor.

"Umm." Kimmy scrunched her face as she went wild with the yellow crayon. "The one that has the good rocks."

Malorie raised her eyebrows at her daughter. "And which one is that?"

"The one that is *way* better than the ugly rock beach," Kimmy said definitively as she fished for the nub of orange crayon at the bottom of the box.

Malorie tapped her foot, trying to decipher her five-year-old's code. She shook her head in defeat. She'd have to wing it instead.

"All right, honey," Malorie said, loading up her arms with a tote bag, soccer duffle, and child-sized *Hello Kitty* suitcase. "Let's go. We'll pick up your brother on the way."

"One more minute," Kimmy said, sticking her tongue out the side of her mouth in concentration. "I just need to finish the scales of the Bad Dragon."

The girl looked into her crayon box, knowing the exact color a 'bad dragon' should be. Her mouth dropped open in horror. *"Barf Green* is gone!" she yelped, looking quickly at her mother. "Did you take it?"

"Don't look at me," Malorie said, trying to hold the front door open with her foot. She huffed. "Maybe it's wherever your brother is."

Kimmy scrunched up her face as she gathered her crayons and half-colored picture. "Felix stole it then! He better watch out," she threatened as she hopped toward her mom. "Or the Bad Dragon will *eat* him!"

The closest beach was less than a mile away, making it the most likely place to look for the seventeen-year-old. The parking lot was empty, save for a Power Bar wrapper, its shiny silver interior reflecting the morning sun in a blinding white ray. Malorie swung into a spot at the front, leaning forward to look along the beach. The sand dipped out of view, blocking most of the beach from this spot.

"I'll be right back, Kimmy," she said, looking back at the girl who was fully invested in a debate with her stuffed lion. Something about the pros and cons of sparkles.

Malorie left the windows down, letting the sea breeze drift into the minivan in soft puffs. It rustled Kimmy's auburn pigtails and made her giggle.

Malorie smiled, clicking the lock button an extra time for good measure as she walked toward the beach. Her eyes squinted against the glare that rolled and somersaulted down the swells of the incoming surf before the light shattered into a splat of foam. Hand on hip, Malorie searched the beach. Far along the sand, something caught her eye. It was hard to make out. A speck of heather gray, masked by a salty haze. Felix's *Game of Thrones* sweatshirt.

The woman sighed, as she made her way toward it. Her clogs sunk into the loose sand.

"Felix!" she called. "Felix, come on! It's time to go."

Malorie huffed, hoisting up her heavy feet. It was always like pulling teeth trying to get the kid to leave. She rolled up her sleeves, ready to drag Felix back to Washington by the scruff of the neck if need be.

She wasn't close enough to spot the speckles of red on the grey sweatshirt. Or the crimson stream that stained the leather bracelet around the boy's wrist.

Or the blood-drenched crayon, that would never again be the color of *Barf Green*.

9

ELLE

The station was in complete chaos after Felix Walker was found dead on Winslow Beach. The case was the same as the others. A teenager. Innocent. Throat slashed. No witnesses. No evidence. Nothing.

His family was brought in for questioning right away, and I had to bite my tongue when Felix's little sister was interviewed by the police. She was so young she was barely able to register the reality of what had happened. Her green eyes were round and wide, bouncing from police officer to police officer.

"This was found next to the body," Benjie said to Andrew, handing him a plastic bag holding a soaked, partially disintegrated, yellow Post-It.

Andrew took a look and sighed. "I doubt this has anything to do with why he was killed," he muttered. "But ask the mom about the girlfriend just in case. Check it for prints too. Who knows? Maybe we'll get lucky."

We didn't. There wasn't a print on anything.

I could feel everyone's frustration growing with each passing hour. Every 'lead' turned out to be nothing. Every explanation seemed to be empty and useless.

And then there was the issue of the upcoming summer. Mayor

Sully was in the precinct every other day asking for an update. His priority was clear: keep the beaches open. He threw a fit when Chief Ramos blocked off the areas where the bodies had been found. "Do you want to give people a reason not to come here?" the mayor had yelled at Ramos.

Keith Sully was the youngest Mayor in Cape August history and was eager to continue his trajectory. With re-election coming up in the fall, it was no wonder he was eager to resolve this issue. Nothing said bad publicity like a string of unexplained murders. And nothing said *catastrophe* like having the town's revenue dip with a loss of tourism dollars. I could only imagine his reaction if every beach needed to be shut down.

I had actively been avoiding him, mostly because he was rather unpleasant. But the more I helped the station with their public interface, the more I risked being noticed. So, when Mayor Sully strutted over during one of his visits with his perfectly moussed hair and too-wide smile, I wasn't surprised.

"Our very own Elle Wolfe!" he greeted, clapping me on the shoulder so hard that it almost sent me face-first into my computer.

"Mayor Sully," I said with a forced smile. "Good to see you."

"And you! Say, I hear you're working for *Point*. Good magazine. Lots of readers."

"Yes . . . *Sir*," I agreed, almost forgetting to add the title. It was still odd to see Sully in a position of power. He had been a senior at my high school when I was a freshman. I still saw him as the smarmy, albeit handsome, debate team leader.

"And I'm sure you're here to cover the . . . strangeness of the past couple weeks?" Sully asked with surprising casualness.

"Erm, yes," I said again, fiddling with my hands out of habit. "But I can assure you Chief Ramos approved it."

"Oh, of course," he said with a toothy grin. His teeth were a little too perfect. "I just want to make sure that you and I are on the same page. In terms of *wording* . . . If you catch my drift."

"Meaning . . .?" I started, feeling dread in the pit of my stomach.

"You see, I think journalists have been too quick in assuming these are *murders*," Sully said, looking at me hard. "I don't think there's nearly enough evidence to call them something so hideous. Wouldn't you agree?"

"Well, I'm not an expert," I said.

"Right-y-o!" Sully exclaimed. "I would hate for your article to make you look incompetent."

"Yes, except—"

"Wonderful!" the man crowed. "I'm so glad you agree! Would hate for you to get into any kind of trouble. Especially when it's so easily avoided. Writers are being fired for every little thing these days." There was an unmistakable glint of warning in his eyes before he gave a wave. "Have a glorious day, Ellie!"

I gaped after him as he slipped out the door. "That's just great," I grumbled to myself, looking at the article I'd already written. I sighed. Sully had a lot of connections. Not to mention the most obvious one of his father, the Senator of Massachusetts. No doubt he could make my life difficult if I didn't play by his rules. Who knows? My story could even get pulled altogether, and then I could *still* be fired.

Shaking my head, I used the cursor to pull the document to the trash on my desktop. Back to the drawing board.

10

ROSLYN

The burn of the gin brought instant relief, helping to ease the tension of the day. I stood at my kitchen counter, daring to close my eyes for a fraction of a second. I tried to remember the last time I slept. Part of me didn't want to calculate it.

Jasper had been quick to curl up by my feet while I internally debated which need was more important: food or rest. Opening the fridge would be disappointing. I wasn't home enough for grocery shopping to prove worth it, and the only places that would offer take-out at this hour sounded nauseating. Boston had its limits.

I brought the glass to my lips and took a long draw. Despite my thin frame, I could handle my liquor. It had been helpful on a handful of occasions. I refilled the glass with half the amount as before. Not enough to accomplish a buzz, but enough to hopefully take the edge off.

Or, at the very least, dull the memory of the wolfish looks a guy in the finance department gave me today . . . Not that I wasn't used to it. I was objectively attractive, something that historically made a job surrounded by men more difficult. Accepting the simple fact, I had found a hidden power in it a long time ago.

I had still visualized throwing that FBI accountant out the window after a *particularly* suggestive comment. Mostly because it was so moronically phrased. If someone was going to be inappropriate, they should at least have the decency to make it anatomically accurate. "Imbecilic neanderthal," I muttered to myself.

I sighed, feeling the beginnings of a headache behind my eyes. It helped me make my decision. Finishing the gin, I started to make my way through the dimly lit apartment. Jasper was awake quickly, padding by my side through the small, neat space. It was practical, even if it might seem sterile to the few that I allowed through the front door.

Perhaps the absence of personal photos or mementos had something to do with that.

I stripped my clothes robotically, shedding everything. Well, almost everything. I glanced at the small silver bracelet still fastened to my wrist. I couldn't help but run my finger along the back of it, feeling what was etched in the metal. It was the only thing that I never took off. The only thing that was as much a part of my body as any limb. I glared at it. It was ridiculous to feel such animosity for an inanimate object, and yet I couldn't separate myself from the loathing I felt for it. Especially after today . . .

I pulled my finger away as if burned, before heading for the shower. The water was cool. Soothing, almost. It took everything in me not to fall asleep standing up.

I'd managed it once before.

I dried off robotically, not feeling the softness of the towel. Finally slipping between bed sheets, I leaned over to turn off the lamp. My fingers hesitated on the switch and I bit the inside of my cheek. It didn't give much light. Just enough to chase the shadows to the borders of the small room, deluding the intensity of the dark. I growled, forcing my hand to shut it off. I wasn't going to cater to myself. The dreams would come regardless.

It was a couple of hours before my mind allowed me to sleep, and even then it was brief. A buzz dragged me back into consciousness and I shot my hand out to answer the phone.

"Hunt," I said, instantly alert. I looked at the clock. It was 5:16 am. Only one person would be awake and calling me now.

"I hope I didn't wake you," Oliver said, sounding nervous. "I know you're usually up by now." It was almost impressive that he had memorized my sleep schedule. There was no need to tell him that this morning was an exception.

"I was awake," I lied. "What happened?"

"I was looking through the requests and saw that we got one from Cape August last night. You told me to keep an eye out for it."

"Took them long enough," I muttered, more to myself than to Oliver. "Have we been approved?"

"The Director just gave us the go-ahead. I called you right away."

I was already moving toward my closet. "Print out the details of the case so we can debrief the team on the way. I want to be on the road within the hour."

"I'll call the others," Oliver said.

"Tell Bonnie that if we have to wait for her again, she'll be transferred to Human Resources," I warned.

Oliver paused on the line. "Ummm . . . Do you want me to use those exact words?" His voice squeaked higher.

"Unless you'd rather have me call her . . ." I said, my tone taking a dangerous dip.

"No," he said quickly. "I'll have them all meet you at the office."

Within fifteen minutes I was packed and ready. Jasper sat obediently, his brown eyes watching as I holstered my Glock 17.

"Ready?" I asked the Dutch shepherd, who gave me a small woof in response. "Let's go."

11

ELLE

The next Monday marked three weeks since Molly's death, and still they were no closer to finding the murderer.

The upcoming tourist season only added to the pressure. With summer right around the corner, business owners were frantic about how this would affect profits. Natalie Baker called eight times a day with innocent questions about her flower shop, and Randy Davis, the owner of the surf shop, had all but camped out on the steps of the station.

The media was certainly not helping matters. Almost every morning there was a new reporter asking the same questions in the same crazed, frantic way. Fulfilling my unofficial role as 'station liaison,' I tried to play mediator. It sucked a lot of the time I should have been using to write my own stories, and Tony had started to notice.

Having just listened to a strongly-worded voicemail about that particular issue, I stared at the blank Word document on my screen. The cursor blinked, mocking me. I'd been at this for the last three hours, and still I had nothing. This was starting to become a nightly routine.

With a groan that was a little too loud, I smacked my head down, not caring that I landed on my keyboard. The reason I hadn't produced anything had nothing to do with the fact that I was stretched too thin. The truth of the matter was that I wasn't sure how to even start the story anymore, let alone how to word what came after. The last thing I wanted to do was to exploit flaws in the system here, but in reality, the Cape August cops were simply not equipped for something of this caliber. But how would exposing that help anyone? It would only produce more panic and fear, and potentially fuel the media storm already raining down.

But I couldn't lie either. I muttered choice words into the spacebar of my laptop.

Andrew growled in frustration next to me, running his hands over his face.

"Where the fuck is this guy?" he muttered to himself. He had been staring at the same crime scene pictures for the last five hours.

"Everyone, I have an announcement."

We all looked up as Chief Ramos walked to the middle of the room.

"I've called for reinforcements," Ramos said.

A murmur swept around the station.

"Reinforcements?" Benjie squeaked.

"The FBI," Ramos said, and the room broke into chaos. Phil's chair toppled over as he leaped up, shouting a protest. Jay groaned. Benjie let out a small yelp. Other Station Boys fought over one another to be heard.

Beside me, Andrew was silent. I looked over and saw his mouth was pressed into a thin line, his eyes darkening by the second.

"Enough!" Ramos bellowed, silencing the commotion. "This is not up for debate. We'll still be leading the investigation. It's still our case. They'll just be supporting us."

"They'll scare the crap out of every tourist!" Phil protested. His hunched stance and balled-up fists made him look caveman-esque. "Say goodbye to the Fourth of July. No one will come to this publicly dubbed death trap!"

To his credit, Ramos remained unphased. "I talked to their Unit Chief. They'll be as discreet as possible," he said. "But we need help. If this continues—"

"It won't," Andrew piped up. His voice was low, but it cut through Ramos' with surprising clarity. "We're handling it. I think we've made some good progress—"

"It's not enough," Ramos interrupted.

I held back my sigh of relief. I agreed with Ramos. It wasn't enough. Not at this point.

"They are more equipped to deal with something like this," he continued.

"In a city, sure," Andrew said. "But this is a small town. No one is going to like having to deal with the feds. Hell, I don't want to deal with them."

There was a general mutter of agreement.

"This is what they do," Ramos continued, raising his voice. "They will be here soon and I expect all of you to be on your best behavior. We all have the same goal. Now, let's get it done."

No one spoke over the next few hours; everyone seemed to be in their own world of anticipation. Waiting for the inevitable.

Until the time finally slipped away.

"The FBI just pulled up," Benjie announced.

Andrew stiffened. "Here we go," he groaned, getting up from his chair. "Might as well see who we're dealing with. Shall we?"

I nodded, trying to keep the excitement from erupting out of me. Obviously, I hated the circumstances surrounding it, and I didn't like the fact that their assistance was required, but I had always been curious about federal investigations – how they worked, the protocol, and how closely the real thing resembled crime shows.

"Let's greet the calvary," I joked, trying to lighten the mood. Andrew cracked a smile.

I followed him to the front of the station where a black SUV had just pulled up. The vehicle was huge, probably able to fit at least eight people if needed, and was so clean that the sun reflected in blinding prisms off the surface.

The driver got out first. He was handsome, probably in his late thirties, tall, with messy black hair that looked purposefully tousled. He had a perfectly symmetrical face, and a strong jawline dusted in a five-o'clock shadow. His very stance – shoulders rolled back and a small smile playing on his lips – made confidence, and maybe a hint of arrogance, roll off of him in waves.

If he was one side of the coin, his companion, struggling to climb out of the back, was the other. This man looked to be the same age but had a softer, pudgier look. He had thin, mousy hair and wore glasses that seemed too small for his round face. His cheeks had a rosy complexion as if he had just sprinted around the block twice, and he fumbled with his belongings (several folders, a cell phone, and a notebook) as he stumbled out of the SUV. As soon as he stepped onto the pavement, it became evident that his gray slacks were too long for his short legs by several inches.

Climbing out after him was a curvy woman with bright red lips twisted into a scowl. Her wild hair had clearly gotten ruffled up during the drive. She muttered in irritation as she attempted to tame the ball of frizz.

Behind her, a petite woman leaped out from the lowered backseat with a surprising amount of energy. She must have been no more than five foot two, even shorter than me. Tightly curled black hair framed her smiling face. At a distance, I could see a series of brightly colored pins attached to her blazer.

An older man, probably entering his fifties, circled around the back of the SUV from the other side. His hair was a neat silvery-gray, and his face was serious, with a well-trimmed beard and mustache to match.

But it was the person stepping from the front passenger's side that seemed to hold the attention of the onlookers. To say she was strikingly beautiful would have been an understatement. She was young, perhaps in her late twenties or early thirties. She was on the taller side, probably around five foot nine, with a slim figure and long legs. Her pale, golden-blonde hair was neatly tied into a bun with a few hairs allowed to fall elegantly around her face. Even from here, I could see the natural highlights interwoven in the locks, adding depth and complexity to the color. Her eyes were such a piercing blue-green that they seemed to flash even from a distance. Her high, prominent cheekbones and thin nose gave her face a delicately angular look, while still maintaining a softness of conventional beauty.

She dressed conservatively in a white, button-down shirt, tucked into black slacks and a matching black blazer. They looked tailored just for her, hugging her slim body to accent her femininity, without overly sexualizing herself. She stood with perfect posture, natural grace, and elegance, without the arrogance that the driver seemed to have. As she moved, she took long, authoritative strides which seemed even more impressive when I realized the tasteful, yet practical, black heels she was wearing. She didn't seem to walk, so much as glide, toward the station.

All eyes were glued to her, but if she knew it, she didn't let on. She let out a low whistle as she rounded the car and the last of the passengers jumped from the very back: a dark, lean, medium-sized dog with a long snout and pointed ears. The dog fell into step with her. They seemed to move as one, in perfect synchronization. It was both impressive and intimidating.

To everyone's surprise, it was this woman that took her place at the front of the group, making a beeline for Chief Ramos himself.

"No way," I heard Benjie murmur to Andrew. "*She's* in charge?"

"We don't know that yet," another cop whispered. "She might be their contact person or something."

Andrew stayed silent, but his eyes followed her like a guard dog ready to attack.

"Chief Ramos?" the woman asked politely, checking his name tag as she held out her hand. Her voice was crisp and clear. "SSA Roslyn Hunt," she introduced herself. She stood back and gestured to each of the other agents in turn.

"This is SSA Jason Dalton," she said as she gestured to the tall, fit man who took the chief's hand with a dashing smile, "Oliver Griffin," —the short, pudgy man nervously shifted his things under one arm to shake hands— "Harold Hopper," —the gray-haired man gave a tight-lipped smile— "Bonnie Fischer," —the crazy-haired, scowling woman forced a smile, which looked more like a grimace— "and Matilda Goodwin," —the pin-woman enthusiastically shook Ramos' hand with both of her own.

"Well, welcome everybody," Chief Ramos greeted, flexing his fingers after Agent Goodwin's handshake. "I really appreciate you bringing your entire team all this way," he said, addressing Agent Hunt.

Her team. So, she was the one in charge after all. Several cops murmured behind me.

"Of course," Hunt said with a polite nod and an unreadable expression. "I hope you don't mind the dog. He's with us." She said it in a way that made it impossible to refute.

"Not at all," Ramos assured, looking down at the canine who sat obediently at Hunt's feet. "If you all can follow me, I'll introduce you to my men." He led the group up a couple of steps to the station doors where Andrew and I stood with the others.

"You've got to be kidding me," Andrew muttered under his breath, his eyes trained on SSA Roslyn Hunt. "They think 'America's Next Top Model' is going to help us here?" He crossed his arms tightly across his broad chest as he glared at her.

"They're just here to help," I whispered to him.

With the FBI group right in front of us, Chief Ramos stopped for introductions. "This here is Lieutenant Andrew Wells, the officer that was dispatched to each of the crime scenes."

Andrew mechanically held out his hand to shake each of theirs. At least he *tried* to smile.

"And this is our station mascot," Chief Ramos chuckled as he put his hand on my shoulder. "Miss Elle Wolfe has been helping us with some of the public outreach. She works for a magazine. What was it called again? *People Magazine?*"

"So close," I laughed. "I'm a writer for *Point Magazine* based in Providence. I'm currently writing a story about how a small community copes with suddenly being in the spotlight. I would love to talk to you while you're here." I was dying to hear about what their lives were like, how they solved cases, any little detail at all. Andrew and the others might be apprehensive to have the feds around, but I saw endless opportunities.

"We won't have time," Agent Hunt dismissed politely. I wasn't surprised by her lack of enthusiasm. Anyone that worked for the government was often a tough nut to crack. "We need to focus on the task at hand."

"Oh, of course—" I started, only to have her cut me off smoothly.

"In fact, I'm not thrilled with the idea of someone from the media being around at all. Especially during an investigation like this one." The woman's gaze held me to my place, her intense blue-green eyes staring me down and sizing me up. The look was so forceful that I had to resist the urge to take a step back.

"Naturally," I said quickly. "I'll make myself as scarce as possible. Chief Ramos and my father go way back. He would never have let me work in the station if he thought it was going to be a problem." I smiled as her eyes narrowed. If looks could kill, I think anyone within a thirty-mile radius would have burst into flames.

An instant later, she looked back at Ramos.

"Shall we?" she said, her voice cool and her face a neutral mask.

As we entered the building, I made sure to create some distance between me and the lead agent.

"I love that magazine . . ." Agent Goodwin whispered to me, beaming. "The piece about how Komodo dragons are capable of virgin births was fascinating!" She gave me such a genuine smile that I couldn't help but return it, although I had no idea what article she was talking about.

Once inside, Ramos led the team to a room at the back of the station. As they walked through, the police officers talked in hush voices to one another.

"I don' like it," Phil said. "No one around 'ere is going to tell 'em shit."

It irked me that he sounded so pleased about it. I opened my mouth to retort, but Andrew shot me a look.

I grumbled under my breath instead.

"They're of no use 'ere,'" Phil went on. "The sooner they realize that, the better. And that li'l darlin' that they got leading 'em . . ." He chuckled as he looked at Roslyn Hunt. "She'll be kissin' our asses in no time. Not that I'd mind that." He gave the agents one final sneer before turning his back and returning to his desk.

I looked at Andrew after Phil was out of earshot. "Aren't you going to say something to him?" I asked.

"You don't understand," Andrew said, his tone lightly dismissive. "Phil's right. They're just going to get in our way. They're outsiders."

"But don't you think that if you work with them, they might be able to—"

"Anything they can do, we can do," Andrew snapped, but then his expression softened when he turned his full attention to me. "Look, I know you're worried. I am too. But trust me, we got this." He smiled gently and while I wanted to believe him, I wasn't convinced. I tried to return the smile anyway.

"Now, I was going to swing by the first crime scene and see if we missed anything," Andrew went on. "Wanna tag along, Nancy Drew?" He gave me a knowing smile.

Well, duh.

"I just want to grab some extra batteries for the radio," he said, walking toward the back room with all of the agents. I followed him like a moth to the flame.

"Is this everything you have?" I heard Hunt ask. Peeking around the corner, I saw her flipping through three sets of files. Her eyes flashed across each page as if taking a mental picture of the information.

"So far," Ramos admitted. "We're kinda in over our heads."

"That's what we're here for," Goodwin said kindly, having to tilt her head way back to look at him.

"We'll have to take another look at the crime scenes," Hunt said. "Would one of your officers direct us?"

"I believe Lieutenant Wells was just about to go to where the first girl was found," Ramos said, looking at Andrew as he entered. "We took pictures right away and have already stripped the place of any evidence. I doubt you'll find anything else. It's been a couple of weeks now."

"It'll still be useful to see the landscape," Hunt said.

"Alrighty then," Ramos said. "Wells can give you an escort."

Andrew looked like he had just bitten into a rotten apple. "Erm, yeah. Sure."

The FBI Unit Chief gave him nothing more than a quick nod before addressing her team. "I'll accompany Lieutenant Wells to the first site. Fischer and Dalton, I want you two to stay here and start compiling what we know. Griffin, I want you to talk to the press. Get them to back off. I don't care what you have to say, but I want them to give this a wide berth. Hopper and Goodwin, go to the second crime scene. Is an officer available to escort them?" Hunt flashed her eyes at Ramos with the question.

"I can take them myself. I'll just grab my keys in my office," Ramos said.

Hunt turned to her team. "Remember the kind of person we're likely dealing with here. Clean. Efficient—" Hunt stopped short when she spotted me in the entryway.

"You. What are you doing in here?" she demanded harshly.

"I-I was just—" I struggled under the power of her gaze.

"She's with me," Andrew stepped in.

"I will not have the media hearing confidential information," Hunt said.

"We've signed off on her," Andrew argued, his body tense.

"And that's wonderful for you," she retorted with cool sarcasm. "But I will not allow a *reporter* to listen in on the details of an ongoing investigation until we have a sound profile. Right now, we're only going to have theories and speculations. Those shift all the time. We wouldn't want to confuse your journalist." She said it so politely that the bite of her words was almost unintelligible as she essentially called me stupid.

I opened my mouth indignantly, but any retort I had was cut off as her piercing eyes fastened on me. I swallowed hard.

"In my experience, reporters often have difficulty distinguishing the difference between theories and facts," she breathed. Her tone was deathly cold with her warning as if daring me to cross her.

Andrew seethed for me. "That is hardly your place to—"

"It's exactly my place," Hunt cut him off curtly. "I'm sorry, but my answer is no. Ms. Wolfe, this room is off-limits."

"Well, she's coming when I take you to the crime scene," Andrew challenged, and I saw Hunt's mouth twitch with a withheld sneer.

"She will be doing no such thing." She turned sharply to her team. "You are all dismissed."

Without any hesitation, they dispersed to fulfill their tasks. Ramos paused, looking from Andrew to Hunt. The tension was palpable between them, making me shift uncomfortably.

"Thank you, Chief Ramos. I appreciate your cooperation," Hunt said.

Ramos looked at Andrew hard before inclining his head to Hunt and taking his leave.

"It's public property," Andrew continued at a harsh whisper once Ramos had left the room. "She's allowed to be on the beach in the summer."

I opened my mouth to step in, not wanting to be the reason for a misunderstanding so early on in their collaboration.

Before I could, Hunt sneered a response. "Then you can drive her to the beach," she practically hissed, "but she will stay far away from me and the investigation area. Isn't that right, Ms. Wolfe?"

"Right," I squeaked.

"Good," Hunt approved with sarcastic sweetness. "Now, Lieutenant. If you'd be so kind."

It only took fifteen minutes to get to Lovell's Landing, but the tension between Andrew and Hunt made it feel like an hour. Ironically enough, that tension seemed to be pretty one-sided. As Andrew stewed, his knuckles tight on the steering wheel and his face barely able to hold back a snarl (or a pout), Hunt seemed indifferent to our company, focusing instead on flipping through files. She would occasionally address Andrew to ask a question, but her voice remained neutral. Robotic almost. It matched how she sat in the seat, her posture straight and rigid. The FBI dog, that she had insisted on bringing along, seemed to mimic a similar position. It was a little unnerving sitting next to him in the back.

As we pulled into the beach parking lot, there were only a handful of cars. It was early enough in the season that the tourists hadn't fully begun the migration to the shores. Hunt got out of the car first, her eyes scanning the area before opening up the back to let the dog out. She didn't even glance in my direction.

"She's a peach . . ." Andrew muttered to me when it was just us in the car. He watched Hunt head to the beach steps.

"Eh . . . more like a pineapple," I mused, trying to lighten the mood.

"A little prickly around the edges." I inwardly cringed, but Andrew chuckled anyway.

"I think that was the worst joke you've ever made . . . And that's saying something," he snorted.

"All right, all right." I held my hands up in mock surrender before putting one hand over my mouth and whispering, "Maybe more like a dragon fruit . . . Those are a little more controversial." He laughed, some of the agitation easing from his face. I didn't mind compromising my pride if it was able to brighten him.

Hunt was long gone by the time we reached the beach steps. I paused at the top. She'd given me strict instructions not to get anywhere near her.

"You coming?" Andrew asked as he passed me.

"Won't she get mad?" I whispered as if Hunt was somehow listening in. Honestly, she seemed like the type to have supersonic hearing.

"She'll get over it," Andrew said with a shrug.

I followed despite my better judgment, unable to stop my burning curiosity from leading the way. Even so, I tried to stay out of Hunt's direct line of sight.

She can probably smell my fear, I thought dryly.

Once we were a stone's throw away, I decided that I shouldn't push my luck further and stopped. The day was bright, and I had to squint to see anything. As I should have figured, the spot that had once been the crime scene didn't give any dramatic insight as to the events that had occurred there. Instead, it looked exactly like the rest of the beach. Just as sandy and just as anticlimactic.

At the same time, I couldn't help but feel goosebumps begin to form on my skin, despite the warm summer sun beating down overhead. The beach had seen everything the night of Molly's death, and only those grains of sand knew how events had transpired.

Andrew approached Hunt, but she didn't bother to look up. Not even when he was right next to her. She studied the steep, sandy cliffs overhead. Her face was serious and contemplative. I wondered what kinds of scenarios were running through her mind as she surveyed the scene. If only I could ask.

I followed her gaze, trying to fill in some of the blanks for myself. It would have been difficult for anyone to get down the beach from the cliffs, especially with a body in their arms. And we were a good way down the beach. So, whoever killed Molly was either strong or had brought her here alive. Unless Molly was here on her own that night?

I sighed, looking back at the sand. The only witness that knew all those answers, but refused to give them up.

12

ELLE

We didn't stay on the beach for long. When Hunt was finished investigating the area, she stalked wordlessly past me. She barely spoke on the ride back to the station. When she had to say anything at all, I noticed how few words she was able to use. It was a very concise, efficient method of communication, and would have sounded curt if her tone wasn't so professionally polite.

Back at the station, Hunt made a beeline for the conference room where the rest of her team waited. I inched forward despite myself.

Maybe I could just take a teeny tiny look—

"Bad idea," Andrew whispered, putting a hand on my shoulder. I sighed. He was probably right. No one except the FBI seemed to be using that room at all now. Not that there was any reason that the Cape August cops couldn't, but the Station Boys seemed to be acting like it was tainted, giving it a wide berth whenever they needed to pass it. Only Chief Ramos seemed oblivious to the imaginary barrier and entered freely.

As the sun began to sink behind the station windows, Andrew got up and stretched.

"I think I'm going to call it a night," Andrew said, looking down at me when I remained rooted to the spot. "You staying?"

"Yeah," I said, looking at the blank Word Document on my screen. I had wanted to at least get an outline of a story done today . . . And yet here I was.

"Well, try to get some sleep," Andrew said, before offering a wink. "See you tomorrow, Nancy Drew."

The other officers began to trickle out of the station soon after, and within another hour, only I remained. Before long, most of the FBI members had begun to show themselves out too. As they passed, they'd offer a half-hearted goodnight or incline of their head.

Goodwin was the only one to break the pattern. As her big eyes spotted me huddled in the corner, she almost ran over.

"Hello," Goodwin said with a grin. "We were going to get a quick bite to eat somewhere. Would you like to join us?"

I almost jumped at the chance but hesitated. I doubted her colleagues would approve of her extending the invitation.

Before I could say anything, a certain voice sliced through the air. "Ms. Wolfe. A word."

I gulped when I recognized the owner. There was no mistaking it. Looking up, I saw that Hunt was staring at me from the doorway of the conference room. She stood with her arms crossed and her face blank.

I looked to Goodwin for help.

"You'd better handle that first," she whispered.

I walked stiffly, feeling a kind of impending doom with each step. Before I could reach her, Hunt disappeared through the entryway, stalking deeper into her domain.

Peeking into the room, my eyes had to adjust to the lack of light. Only one lamp had been left on, barely illuminating Hunt's outline. It made her seem phantom-like, the darkness accentuating the glow of her eyes.

"Please close the door," she said coolly, "if you would be so kind."

It wasn't a suggestion, more a direct order.

This is probably the part where she sucks out my soul.

Despite the overwhelming feeling of dread, I inched inside, closing the door behind me. It clicked with a sound of finality, locking me in and sealing my fate with it. I allowed my eyes to sweep the dim room. Lining the walls were large whiteboards, full of pictures and notes from dry erase markers. The desks surrounding them were piled high with boxes and notebooks. The black dog lay in the corner, staring at me. Chancing a look at Hunt, I saw that she was regarding me just as carefully.

I gulped.

"Please," she said, motioning to the chair in front of her. Again, I knew it wasn't an offer, so much as a polite demand. I took a shaky breath before perching on the edge of the seat. I fought the need to fiddle with my hands. Hunt remained standing a few feet away, despite the many chairs around her. It gave the illusion that she towered over me. The power move was definitely intentional.

"Do you know what my job is?" Hunt asked. She sounded casual. Flippant.

Was this a trick question?

"Yes . . ." I answered, cautious as I wondered how she might be setting me up. She stared, clearly waiting for me to continue.

"Your job is to catch criminals," I went on.

"Correct," she sneered. "My job is to stop the people responsible for maiming and butchering innocent people." She looked at me with cold indifference, which somehow matched the scorching blaze of contempt in her eyes. It was a deadly combination of fire and ice, and it forced me to repress a shiver.

"Would you please explain the purpose of your job?" she asked, her tone laced with patronization.

"To report the truth," I said, squaring my shoulders.

"No," she corrected. "That is what your job *should* be. It's not the reality of it."

"Please. Enlighten me," I retorted before I could stop myself. A muscle in her face twitched when I mimicked her tone. I bit my tongue.

"The reality of *your* job," she went on, "is that the more information you can sensationalize, the more you are rewarded for it." She began to circle around my chair, looking at me like I was prey. Waiting for a sign of weakness before she went in for the kill. I felt frozen to my seat, my heart hammering in my chest. "Do you know what makes my job that much harder?"

"I have a funny feeling you're going to tell me," I muttered mostly under my breath.

"Sensationalized publicity," she hummed, ignoring my statement.

"Well, it's a good thing that's not the kind of stuff I write," I said, keeping my head high.

She stopped short, crossing her arms lightly over her chest. It was almost casual, except her stance was anything but. She had a powerful presence despite her willowy frame.

"I don't like how close you are to this investigation," Hunt said. "If it was completely up to me, you would be as far away from all of this as possible."

A hint of a snarl crossed over her face.

"Let me put this in a way you can understand, Ms. Wolfe," she almost growled. "The time and energy I waste keeping an eye on you is valuable time and energy that I could be using to find a killer. Now, personally, I would like to think that my time is much more suited to investigating the case, but here we are instead. I am spending it here. With you." She looked down her nose at me and I felt myself shrinking in my seat, lowering my head under the weight of her words. If she was trying to make me feel guilty, it was working.

"That being said," she went on. "I talked with Chief Ramos. Fortunately for you, he made a compelling argument on your behalf. It seems like you provide a 'morale boost' for the office. Something about you having the ability to 'rally the troops.'" She said the words skeptically, clearly not believing them. "Out of respect for him, and because, technically speaking, local law enforcement has the final say here, I've decided to stomach your *presence*, but not, under any circumstances, will I tolerate your *participation*." Her expression was knife-like. Just as rigid, and equally sharp.

"This will be the last time you enter this particular room," Hunt said. "You will stay out of my way, and if I see you sneaking around, hampering the investigation, or writing any slander or exposé of any kind, you will find that I am not normally so . . . *open-minded*." She leaned forward as if she was ready to pounce. My mouth felt like it was coated in chalk.

When she straightened, she looked neutral once again. However, the carnivorous glint in her eye never faded.

With a thick gulp, I found my voice. "I'm sorry, I know you don't know me—"

"And I have no desire to," Hunt sliced through my sentence. "What I want is for you to give us the space we need to do our job. We didn't come here to babysit a journalist, and I will not hesitate to insist on your immediate removal. You would do well to act accordingly."

"I—"

"There is no need to discuss this further. I am glad that we have come to an understanding." Hunt motioned to the door, dismissing me. Stunned by the abrupt end to the 'discussion,' any response I had evaporated.

I got up to make my way toward the door. My legs felt like jelly.

"And Ms. Wolfe," Hunt breathed. I froze, feeling a chill in the air as the last of her words drifted to my ear.

"Have a pleasant evening."

13

ROSLYN

It was much-needed relief when everyone left the station. Finally, in the muggy room with nothing but the loud fan and the silent dog for company, I could hear myself think.

I looked up at the whiteboard displaying the pictures of the victims before and after their deaths. I glanced at a smiling Molly Edgars, caught with a novel in her hand at her father's bookstore. A smug Jamie Kane sporting a backward baseball cap and his number 53 football uniform. A rattled Felix Walker who had clearly not expected to be caught playing a beat-up guitar . . . The three had nothing in common apart from the fact that they were all teenagers. From looking at their files, I learned they had never met, which was hardly surprising. Even though it was a small town, Molly was the only local, with Jamie living in New York during the year and Felix being in Seattle. Their families had never intersected in any way. They didn't have connecting interests or personality traits. The quiet introvert, a high-school jock, and an awkward musician. The only thing they shared was how they died.

I glanced at the clock, sighing. Nine thirty. I went to my bag and pulled out the useless pill bottle, popping what I already knew would do next to nothing. I swallowed it dry.

Jasper watched, cocking his head to one side. I raised my eyebrows at him, giving the bottle a little shake.

"Just for show," I said with a humorless chuckle.

I knew I was just going through the motions with these, but until I had an alternative...

I shoved the orange bottle deep into my bag so that I wouldn't have to look at it and glanced back at the board.

The cut marks on Molly Edgars' neck caught my eye. There were hesitation marks. Hints of where the knife had grazed the surface of the skin, without causing real damage. It spoke to inexperience. Looking at the necks of Jamie Kane and Felix Walker showed one, clean cut. The killer was growing in confidence. Becoming more lethal and efficient.

I brought up a finger to massage my temple.

It wasn't just the evolution of knife strokes that spoke to a certain level of sophistication and competence. It was everything else too. The killer hadn't left a single witness. Not a shred of evidence.

I took a step closer to the whiteboard.

Each victim had been almost fully submerged by the waves by the time they were found. The high tide could very well have washed away any mistakes our guy made.

My phone buzzed in my back pocket.

I pulled it out and answered, "Hunt."

"Evening," a deep voice said. "I'm returning your call."

It's about fucking time.

"Director Weaver," I greeted. "Yes. Thank you." I paused, deciding to skip the small talk altogether. "I think you need to pull me from the case."

"What?" the voice on the line asked sharply. "Why?"

"You know why."

"You were cleared by medical personnel," he argued.

I almost laughed. Not that any of it was funny. I was fairly certain it was the Director who had told the examiner to clear me . . . Something about '*not wanting to bench his quarterback during the Superbowl*' or whatever the fuck the metaphor was.

"I'm still having some problems with my new medication," I said, hating to hear the words out loud.

"What kind of problems?"

"Do you really want to know the details?" I asked. I had to assume the silence on the other end was a no.

"Have you had an incident since last week?" he asked instead.

"No . . ." I said.

"Then, it sounds like you have it under control."

"That's not exactly how this works," I said as forcefully as I could get away with.

"I need you there, Hunt."

I ground my teeth. "Sir—"

"I understand it's not ideal," his voice cut me off. "But you're more than capable, and to be honest, I don't have the capacity to sanction another agent there right now."

My fingers clenched around the phone, already knowing the answer to my question before I even asked. "Is this an order then?"

"Only if you need me to make it one."

I forced a breath through my nose. I didn't have a choice.

"Understood," I said. "But I'm going to need to tell the Cape August officers about the situation."

"No." His voice was firm. Final.

I paused. "Excuse me?"

"No," he repeated. "Your team knows. That's enough."

My face twitched in irritation. "With all due respect—"

"If you tell the officers, it will only become a distraction for everyone," he said. "Who does that help?"

I held my tongue. He had half a point.

"Keep that dog of yours close, work the case as quickly as possible, and then come back to the city. It's that simple," Weaver said. I thought he had hung up before I heard him add: "You're the best we've got for this."

"Yes, sir," I muttered before the line went dead. My fingers closed into a tight fist around the phone.

"Shit," I said, running a hand through my hair. I thought back to the little orange bottle.

"Miss Roslyn," a sugary voice greeted, almost making me jump. I turned to see a young man with a Cheshire cat grin entering the room. I could smell his hair product from here.

"Mayor Sully," I breathed, recognizing the voice from the eleven voicemails on my phone, all of which I had chosen to ignore. "To what do I owe the pleasure?"

"I just came to see how you and your team were settling in," he said, drumming his fingers on the nearest desk. He was well dressed, in a royal-blue button-down that must have cost at least $300, and a pair of slacks worth even more. Designer. Limited edition. I recognized the thread pattern of the seams.

"You're too kind," I forced, watching the man carefully.

"Well, that's this town for you," Sully exclaimed with a far-from-genuine smile. "Willing to do anything and everything for its guests! Especially this time of year."

Ah, I thought to myself. *'Miss Roslyn' knows where this is going.*

"Speaking of which, we should probably go over those kinds of details," Sully said as if the thought had suddenly popped into his overly styled head. I raised my eyebrows. "As you may have heard in any one of my voicemails," he said with a pointed look, "here on Cape August, we depend on our tourism in the summer to keep us afloat for the rest of the year. No pun intended!" He chuckled heartily, slapping his hand on the desk near him. I repressed a growl as he touched some of the carefully organized notes.

"There have been some valid concerns about how your presence will affect our businesses," he continued. "Our vendors are concerned, and for good reason, if I do say so myself. I mean, you can't deny that the FBI's presence is going to be a little unsettling to our visitors."

"I would be more unsettled by a serial killer running around," I noted coolly. "Personally. But maybe that's just me."

His smile faltered before he pursed his lips. "You mean *alleged* serial killer," he corrected.

My eyes narrowed. "Excuse me?"

"We hardly know it's something as drastic as that yet," he said, glowering from behind a new plastic smile. "We wouldn't want to cause unnecessary panic."

I took a beat of silence, staring at the man.

"I've heard excellent things about you," he went on. "Not just a pretty face, eh?" Sully beamed, but the glint in his eye was hardly friendly. He lounged against the desk behind him.

"It's just that we wouldn't want to ruin a perfectly good summer under false pretenses," he said. "Especially if this could all just be a misunderstanding." It was everything I could do not to throttle him then and there.

"A misunderstanding," I repeated, rolling my shoulders back.

"Maybe a misinterpretation is a better term for it," he chirped.

A muscle in my jaw tightened, but I forced my expression to stay neutral. "I think it's pretty hard to misinterpret three bodies with their throats slashed," I said, before directing my eyes to the door. He either ignored or missed the dismissal.

"But we don't really know what killed them," the man said, wagging his finger in the air. "Could have been anything really. Boat accident, perhaps. Hell, maybe even a shark attack. We had one of those a couple of years back."

I felt my mouth open with the shock of seeing such pure stupidity up close. I would have found it fascinating if it wasn't so terrifying.

"Shark attack . . ." I said. "That's what you're going with?"

"Sounds better than a murderer," Sully said. "I talked to the coroner this morning, in fact. He's willing to retract his previous statements and sign off that these events were the work of a rogue shark."

"I see . . ." I said. "Well, excuse me if *I* won't 'sign off' on that." I turned, working to end the conversation. It was going to make my ears bleed. "Now, if you'll excuse me—"

"Rosie," Sully said, touching my arm. "May I call you that?"

I pulled my arm away as politely as possible. "Absolutely not."

He ignored me.

"I just want to remind you that the FBI is only allowed to assist. You had to be invited into this town if I recall," he said, putting his hands behind his back as he began to walk around me. "Federal jurisdiction only goes so far."

Of course, I knew the limitations of my position, and of course, he knew that I knew that. And yet . . .

"Your point being?" I asked.

"No point," he said with a light little shrug, continuing to circle. "I'm simply saying that it's the local authorities that have the power here, and as they work in tandem with *me* . . . Well, you'll just need to run certain things by me. Chief Ramos, rather. But that shouldn't be a problem, of course. I'm happy to cooperate. I just want to make sure we understand each other."

I stayed silent for a moment, watching as Sully made to walk behind me one more time. I took a step back, cutting off his path and forcing him to stop short. He tripped on his $700 shoes.

"Yes," I said with a sweet smile. "I think I understand just fine."

14

ELLE

The FBI and the Station Boys were like oil and water: they could not and would not mix. Hunt and her team had only been on Cape August for a few days, but it felt like an eternity. It didn't help that the entire town was now aware of their presence. With the summer looming, the FBI team was instantly ostracized by the locals. Being seen talking to them seemed equivalent to admitting that there was a genuine reason for their presence, so everyone was desperate to avoid them at all costs, shying away from their questions or refusing to answer anything at all. I had to admit, it made sense from a marketing standpoint. No shopkeeper wanted to be seen talking about a triple homicide case. It was bad for business.

The town's cops seemed to be taking advantage of the situation, and I even overheard Phil advising the coffee shop owner to only come to the 'local boys' if there was any information regarding the case. Even in the station, many seemed to be going out of their way to make it difficult for the FBI team, from not telling them the Wi-Fi password, to 'misplacing' files that I had clearly seen a couple of days prior. It wasn't that they didn't want the case solved, they just didn't want the FBI to be the ones to do it.

It was starting to get ridiculous and it took every ounce of my willpower not to say something. As Hunt had reminded me, it wasn't my place to get involved. Still, it was hard to watch; I had chewed my fingernails down to the nubs.

With all of this going on, I was careful not to have another one-on-one encounter with the terrifying Roslyn Hunt. Especially considering the fact that the local cops were doing everything in their power to get in her way already. It wasn't long before she stopped asking the Station Boys for anything, using the tech woman (Bonnie Fischer) to bypass their roadblocks. That included getting in contact with Nelson Edgars to bring him back into the precinct.

Andrew was steaming about it as he snuck me into the side room so that I could watch the interview take place through the one-way glass. It was an added feature that had seemed altogether unnecessary for the limited police station but was proving useful now. Peering through, I could see an older, haggard-looking Nelson Edgars. I had seen him just last Christmas as I browsed his bookstore, but he looked like he had aged ten years in that time. His hair was grayer, thinner, and weaker, which matched his overall deathly appearance. It made my chest ache.

Even with a wall of glass between us, I could hear Hunt's voice perfectly as she questioned him.

"And where were you the night Molly was killed?" Hunt asked.

"Picking up some first editions for the bookstore," Nelson said, grief making his shoulders sag. "I always do it myself. Limits the hands that touch them."

"Where?"

"Portsmith. Was going to stay the weekend until . . . Well, until I got the call."

"And it was just you and Molly?" Hunt asked.

"Ever since her mother died when she was two," Nelson said.

"And you haven't dated anyone else in that time?"

"No one of consequence." Nelson twirled his wedding ring around his finger.

"What about other family?" Hunt asked. "Anyone Molly was close to?"

"It was just me and her mostly," Nelson muttered. "Except for my brother on the odd occasion."

"When was the last time you saw him?"

"Not for years," he sighed, resting his chin in his hand. His eyes drifted past Hunt, focusing on a spot in the far corner of the room.

"Not even for Molly's funeral?" Hunt asked.

Nelson shook his head. "He . . . doesn't handle grief well." He rubbed a hand down his face.

Hunt raised her eyebrows. "Not even to support his own brother?"

"We had a bit of a falling out," Nelson admitted.

"How was his relationship with Molly?"

"Pretty good, all things considered," Nelson said with a shrug. "They would talk on the phone. For birthdays and holidays. That kind of thing."

Hunt paused for a moment, thinking, before giving a small nod and continuing on with her questions.

Next to me, Andrew shook his head. "I can't believe this," he seethed. "She's drilling him after he just lost his daughter."

"What choice does she have?" I argued at a whisper, afraid to disturb the questioning on the other side of the thick glass.

"To trust us. We already asked Nelson all of this," Andrew growled.

"Well, you aren't exactly cooperating with her," I mumbled, unable to keep my
irritation inside any longer.

He looked at me quickly. "What do you mean?"

"Everyone here is going out of their way to make the agents' lives more difficult."

"That's not true. They just don't understand the nuances of this town."

"Then why aren't you helping them to understand?" I asked.

Andrew just shook his head, refusing or unwilling to give me a legitimate answer. Maybe because there wasn't one.

And it wasn't just the cops and shopkeepers that were proving problematic. Later that day, a swarm of reporters surrounded the station, armed to the teeth with their recorders, cameras, and notebooks.

Benjie and Jay watched from the window.

"What do we do?" Benjie squeaked.

"Ignore 'em," Phil growled from his desk. "They'll go away."

"No, they won't," I said, peering out. There were at least three different news stations out there, and I could tell that they were prepared to wait. I recognized the determined glint in their eyes. I once had that same look.

"I can talk to them," I offered, steeling my nerves. I'd dealt with a few over the last week, but not a rabid pack. Being on the receiving end was very different than being *part* of the mob. I gulped, looking at Andrew. "What should I say?"

He opened his mouth, but someone else's voice beat him to it.

"You will say absolutely nothing," Hunt said from across the room. She stalked smoothly toward us, Oliver Griffin hurrying behind in his too-long slacks.

"Then, what do you expect us to do?" Andrew demanded as Hunt looked out the window herself, quickly assessing the situation.

"Nothing," she repeated. She looked to Oliver. "Do you have a statement for me?"

"Yes," he squeaked, shoving his too-small glasses further onto his face as he handed her a flashcard. Her eyes darted across it.

"This will work," she breathed. "While I'm out there, I want you to get Nelson Edgars out around back. Make sure he gets to his car without being swarmed."

Andrew balked. "You're going out there?"

"The media has the station completely surrounded, Lieutenant," Hunt said. "If you have another way of getting Mr. Edgars out of here quietly, please let me know."

Andrew opened his mouth, but any suggestion dried up in his throat.

Hunt gave him a pointed look. "Exactly," she muttered, adjusting the collar of her pale-blue shirt. She looked back at Oliver. "Go."

With that, Hunt walked out, closing the door with a forceful thud. Reporters practically flung themselves at her, desperate to get the scoop. I could hear the buzz of their questions through the crack of the door as they threatened to swallow her whole.

I couldn't help myself. I slipped out the door, hugging the outside of the building. I caught the end of Hunt's statement.

". . . and will provide updates as new information becomes available."

Questions hurled through the air, swirling into a jumbled mess of noise. From behind the mass, TV reporters talked to their cameras.

"I'm standing here in front of the Cape August Police Station, where people fear a violent maniac is on the loose—" one ABC reporter said.

"Rebecca Holmes reporting live from the town where Jamie Kane was found brutally murdered—"

"Something is hunting swimmers on the shores of Cape August, but it's not a shark—"

"The scariest thing since *Jaws* has come to fruition—"

All the while, Hunt kept her expression calm and collected.

"Once again, it is too soon to say what we are dealing with at the present time," she said. "We will release an official statement when we have enough information."

"Will he strike again?"

"Is he mimicking the behavior of a shark?"

"Is he *eating* his victims?"

I shivered at that particular image.

From the corner of my eye, Oliver Griffin peaked out the door, whispering Hunt's name. Somehow through all the ruckus, she heard him and turned. The two made brief eye contact before Hunt turned back to the reporters.

"Unfortunately," she said, her voice cutting through the noise, "we are not taking any more questions at this time. Once again, we would like to express our deepest condolences to the families and friends of Molly Edgars, Jamie Kane, and Felix Walker. The FBI is working tirelessly with local law enforcement to respond to the situation in the fastest, most appropriate, way possible, and we will keep the public informed as updates emerge. Thank you." With that, Hunt turned on her heels, leaving the reporters thrusting their mics into the open air. As she passed, she glanced in my direction. Her mouth was tight, pressed into a thin line.

But she didn't say anything.

Instead, she swept into the station, directing her next words to Phil. "Jamie Kane's family rented a house off of Quint Avenue, correct?"

"Something like that . . ." Phil muttered, eyeing Hunt with irritation.

"I want to ask his mother a couple of follow-up questions," Hunt said. "Do you have her specific address?"

Phil crossed his arms over his chest. "I might."

Everyone waited for Phil to move toward his desk, but he continued to stare at her. I nudged Andrew in the hope he would intervene, but he just watched with a silent snarl.

"Could you please give it to me?" Hunt asked.

"I could," Phil muttered, planting his feet firmly on the station's wooden floor.

Hunt's face remained unchanged, but something in her eyes flashed as she regarded Andrew instead.

"If you would be so kind as to forward me those details. I would hate to waste time having our analyst track down information that you already have." She shot Andrew a sharp look from beneath her cold, polite exterior, before turning on her heels and heading to the back of the station.

"I'll give her ta the end of the week," Phil muttered with a satisfied smirk as she drifted away. "Then, she and that team will leave us the hell alone."

"Nah," another man said. "I'm sayin' at least a month."

"Ha!" Phil chided. "I'll take tha' wager."

"You're both wrong," Andrew said. "Two weeks. Max."

The conversation made my blood boil. Before I said something I couldn't take back, I grabbed my laptop and walked out. This rivalry needed to end. It was totally unproductive, not to mention childlike and petty.

I started to cultivate my budding plan on the drive home. It needed to be well thought out. Detailed. Roslyn Hunt would allow nothing less when I proposed it to her. I needed to make her see that at the moment, I might be the only one on Cape August that would help them. The only ally to bridge the gap between their team and the town.

I just hoped it wouldn't bite me in the butt.

15

ROSLYN

"I already told you. The production of that particular medication has been paused. You can't refill something that doesn't *exist*," I seethed into the phone. Next to me, Oliver gave me a careful glance but quickly focused back on the road. His sweaty fingers slipped on the steering wheel.

"Right! I forgot about that," my doctor said through the speaker.

"Funny how that happens when drugs go generic, eh?"

"Hysterical," I muttered.

"How about you come in tomorrow afternoon for some blood work?" he suggested. "Then, we can—"

"I'm out of town for work," I said. "As I've already mentioned . . ."

"Oh, right," he said. "And the Phenobarbital wasn't effective for you?"

"Correct," I repeated for the seventh time.

"That's unfortunate."

"Yeah . . . well . . ." I started, clenching my teeth. My eyes flashed at the street names. I didn't have time to let Oliver miss it.

"Let's try a low dose of Valproate then," the voice in my ear said happily. "See how that works."

"Great," I said, as we turned onto Quint Avenue. I hung up as soon as the car pulled up to 342. The house was large and freshly painted, sitting on a lush green lawn. Down the street, rentals and year-round homes sandwiched one another in various states of upkeep. Some had neatly manicured yards, while others were more . . . wild looking.

I left Oliver in the car to make some calls, while I took Jasper out with me.

"You can't park there, dear," a voice called as I started toward the house. I turned to see an elderly woman, curved with age, hobbling down the street. She was still remarkably fast as she scurried toward me. Her big eyes blinked behind thick, tortoise-shell spectacles.

I looked back at where we had parked: right between a minivan and a red sports car. It was identical to every other spot.

"I beg your pardon?" I asked.

"You can't park there," the woman repeated, smiling a little too hard. It was making her eyes bulge. "You have to park on the other side of the street."

My gaze followed her long, bony finger that was pointing at a matching spot. I raised my eyebrows.

"I don't understand," I said, before looking at the house. "This is number 342, correct?"

"Yes. But you have to park in front of number 361 if you want to see anyone at 342," she said sweetly. I scoffed, thinking it had to be a joke.

But the woman just blinked.

I pursed my lips. "There aren't any signs that say that."

"Oh, of course not!" She laughed as if the very idea was absurd. "You just have to know. Everyone in the neighborhood knows, naturally. And the renters are informed the day they move in."

I did not have time for this.

"There are other cars parked on this side of the street . . ." I noted.

"Indeed! But not in that particular spot," the woman said with a knowing grin. She wiggled her nose to keep her glasses from sliding.

"And there isn't a fire hydrant," I went on.

"Nope," the woman agreed, bouncing on her toes.

"So . . . We agree that it would *appear* to be an *open* spot," I said, working to keep the snark out of my tone.

"Well, I suppose. Yes!" The woman beamed.

"Wonderful." I took another step toward the door. "My colleague is staying with the car, so—"

"But you still can't park there," she called.

I felt a muscle in my eye twitch. It took an obscene amount of effort to keep my face calm as I turned back around.

"Why?" I asked through partially gritted teeth.

"Well . . ." the old woman said, stopping to think. "I can't quite recall the specific reason. But it's just not done, dear."

All my patience. She was sucking out *all* of my patience.

"I promise, I'll only be a minute," I said, turning on my heel toward the house for the third time. I had managed to take a whole three steps before . . .

"Maybe your friend could just move the car first," she chirped. "Just a smidge."

I glanced at Oliver fumbling with his notebook, cellphone squashed to his ear. He was too busy to deal with this bullshit. I pursed my lips.

"I don't believe I caught your name," I said.

"Oh, deary me!" the woman cried. "Marigold Buzbee, at your service."

I summoned up the sweetest smile I could muster.

"Pleasure," I said through my clenched expression. "My name is Roslyn A. Hunt with the Federal Bureau of Investiga—"

"Oh!" Marigold Buzbee exclaimed. "The one investigating that murder or something!"

"Yes . . . or something," I said, taking another backward step. "It was lovely meeting you, Ms. Buzbee." I knocked on the rental door twice.

"You too, dear!" Marigold Buzbee said as Mrs. Kane answered and allowed Jasper into the house.

"Oh, dear!" Marigold Buzbee cried as I stepped over the threshold. "Missy Hunt! What about your c—"

I closed the door with a resounding *thud*.

"Mrs. Kane," I greeted. "Thank you for meeting me. I wish it was under different circumstances."

"Thank you. Did you find the place all right?" Mrs. Kane asked. Her hair was stringy and needed a wash, her face was gaunt, and her lips were stained from last night's red wine. She was wearing an oversized sweater that looked as though it belonged to someone three sizes larger than her, and two mismatched slippers that poked out underneath stained sweatpants.

"Just fine," I assured her. "We parked right in front if that's all right.

Mrs. Kane rolled her red, bloodshot eyes. "That's fine by me. Please, come in."

She led me deeper into the rental house. It was impersonally beach-themed, with large windows in every room. All the light clashed with the grim, desolate feeling that hung around the seashell decor. Tissues were strewn about and shoved in the corners of the couch, dishes were piled high in the sink, and there was a chill in the air that had nothing to do with the overactive fan.

"Is the rest of the family here?" I asked, sitting down at the dining room table littered with stale cereal that had spilled from a fallen box. No one had bothered righting it.

"No," she said. "They went to a movie. Trying to keep the kids busy . . ." Mrs. Kane trailed off, staring into space. She scratched at a spot on her neck that was raw and irritated.

"I understand," I said. "It's good for them to get out of the house."

"They were supposed to be gone a week ago . . . But everyone stayed," she went on. "The cousins. Grandpa Rick. Uncles. Aunts . . . Everyone. They stayed." There was an odd tone of surprise coloring her words.

"We're not that kind of family," she explained before I asked. "We love each other of course, but from a distance. We see each other once a year. Bicker and fight. Then we go our separate ways for another fifty-one weeks. I didn't think . . . I just figured they would have left by now."

"It's important to have a support system," I said. Mrs. Kane nodded but looked away.

"I think they don't know what to do with themselves," she murmured, her eyes glazing over. It dulled the redness of them a little. "It's not like they didn't have excuses to go. Uncle Billie was supposed to go back to work days ago. Aunt Cynthia had a wedding to be at. I would have left if I were them. Tried to do something else. Anything else. As long as it was away from here." She cocked her head to one side as if studying something I couldn't see. "I think . . . I think they don't know how. To leave, I mean. To move on."

"No one does," I said. "This is an impossible situation."

Mrs. Kane nodded again, her mouth opening, but not making an effort to say any words. I waited, giving her time to compose herself. At my feet, Jasper settled back onto his haunches. A clock dinged somewhere in the large, empty house.

"Did Jamie make a habit of leaving late at night?" I finally asked.

Mrs. Kane gave a watery chuckle. "He is an eighteen-year-old boy. Of course, he does." Her eyes widened with her mistake. She swallowed hard. "Of course, he *did*."

"Have you noticed anyone hanging around?" I asked. "Someone that always happens to be at the street corner at a certain time, or anyone who doesn't quite belong?"

"No. Nothing like that."

"Was there anyone who would want to hurt your son?"

"No," Mrs. Kane said. "He was a little arrogant sometimes, but never meant anything by it."

"What do you know about the friend he met up with that night? Alton Piperon."

"Alt?" Mrs. Kane clarified. "I didn't know him well. He was one of Jamie's summer friends."

"How close were they?"

"I don't know. Not very. Why?" Mrs. Kane leaned forward, her eyes suddenly blazing. "Could he have something to do with it?"

I shook my head. "I doubt it. I'm just trying to get a picture of what happened that night."

Mrs. Kane's shoulders deflated. "Oh."

I looked toward the stairs. "Can I take a look at Jamie's room?"

It was at the farthest end of the second floor, no doubt chosen in an attempt to be away from the family commotion. Next to the bed, an open suitcase sat overflowing with football jerseys and wrinkled button-downs. The room reeked of cologne and dirty cleats. Hair products lined the windowsill.

In the corner was a book with charcoal pencils scattered around it. I crossed the wooden floor and flipped it open. I raised my eyebrows at the detailed sketches of a bird. The texture of the feathers had been added with a careful hand, and the label of *Cape Oystercatcher* was written neatly in the corner. I turned the page. Another bird. The book was full of them.

"He never let me look at those," Mrs. Kane said over my shoulder. "I think he was embarrassed."

"He had talent," I noted.

Mrs. Kane smiled. "He wasn't the dumb jock he wanted everyone to see."

She took a shuddering breath and began to wring her hands. "He was my only one you know," she murmured so quietly I wasn't sure I was even supposed to hear it. "I wasn't even sure I wanted kids until he came along. When Jamie was born, I realized how stupid I had been. I wanted him to have brothers and sisters. A whole family. You know, like I did. But I couldn't."

She looked up at me, the devastation so potent in her expression that it made me freeze. Seeing death was one thing. It was cold. Easy to compartmentalize. But raw emotion like this . . .

I bit the inside of my cheek, forcing myself not to look away.

"I'm never going to have a child again," she whispered, looking at me as if it was some sort of question. As if she wanted me to tell her that there was some chance to the contrary. Jasper shifted uncomfortably next to me.

I left the house shortly after, only to find a passive-aggressive note tucked under the windshield wiper of the SUV. It looked like a mock parking ticket and was signed ~*M.B.*

"What the hell?" I muttered, shaking my head. Oliver's eyes widened when he saw it.

"Did we do something wrong?" he asked, shoving his glasses further onto his face.

I crumpled the note in my hand. "No."

16

ELLE

She was harder to find than I would have thought, especially since the bar was practically empty. Looking around, I couldn't help but feel it was an odd choice for Agent Hunt. Its worn wooden tables and ancient red rug were begging for an update. It smelled of cheap vodka, grenadine, and stale wonton wrappers. It was a local joint: Chinese restaurant by day, and dive bar by night.

Only locals would be here this late or tolerate the mediocrity of it. It made it that much more confusing to find this particular woman *here*.

Roslyn Hunt was in the farthest corner at the bar, skillfully hidden from the front door so that I had to do a full sweep of the room to spot her. She was pouring over a neatly stacked file of papers, making quick, decisive notes on a pad next to her. She still managed to keep her back rigidly straight. Regal somehow.

I pushed myself forward, keeping a stool between us as a buffer so as not to totally invade her personal space.

She paused her pen before deciding to ignore my presence and continue her notes. Underneath her seat, the black dog watched me without blinking.

I took a moment to steady myself as the bartender approached.

"Can I get an Old Fashioned?" I asked, making sure my voice was loud enough for Hunt to hear. The bartender gave a small smile before wordlessly hobbling toward the glasses. He had owned the bar for the last forty years, but a stroke had left him practically speechless.

I chanced a tentative glance at the woman feverishly scribbling.

"The answer is still no," Hunt said dismissively as if feeling my eyes on her. She didn't bother to look up from the pile of paperwork as she addressed me.

"I'm not asking for an interview ... this time," I replied, watching as the bartender shakily poured the whisky into my drink. He was giving me a heart attack holding the heavy glass bottle with a single, withered hand.

"Well, the answer to whatever else you might want is no," Hunt muttered.

"They're taking bets, you know," I blurted before I lost my nerve. "On how long you'll last." I didn't have to clarify who I was talking about. She knew. I was surprised to see a small smirk forming on her lips. She kept her eyes on the papers in front of her, but her pen had slowed.

"Is that so?" She sounded almost amused by the news. "And what's the consensus?"

"Two weeks," I said. She raised an eyebrow.

"It seems like I'm already halfway there," Hunt mused. She flipped the page, adjusting it to utilize the dim light.

"I also know that they're blocking you out," I continued. "I know that they want this to be taken care of in-house and that most people in town feel the same way."

"Shocking. The local community not liking a government entity butting into their personal business?" Hunt breathed sarcastically. "Can't imagine what their problem is."

"Well, I don't agree with how they are handling it," I said, turning my body to face her.

"And here I thought we had nothing in common," Hunt deadpanned.

"I'm serious," I said.

She sighed and put down her pen, resigned to the fact that she would have to deal with me directly. "What do you want, Ms. Wolfe?" she asked.

"To help you."

She pressed her lips together as if to keep from sneering. I could still see the cruel mirth swirling in her eyes.

"If you really want to help, try to rein in your friends from ABC," she muttered, picking up her pen as if the discussion were over.

I grimaced. ABC had been particularly insufferable. "That's not the kind of help I was referring to. You have bigger problems," I pointed out.

Her gaze snapped back. Her blue-green eyes stared with such intensity that it felt like they could burn a hole through my skull.

"You're an outsider," I went on. "Nobody here trusts you. Locals are only going to open up to other locals, which in this case means the guys at the station. The same people who happen to be trashing you and your team every chance they get. It doesn't matter how many cases you've solved, or how good you are, your chicken is already cooked . . ."

The corners of her mouth twitched at that. I fought a blush as I pressed on. "You have no credibility with them because they don't know you. You don't have an in. But I do. I grew up here. Everyone knows me and trusts me. My dad was a firefighter for twenty-five years here and my mother is still a third-grade teacher at the school down the street. I have the connections you need. I can get you in the door."

Despite the power of her gaze, I forced myself to look right back. A long time passed.

Doesn't she need to blink?

"Besides . . ." I continued, unable to take the suspense anymore. "It's not like you have many options here."

Hunt's face hardened. "What's in it for you?" she asked, making it sound more like an accusation than a question. Her eyes stayed fastened on my face as she waited for my response, scrutinizing every twitch or break of eye contact I dared to make. It was like looking at a human lie detector.

"I get to report on it all," I said. She pursed her lips. I hurried on before she had the chance to shut it down. "I will run everything by you first before I send it to my editor. I'm not a news reporter, so I can take more time getting the details right. I can tell the story you would want told anyway."

"You make it sound like you're doing me a favor."

"I am," I said.

Hunt looked unimpressed. "Ms. Wolfe, if it were up to me, the media would stay away from this altogether, so I don't see how—"

"But that's not going to happen, and you know it." I saw mild shock in her expression as I cut her off. She wasn't the kind of person someone cut off. Ever. I gulped around the lump in my throat, trying to look braver than I felt. There was a moment of tense silence, but she just looked at me expectantly until I continued.

"You might be able to banish *me*, but reporters are all over this, and it's just going to get worse," I said. "You've been through this before. They will bombard you with questions, and if you refuse to answer, they will fill in the blanks themselves. They will go around you, asking locals, going to the other cops, and listening in on conversations that they shouldn't be hearing. Theories and conspiracies will be written and reported on like they are facts. You know how dangerous that is."

Her body stiffened, but she didn't speak.

"With me reporting on the situation, you can make sure I get it right. You would have the power and opportunity to fact-check before the masses get their hands on it. How many times do you get that chance?" I was her best shot. I searched her face for a hint of what she was thinking.

Her expression remained unchanged.

"Besides," I continued, desperately wanting to ease the tension even a smidge. "This is my hometown. I want to protect it the only way I know how. That means getting the right information out at the right time." I felt my heart swell with purpose as I said it, holding my head higher under her scrutinizing gaze. "That also means facilitating the best team possible. And that would be you."

She pursed her lips.

"I Googled you," I admitted. "You graduated top of your class at UPenn before joining the FBI. You worked in Chicago for a year, proving to be instrumental in the Cop Strangler case, before transferring to Boston. You became the unit chief a year ago, and at twenty-nine you're the youngest to ever earn that title.

"That also made it a controversial decision," I said, "and it was put to the test six months ago. Your team was called in as backup when a terrorist group threatened to blow up Fenway Park. It was you who tracked them down."

Hunt leaned back and lowered the intensity of her gaze, as one might lower the volume on the radio. I'd left out a bunch of other details. Details that she probably figured I knew if I had gathered this much information already. Like her other issue with the media . . .

The press had historically had a field day with her, using her looks as a platform for furthering their own agendas or exploiting it as a way to boost their viewership. The more unsavory news outlets had paraded footage and photos of her, highlighting her physical attributes while pushing her qualifications to the wayside. It only got worse when she was thrust into the spotlight. These same news outlets flaunted close-ups, pushing cameras in her face, and trailing the lines of her body. I had watched the clips, and they weren't just objectifying. They were downright degrading. It hadn't helped that the news cycle had been especially slow that week.

Taking this into consideration, it didn't take a rocket scientist to figure out why she was so wary of my presence. I just had to prove that she could trust me, or at least that it was worth taking the risk.

"You've done your homework," she finally said.

"I wanted to be prepared."

For a moment, I thought she was about to smile, but it must have been a trick of the light because a millisecond later, the look was gone. With a low sigh, she broke my gaze and took a delicate sip of her drink. I took the opportunity to take a deep draw from mine.

"Okay," I heard her cool voice say. I choked when I heard the word.

"What?" I croaked, not daring to believe my ears. I hadn't really thought she would agree.

"I said 'okay,'" she repeated calmly, though her tone sounded annoyed. I had to fight the urge to leap up in excitement.

"Really? Great! So, when should I—"

"But there are rules." Her voice cut through my excitement like an ice ax: cold, precise, and brutal. It wasn't enough to deflate me.

"I figured there would be," I said, trying not to squeal with delight.

"If you break even one, you're done. No second chances. No warnings. Done." Her face was an emotionless mask.

"That's fair," I reasoned, almost bouncing in my seat.

"You touch nothing. Not evidence, not a gun, not a badge, not even a stapler. You will stay out of the way. That means being silent during the questioning of witnesses. Any concerns you have can be voiced after. Not during. If you so much as breathe too loudly, you're out."

I would have laughed if she didn't sound so terminal.

"You will interview no one on this subject without a supervisor," she ordered. I opened my mouth to protest, but she beat me to it. "No exceptions."

I nodded. "Okay."

"You will not ask questions while we are at the station. That is not the time for you to be 'digging' for your little stories. When in the precinct, you will be seen and not heard." I tried to look neutral as my heart leaped with excitement. The fact that I could observe as they worked would be a surreal experience.

"You share the details of the case with no one. I mean no one," she commanded. "Not your editor. Not a friend. Not anyone." Her eyes darkened. "And above all, you will do as I say, when I say, how I say. There will not be a moment's hesitation and there will be no argument." Her tone was final. This wasn't a debate.

"Is that clear?" she asked.

"Yes. Very clear," I answered quickly.

She gave a curt nod and returned to look at the file in front of her. She didn't bother to look up again when she went on. "I will see you at six-thirty at the station tomorrow morning. You may bring a notepad, a laptop, and your cell phone. They will all be searched, so keep that in mind. You will agree to a full background check and drug test. Our analyst will be looking closely at any and all records . . . so if there is anything you'd like to share, now would be the time . . ." her eyes glanced sideways at me, raising a perfect eyebrow.

"Erm . . . there's a speeding ticket from three years ago," I said, trying to think if there was anything else I should be mentioning. "And I smoked pot in college . . . Oh, and there was that time that I—"

"I mean anything of substance," she huffed, irritated.

I beamed. "No. I'm clean as a whistle."

"Mmm," she murmured, resuming her notes.

"So . . . is . . . is that it?" I asked.

"For now," she said, clearly dismissing me.

"Thank you. This is a good decision. You won't regret it," I vowed.

"Too late," Hunt muttered.

I chuckled at the joke, choosing to believe she was kidding.

She didn't look amused.

17

ELLE

I woke up giddy the next morning. I had always been fascinated with criminal investigations, reading every Nancy Drew and Agatha Christie novel before I finished high school. I had to remind myself that this wasn't fiction. This was real, with real lives at risk.

The smile faded from my face as I rummaged for clothes. I dressed professionally in a white skirt and light green button-down shirt. I even added a pair of cream heels from my mother's closet.

As I drove to the station, the sun was just beginning to peak shyly around the corners of the buildings. It was still early, and the streets were empty, save for a few ambitious runners. There were only a handful of cars in the precinct lot. Most of the cops hadn't gotten there yet, which was probably just as well. I already knew that Andrew wouldn't approve of the arrangement I had made with Hunt. I figured the rest of the Station Boys would side with him. Maybe I could get a cup of coffee in my system before having to explain myself. Regardless of the scrutiny I might have to face, I stood by my choice.

Inside, the only light came from the back room that the FBI team had commandeered. I crept nervously toward it, my mind racing as fast as my heart. I peeked around the doorway.

"Come in," a smooth voice called. I had to suppress a shiver. It was

Hunt. I saw her standing by the whiteboard, her back to me. I wondered how she knew I was there.

"Erm, hi," I greeted lamely as I walked into the room. It was just the two of us.

She didn't even bother to tilt her head in my direction. I shifted my weight between my feet. Did she want me to speak, or to stay silent? I fought the urge to chatter, watching her back and waiting for her to turn instead.

She was wearing light-gray fitted slacks and a cream dress shirt that had been perfectly tucked. Her hair was tied back neatly into what was becoming its signature loose bun. Say what you will, but she'd mastered professional elegance.

At last, she turned to face me.

"Did you bring the required identification?" she asked unceremoniously. I nodded, swinging my overstuffed bag to try and fish them out. I could feel her gaze as I fumbled with my belongings.

"Put them on my desk when you find them," she said, already sounding exasperated. "Over there are the forms for you to fill out." I looked up to see her motion to a desk on my left. It was piled high with paperwork. I opened my mouth to ask, but she beat me to it.

"Contracts and liability forms," she explained. "If you end up dead, I would hate to waste my time with a lawsuit."

I chuckled at the dark humor, swallowing hard when I realized that she wasn't joking.

She didn't say another word and I took that as my cue to get started. The contracts were thorough and precise, so much so that I wondered if she had drafted some of them herself last night.

It was another hour before the rest of her team entered the station. Handsome Jason Dalton looked at me curiously while a scowling Bonnie Fischer rolled her eyes. The plump Oliver Griffin was too busy to even notice I was there, and the older gentleman (was his name Harry or Harold?) simply ignored my presence altogether.

Only Matilda seemed pleased. "Oh! You're here!" she cried happily, bouncing on the balls of her feet.

"I am," I smiled, appreciating the positive feedback from at least one of the agents.

"And that would be because . . .?" Jason Dalton started, loudly enough for everyone in the room to hear. He looked to Hunt for an explanation.

Without taking her eyes away from her work, Hunt dryly explained the agreement. When she finished, the members of her team seemed to accept my presence without question. I was surprised that they didn't object, but I supposed that if their boss, who was as rigid as anyone, was allowing it, who were they to say otherwise?

It wasn't long before Matilda and Dalton were sitting on either side of me.

"So," Dalton started, leaning back in his chair as he regarded me. His eyes twinkled with curiosity. "How exactly did you swing this?"

"What are you talking about?" I asked. He shot a glance at his boss, who was talking quietly with Bonnie Fischer.

"She's hated your guts from day one," Dalton pointed out, tousling his thick hair until it was both messy and stylish.

"She's just cautious around journalists," Matilda rushed to whisper.

"For good reason," Dalton said. "Which makes me wonder how you convinced her to let you in."

"I just talked to her," I said, shrugging.

"Let's just hope you can handle it," Dalton said.

"Be nice," Matilda scolded him. "She needs encouragement!"

"Encouragement, huh?" Dalton said with a cheeky smile. "Well, that can be arranged." Matilda threw a pen at him, and he ducked.

"Don't make her uncomfortable. She might think you're being serious!" Matilda yelped.

"Get your mind out of the gutter. I was talking about moral support," Dalton laughed, shooting me a wink. "Besides, I'm taken."

"It amazes me that you've never been reported," a voice came from behind him as Bonnie Fischer joined us.

Dalton chuckled. "That's because I know not to cross the line."

"I would beg to differ," Bonnie muttered.

"Oh, please. You're the one that starts it. You try to drag me across the line," Dalton complained. Bonnie balked.

Matilda leaned over as the two bickered. "Don't mind them. They always do this," she whispered kindly to me, before motioning to Hunt. "And between you and me, I'm glad she let you stay."

"I just don't want to mess it up," I found myself admitting to her. I blushed, worried about disclosing that much.

She just smiled. "You won't mess up if you don't want to," she said with a dreamy tone. For whatever reason, I couldn't help but believe her.

After another hour or so, I decided to risk venturing out of the FBI cave to refill my coffee mug. It was a daunting task, considering I needed to walk through the rest of the station and past everyone there.

I took a deep breath and inched out of the room. Within an instant, every cop had their eyes on me. I smiled, trying to pretend like everything was completely normal. So what if I just came out of the FBI's lair? Jay offered a tentative wave as I walked by, while Phil appeared to have swallowed something incredibly sour.

I got to the break room unscathed, relieved to find it empty. I grabbed the coffee pot, daring to hope that maybe I had avoided confrontation altogether . . . until I saw Andrew stalking toward me.

Fuck.

"What are you doing?" Andrew asked, grabbing my arm, and pulling me out of earshot of the other cops. Coffee sloshed over one side of my cup.

"What do you mean?" I asked innocently.

"What are you doing with them?" Andrew asked, accusation saturating his voice.

"Helping," I offered. It sounded like a question and I cleared my throat.

Andrew shook his head, as if he couldn't, or wouldn't, understand. "Why?" he asked.

"Because the more help they get, the faster this is over," I said.

"*We* can get this guy," Andrew hissed back.

"But you haven't," I said before I could stop myself. Andrew looked at me like I had physically slapped him. Guilt began to fester inside of my chest, and suddenly I was grateful that the rest of the station couldn't hear us.

I rushed to fix it. "I just think everyone should work together."

Andrew wrinkled his nose. "You don't know anything about this," he growled.

"You're right. I don't," I admitted. "So, why aren't you the one working to bridge the gap between them and the rest of the town?"

"No one should be doing it at all!" Andrew said, irritated.

"Someone has to," I countered. "And it seems like everyone here is just too proud to do it themselves. Or they feel some odd sense of loyalty—"

"That's what loyalty is," Andrew cut me off roughly. "Sticking with *your* team."

"There aren't any teams here," I insisted. Why couldn't he see the big picture? Were they too close to it? Too immersed in the town to have any real perspective?

"There are always teams," he argued.

"There should only be one, then. Us. All of us. Against whoever it is that is doing this."

"There is no 'us,' Andrew growled, putting his face closer to mine. "You aren't part of any of this. You're only here because I let you in."

I opened my mouth to argue but realized I couldn't. He wasn't wrong.

"And I appreciate that," I said instead. "But I'm not going to let you hold it over me."

"You said you didn't want to get in the way," Andrew pointed out. "If you're with them, you're officially in the way."

I faltered at the coldness in his tone and expression. It felt wrong. I hardened my stance.

"Then, I'll officially be out of *your* way," I shot back. "But the feds don't seem to think I'm in *their* way at all."

Andrew's eyes widened. He opened his mouth, but I didn't wait. Turning on my heels, I grabbed my cup and hurried into the back room again. I only spilled a quarter of my coffee in the process, which I took as a win.

Rattled, I tried to focus on completing the documents as quickly as possible, but I was distracted by the conversation in the room.

"So, we're assuming it's a *he*," Bonnie clarified, typing away into her keyboard.

"Eighty-five percent of serial killers are male," Harold Hopper said. "And the way the victims are being hunted, I believe it's safe to assume that it's a man."

"There's no sexual component," Bonnie went on. "I'm looking at the coroner reports that were emailed to us, and none of the victims had signs of sexual assault."

"But he's using a knife," Dalton noted. "Yeah, it's quieter than a gun, but it's also more intimate. Maybe that's how he's getting off." He paused. "Ballsy too, considering he's getting right up behind them."

"How do you know he's doing it from behind?" Bonnie asked.

"Look at the cuts," Dalton said, picking up a picture of Jamie Kane's neck and wheeling his chair behind her. "Where they start and end are the deepest part." Dalton brought his arm in front of her throat and pretended to bring it around. "From this angle, it would be the way my arm naturally wants to move." He pushed his chair back around, facing Bonnie from the other side of the desk.

"As opposed to head-on," he went on, pretending to lash out. "It would be more straight across. Or the middle of the neck would be the deepest part."

"So, he sneaks up behind them," Harold Hopper said with a nod. "He must be fit if he has to move that fast before they can turn around. Over the beach too."

"And quiet," Dalton agreed. "Wouldn't someone hear him tromping in the sand otherwise?"

"Not necessarily," Matilda piped up. "The waves might drown out his footsteps."

"But he'd have to think that," Dalton said slowly. "I grew up in the city and I wouldn't have thought the waves could be that loud. Hell, Lovell's Landing only had them in that one spot, which means he'd have to be familiar with that beach. Otherwise, he wouldn't count on that."

"Do we think he's done this before?" Bonnie asked.

"The first murder looks too inexperienced for him to have done it before."

"But he's learning fast," Harold Hopper said, rubbing a hand over his well-trimmed beard. "Between the first and second kill, he seems to have perfected his technique."

"He's getting bolder too," Dalton noted, twirling a pen. "He killed Molly Edgars in the middle of the night. Little chance of being spotted. But there was sunlight this time. Much higher risk."

"Every murder has been on the beach. Why?" Matilda asked, her voice still dreamy as she looked out the window. "There isn't any cover to hide if someone comes along."

"Maybe that's part of the thrill?" Dalton suggested. "How he gets his high?"

"Or maybe because he can see if a target is alone," Harold said.

My eyes darted to each of them, watching as Bonnie pulled herself out of the conversation to type away on a laptop. Oliver was busy scribbling in an overflowing notebook.

Hunt just stared at the pictures of the crime scenes.

Until . . .

"The water washed everything away," she muttered, making the room fall silent. "He killed Molly when she was well below the high-tide mark. The rising tide covered most of her. Check the tides when the other murders happened."

Bonnie quickly typed, her face scrunched. "It was a rising tide every time."

Hunt nodded to herself. "He's coordinating the murders with the tide so that the water will wash over everything. He's covering his ass if he leaves a print or DNA behind. It's intentional."

"That makes sense," Dalton said. "So, he must have some knowledge of the ocean too. Otherwise, he wouldn't have thought to even take that into consideration."

"He must have studied up before coming to Cape August," Bonnie noted from behind her screen. "The tides are a little weird here with the currents and everything."

"He could be local," Hunt said. "It would explain why he feels so comfortable using the beaches as his hunting ground in addition to his knowledge of tides."

I shivered involuntarily at the thought of that. Somehow the idea of someone like this living here made it that much worse.

"He might summer here," Harold suggested. "A lot of the tourists come back annually. He might be one of them."

"Bonnie, check to see if this has happened anywhere else," Hunt directed. "Maybe a failed attempt. Check along the coast of New England first but expand it if you come up short."

"What triggered him to kill Molly Edgars in the first place?" Dalton asked.

"And why Molly?" Harold added.

"The victimology seems random," Matilda added. "He's killing young men and women, but there's no specific demographic."

"They're around the same age," Dalton noted.

"Still," Matilda said. "Usually there's more of a specific target. Why these kids over others?"

"Because they were there," Hunt said, pursing her lips. "An opportunity presented itself, and the killer took it. He kills to kill. Who it is might not matter."

A sober silence filled the room, and I looked at the worried faces of each agent. Dalton shook his head. Harold ran a hand over his face again. Even Matilda looked tense. I felt like I had missed something. Some hidden meaning behind those words.

Only Hunt remained unphased. Her face was calm. Emotionless. Even as she said, "Which means we can't predict who he might target next."

18

A shadow of a person eased over the sand, a tune dancing in their head. Their dark eyes roamed across the black beach, before sweeping over the ocean. The light of the moon flirted with the water's surface, kissing the inky tension. The shadow began to sing.

Farewell and adieu, to you fair Spanish ladies,

The voice was rough, but not unpleasant. It drifted into the air, seeping into the sound of the crashing waves. As if the voice wasn't entirely human at all, but something else entirely.

Farewell and adieu, to you ladies of Spain;

The fingers of foam reached for the shadow's feet, shimmering. Without even looking at the stretching wave, the figure stepped just out of reach as if so in sync with the rhythm of the tide that it heard the whispers of the wet sand between their toes.

For we received orders for to sail back to Boston,

Reaching into their pocket, the shadow brought out a blade. Designed for gutting fish. Stainless steel. Old, but meticulously cared for. It reflected the moonlight just so. Gleaming. A smile pulled on the shadow's lips.

And so nevermore shall we see you again.

19

Clara knew the cross-country trip would be filled with surprises. Flat tires. Missed exits. Food poisoning from sketchy diners. But she figured those surprises were part of the novelty of it all, strengthening the bond with her two best friends before they all went to college in the fall.

The one surprise she hadn't expected was that those same best friends would hook up on day three of the trip . . .

It made sense. The sexual tension had been festering between Siena and Theo ever since the homecoming dance two years ago. Clara had just hoped that it would come to fruition toward the end of their month-long excursion.

Now, she was officially third-wheeling.

She sighed, digging her fingers into the cool sand. She wondered when it would be safe to walk back to their makeshift camp on the beach. The last time Siena and Theo smoked pot, they had gone at it for at least an hour.

Clara figured she had another thirty minutes to go.

A brisk wind made goosebumps crawl across her skin. She wondered if they had at least remembered to keep the fire going. But she wasn't going to get her hopes up. She pulled her knees to her chest. She could tough it out.

Shhhzzt.

A crunch of sand and dry dune grass came from behind her. It made the hair on the back of her neck stand up. She turned but saw nothing in the dense blackness. A shiver went up her spine. It was probably just the wind.

Shhhzzt.

It was louder this time. Closer. It made Clara inch away, fear twisting in her stomach. She swallowed, her mouth suddenly dry.

"H-hello?" she called. Nothing but the swaying grass answered. She shook her head. She was being silly. This beach was completely deserted, and it was too late for anyone to actively—

Shhhzzt.

Louder. Closer.

Clara made a move to get up but stumbled. Her heart beat frantically as she looked around. But she couldn't see anything.

Nothing at all.

Until something leaped out of the darkness. Clara's scream tore through the air, making the grass shudder.

Laughter cut through it.

"Christ, Siena," Clara gasped, hand to her chest.

"What?" Siena chuckled, plopping down to sit next to her. "I didn't mean to scare you. Jeez."

"It's creepy out here," Clara said defensively, rubbing her hands over her arms to comfort herself.

"No shit," Siena said, taking out a joint. "That's why I came looking for you. Wanted to make sure the Boogie Man didn't get you. You're welcome." She chuckled, lighting the joint and offering it to Clara who wrinkled her nose.

"No thanks."

"Suit yourself," Siena shrugged, taking a hit. She watched the smoke ease into the darkness beyond. "Why'd you leave?"

"Maybe because you and Theo were hooking up again," Clara mumbled.

Siena shrugged again. "That doesn't mean you need to leave."

"It does if I don't want to hear it."

"Hey. You're always welcome to join," Siena teased, nudging her friend's shoulder.

Clara laughed. "I have a feeling Theo would beg to differ."

"Oh, please. It's every man's dream," Siena said. "Besides, you're my A-number-one after all."

Clara began to fiddle with a piece of dune grass.

"Until you move eight hours away," Clara mumbled.

"Hey," Siena said, leaning against her. "You know I'll come back to visit."

"Sure."

"I mean it," Siena said. "Whether you want me to or not. You're going to see me so much, you'll be begging me to leave."

Clara chuckled. "That would be a good problem to have."

"You say that now," Siena drawled. "Just you wait."

"In the meantime, I'm going to pee before Theo comes looking for us," Clara said.

"You do that," Siena hummed, getting up and stretching. "I'm going to dip my toes in the water."

While Siena twirled her way toward the ocean, Clara found a nice piece of dune and squatted. The wind had picked up, whipping her hair around her shoulders. But the sudden chill she felt had nothing to do with the breeze.

Clara pulled up her pants.

"Siena?" She peered into the night, squinting. "Theo?"

No one responded, and yet she couldn't shake the feeling. Like someone was there. Just beyond the sandy hill.

"Siena," Clara said again, her voice beginning to shake. She took a careful step forward, feeling drawn toward the sound of the crashing waves.

A harsher gust of wind brought the smell of salt and iron.

Another step.

Until a scream broke the cycle, shattering the rhythm of the night.

20

ELLE

Benjie sprinted through the doors of the station. "Another body was just found."

"Where?" Hunt demanded.

"At the edge of town. A small beach locals call Bigger Boat Bay. Secluded."

"Witnesses?"

"Two friends called it in, but I don't know if they saw anything. Ramos was patrolling close to there. He's bringing them into the station now."

"Has the body been tampered with?"

"No, we were just about to—"

"Don't do anything," Hunt said quickly, looking back at her team. "Hopper, Goodwin, and Dalton. I want you three to go to the scene. Look at the body and see if you can find anything while it's still fresh. Griffin, Fischer, and I will stay here to question the friends and contact the family."

I ducked my head when her eyes passed over me but to my relief, she didn't say anything.

I kept a low profile until the two witnesses were brought in. Peering around the door, I saw Andrew lead them through the station. We made eye contact, but he quickly looked away.

The two kids behind him must have been no older than eighteen. The boy was short, with floppy hair and an angular face. The girl was curvy with long, windswept hair. Her full face was tear-stained and she was trembling.

Hunt walked toward them.

"Theo Brown and Clara Sánchez," Andrew said stiffly, nodding at the two. "They're the ones that found her."

The boy continued to study the ground, while the girl trembled harder.

"I'm Agent Roslyn Hunt," she said gently. "My colleague, Agent Griffin, and I are just going to ask you a couple of questions."

Oliver led Theo away while Hunt took Clara to the main interview room. I slipped inside the adjacent door to watch from behind the one-way glass. I saw Andrew follow me in, but we didn't speak.

"Can I get you anything? Water? Coffee?" Hunt asked the girl, offering her a chair. Clara shook her head, mute.

"I can't imagine what you're going through," Hunt said, her voice low and oddly comforting.

"S-she was just lying there," Clara stuttered. "J-just lying right in front of me." She looked up at Hunt through wide eyes. "We were going to college in the fall. Siena was going to study marine biology. She l-loved whales." Clara stopped, overwhelmed with a sob that shook her entire body.

Hunt pursed her lips ever so slightly at the display. "I'm very sorry for your loss," she said, her tone a little stiff. "But the best thing you can do right now is to try and remember every little detail. Did you hear anything? See anyone else on the beach?"

It took a long moment before Clara regained control over herself.

"It was really dark," she sniffed, shaking her head. "I could barely see . . . B-but . . ." she trailed off as tears streamed down her face.

"But?" Hunt asked, leaning forward.

"I swear it felt like someone was watching," Clara whispered. "And I thought I heard something. Right next to me for a second. I was scared so I went looking for Siena. I walked over the dune . . . A-and then she was lyin' there—" Clara gasped, burying her face in her hands.

"Clara," Hunt said. "I need you to focus. Look at me. Before you saw her, did you see *anything* else?"

Clara sniffed hard, forcing her trembling hands away. "I don't know..."

"I need you to think," Hunt said, her voice a little too forceful to be considered reassuring anymore.

Clara took a breath, her eyes fluttering shut as she thought.

They flew open. "There was a shadow," she almost screamed, fear pushing every other emotion from her face. "Moving away. F-fast."

"Can you describe it?" Hunt pressed.

"Tall-ish. Kinda skinny." Clara's eyes almost bulged out of her head. "That was him ... Wasn't it? That was the guy that killed Siena?"

"It's hard to say," Hunt answered judiciously, but the way a muscle in her jaw tightened, I knew there was no doubt in her mind.

Finally, we had our first witness.

21

ELLE

"Repeat it back to me," Hunt said. "From the beginning."

"First victim. Molly Edgars," Dalton started, flipping through the file. "Sophomore in high school. She and Nelson moved here when she was two from Portland, Maine. She was always quiet. Good grades. Not many friends."

"Every fifteen-year-old needs someone to talk to," Harold noted.

"Her teacher said she was dating Miles Elliot," Dalton said. "Couple years older than her."

"What do we have on him?"

"Nothing much. Seventeen. Loner, like Molly. He's been in the system since his parents died five years ago," Bonnie started. "He barely has an online presence at all, except for some records of photography contests he's entered within the last year. Looks like he deleted any social media though."

"Has anyone talked to him?" Hunt asked.

Dalton and Harold exchanged a look.

"The police did the interview," Harold said slowly. "It was limited at best."

"And we tried to talk to him at his house yesterday," Dalton added. "They wouldn't let us inside without a warrant. I filed for one, but it could take a little while."

"Where is he now?" Hunt demanded.

"It's finals week at school," Bonnie said.

"I doubt they'll even let you into the building," Dalton said dubiously as Hunt grabbed her blazer.

"Oh, they will," Hunt said. Her eyes flashed to me. "I'll bring her."

I froze. "Me?" I asked, my voice rising an octave.

"This is what you signed up for," she said. "Do you know the teachers there?"

"Some of them," I admitted, anxiety tickling the back of my throat. "But—"

"Then, it's time to test your theory," Hunt said. "Let's see if your local blood helps at all."

Within minutes, we were stuck in the car together. Hunt was painfully silent for the entire ride. I searched for topics, finding myself babbling on and on without any reciprocation. Even when I asked her a pointed question, she seemed perfectly content to barely acknowledge my existence.

At least she had me drive, which was helping to distract me.

Cape August High School was small. Only about a hundred kids per grade. It was inland, or as inland as you can get here. Only a mile from the beach, pitch pines, and red oak trees scattered the open campus, and wafts of salty air rustled the needles and leaves. I almost smiled as I remembered all of the times I'd skipped last period to lay on the sand with Andrew.

I recognized the receptionist the moment we walked into the school's office. Her face still looked like she was permanently sucking on something sour, her hair was just as white in its tight bun, and her long acrylic nails were even the same shade of red.

"Ms. Spinner," I said as her beady eyes locked on me. "So nice to see you."

Her tongue poked inside her cheek as she tried to place me.

"Elle Wolfe," I went on, trying to jog her memory. "I used to—"

"Bright-blue converse, knee-high socks, and a poorly done French braid." She nodded. "Always late on Thursdays."

I chuckled. "I'm impressed."

"I remember the nice ones. *You*, I can't place," she said bluntly, eyeing Hunt.

Hunt flashed her badge. "Agent Hunt with the FBI. I'm here to talk to Miles Elliot. Can you tell me where we can find him?"

Ms. Spinner tightly pursed her lip. "Well, hello to you too."

A muscle in Hunt's face twitched. "Good morning . . ."

"You expect me to let you into my school with *that*," Spinner said, eying the gun peeking from behind Hunt's blazer. "Or *that* . . ." The old woman wrinkled her nose at the dog by Hunt's feet.

"I assure you, both are in good hands," Hunt said smoothly.

"Mmm." Spinner looked unconvinced. She gazed back at me as she circled Hunt and the dog with one long, crooked finger. "Are you with all of this . . ."

I nodded. "Yes ma'am."

Spinner clicked her red nails on her desk. "Fine," she said, talking only to me. "Wait here. I'll call him down."

It wasn't long before we were standing face to face with the boy. He was tall for his age but hunched shyly. His hair was dark and thick, his deep-brown eyes shining from under it. When he saw Hunt, he lost the little color he had in his already fair complexion. She led him down the hall, but I still heard most of what was said.

"Miles Elliot," Hunt said. "I'm with the FBI. I wanted to ask you a couple of questions about Molly Edgars."

"Why?" the boy asked, ducking his head. "I don't know anything."

"How long were you two dating?" Hunt asked anyway.

Miles shrugged, avoiding her gaze. "I dunno."

"When was the last time you saw her?"

"That morning, I guess," Miles said, his voice low and timid. "We're on the same bus."

"But not that afternoon?"

"No," he said, yanking at the collar of his oversized sweatshirt. "I stayed late." He studied the floor.

Hunt pursed her lips. "Why?"

The boy shrugged. "I dunno."

"You don't know?"

"I forget."

Hunt's eyes narrowed. "Can I see your cell phone?"

"I don't have one."

"What teenager doesn't have a phone?" Hunt asked.

Miles shook his head. "Can't afford one."

"What about a computer?"

"I use the ones at school."

Hunt raised her eyebrows. "What about your camera? Can I see that?"

The boy looked up at her quickly. "What?"

"You do have one, don't you? You entered a photography contest a few months ago."

"I had one . . ." Miles admitted, yanking on his collar a little harder. "But I lost it."

"Expensive thing to lose," Hunt noted.

"Can I go back to class?" he asked, not meeting Hunt's gaze. "We have finals, so . . ."

Hunt paused, but then nodded once. "All right. Thank you for your time."

The boy hurried away, and she watched him.

"Now what?" I asked. Hunt didn't look away. I waited, shifting my weight back and forth between my feet.

But as she turned for the door, she never said a word.

22

ROSLYN

Elle Wolfe never shut up. Not for a second the entire way to the school, or on the walk back to the car. I lengthened my stride, hoping that physical distance might dissuade the constant chatter, but she just hurried after me, as if worried I would leave without her. She tripped, her shoes too wide for her narrow feet. The flats couldn't have belonged to her, judging by the wear lines. She was much more of an overpronator than whoever had eroded the heels.

Barely catching herself before she fell forward, Wolfe cast a nervous look in my direction to see if I'd noticed. Her relieved smile told me that she thought I hadn't. From the corner of my eye, I caught a hint of a dimple in her cheek, along with the mark of what might have held a nose ring once upon a time. Probably a 'heat-of-the-moment' decision based on how easily it had healed. It looked more like a freckle than anything else.

I walked faster, almost forcing her into a jog.

"Thank you again for letting me come," Wolfe babbled, fumbling with her car keys. Her fingernails bore bits of pale-blue nail polish in the corners, likely having been removed in a rush.

"I really think that this might be really helpful, you know? For both of us. Joining forces, I mean," she went on. She talked fast as if the more words she could cram in would better fill the silence. "I hope I was helpful back there. Ms. Spinner can be a toughie. Funny story about her actually—"

I barely suppressed a groan as I got into the car.

23

ELLE

I swallowed hard, looking at Hunt dubiously later that afternoon.

"You should get it over with," Dalton whispered to me with a grin. "Rip off the Band-Aid."

I continued to stare at Hunt as if she could somehow bite me from across the room. Steeling my nerves, I inched toward her.

"Sorry to bother you," I began, "but have you had the chance to approve my article yet? I wouldn't ask, but my boss is—"

She cut me off by pulling out a folder and presenting it to me without looking up.

"Thank you," I said, relieved. I took the folder and flipped it open. My eyes were overwhelmed by all the red ink. Hunt had crossed out at least ninety-five percent of the article.

"I...You...What is this?" I stuttered.

"Alterations," she said. "Before it will be up to my standards."

"Your standards are impossible!" I yelped.

Hunt shrugged. "You asked for my opinion."

"Hardly," I shot back. "You demanded to shove your opinion down my throat."

"Only if you want it published."

"What's even wrong with it?" I demanded, thrusting the paper back at her. She ignored it.

"I marked the problem areas," she said. "I left you some notes for the second try."

"There aren't any notes," I growled, shoving the pages in front of her face so she could see the evidence. "You just crossed out everything!"

Hunt sighed, glancing at the first page. She pointed. "There. A comment."

"That just says '*NO*,'" I growled.

"I hope you know what that word means," she said casually.

With a huff, I snatched the papers away before she could say anything else. I couldn't believe her, and yet I wasn't sure why I was even surprised.

I tried again, printing out an entirely new version within the hour. It took her all of thirty seconds to tear it to pieces.

And the cycle continued.

My fingers ached by the time Hunt and I had come to some sort of middle ground, which essentially meant I had to make all of the compromises. The finished article was vague at best, but it was better than nothing. Sighing, I attached it to an email to Tony.

"We need to talk to the cops and give them a profile," Hunt muttered to Dalton.

"Are we ready?" Dalton asked with a grimace.

"No," Hunt sighed. "But we don't have a choice."

It wasn't long before she stood in front of a room of disgruntled Cape August officers.

"The man we're looking for is likely white and in his late thirties or forties," Hunt said. "He's tall but wouldn't stand out. Probably a little under six feet. Fit, but not overly muscular. He's organized. Calculated. Neat. When he kills, he doesn't have a specific type. There's no sign of sexual abuse with any of his victims. This tells us that his primary motivation is the kill itself. Every one of these murders has happened on the beach at dead low tide. We believe that this is intentional so that the rising tide can wash away whatever he might leave behind. It is our recommendation that you close the beaches—"

"We can't do that," Phil piped up.

Hunt's mouth tightened. "At least at low tide. This could help disrupt his cycle, making him easier to catch. We're also going to issue a public statement first thing tomorrow morning."

The room erupted into questions and complaints.

"Quiet!" Ramos demanded, taking Hunt's spot at the front of the room "We're going to double the watch near the beaches. No one is allowed on the beaches after closing . . ."

As he continued to list the new protocols, I heard a low whine. I looked to see Hunt's black dog moving anxiously at her feet. It wasn't loud enough for anyone else to hear. Hunt shot the dog a quick glance, her expression hard. With a silent hand signal, she and the canine dissolved into the wall of uniforms. I tried to see where she was going, but it was as if she had melted into the woodwork. There was something about Hunt's expression that was unnerving. A sudden dread underneath her forced calm.

No one else seemed to notice her absence.

It felt like an eternity before Hunt returned. Ramos was fielding the many questions from the group as she drifted, ghost-like, back into existence. She stayed at the edge of the group, clearly trying to keep her distance. There was something off about her. She still seemed perfectly poised. Focused. But there was a slight strain that hadn't been there before. A weariness. It was just as subtle as the change before, barely detectable under her polished presentation.

My eyes must have lingered a moment too long. In an instant, Hunt's gaze snapped to me. I looked away, a blush warming my cheeks. When the meeting ended, I turned to where she had been, but all I saw was an empty wall.

It was another hour before she swept back into view. She was talking to someone on the phone, pinching the bridge of her nose in frustration.

"Is she okay?" I asked, leaning over to Oliver before eyeing Hunt from across the room. The man turned to follow my gaze, before nervously adjusting his glasses. "Of course," he said, a little too quickly. "Why wouldn't she be?"

"She left during the meeting," I started, watching Oliver's expression. He gave a noncommittal shrug, opening his notebook to become engrossed in the first random page he'd flipped to.

"Oliver . . ." I started.

"She's fine," the man said, almost curt. He winced, his expression softening. "Just. . . please leave it alone, Elle. Seriously." Oliver began flipping through the pages of his loopy handwriting, but I had a feeling it was just a way to end the conversation.

The rest of the day, I found my mind wandering back to that look on Hunt's face. As if I could maybe decipher what it meant.

I sighed. I would probably never find out.

24

ROSLYN

Right after giving the press briefing the next morning, I had an officer drop me off in town. The bookstore was right on the corner, shorter than the buildings that huddled around it. Inside, every inch of space was utilized with row upon row of books, from the maple floor to the top of the oak ceiling.

"Mr. Edgars," I said, walking up to the man behind the register. "Beautiful store."

Nelson Edgars offered me a tired smile. "It's not much, but it's mine," he chuckled, cleaning his square glasses with the corner of his shirt. "What can I do for you?"

I walked around, examining the expansive shelves. I glanced at some of the covers. Most of the books near the front of the store were classics.

"I wanted to ask about your daughter's boyfriend, Miles," I said, looking over at Nelson Edgars. "How well do you know him?"

"I would say pretty well, considering he was practically living at my house," Nelson said, beginning to smile before faltering. "Obviously, not anymore . . ."

"He was over that much?" I pressed.

"Ever since April." Edgars opened a box of books from behind the counter. "He moved into a new foster house and felt pretty lost. I think he found some stability at our house."

"So, he and Molly were serious?"

"Very. They've been inseparable for over a year and a half."

I nodded, my eyes wandering to the book in the man's hand as he began to shelve them. I raised my eyebrow. "*Jaws*?" I asked.

Nelson shrugged, his face painfully weary. "It's been requested over a dozen times," he said. He closed his eyes. "I decided it would be easier to just have them stocked so people stop asking."

"Sorry," I muttered.

"Not your fault," he said, rubbing his face behind his glasses. "The media figured out a long time ago that fear sells."

The front door opened with a bang that made me turn. A furious Mayor Sully was stalking through the store.

"Tell me you didn't hold a press conference today saying a serial killer is hunting on our beaches," Sully seethed, practically lunging for me.

"The public deserves to understand the risk," I said.

"Are you trying to ruin our lives?" the young man shrieked. Edgars coughed behind me. "Do you know how much damage control I'm going to have to do now?"

"Mayor Sully—"

"No. Do not interrupt me," he growled, pointing a finger in my face. A muscle in my jaw tightened. "From now on, you will run everything you want to give to the press by me first."

"I don't think you understand how this works," I said as politely as I could through clenched teeth.

"No. *You* don't understand how this works," he hissed, getting his face dangerously close to mine. I could smell the mousse in his hair. It was surprisingly cheap. Off-brand. "Do you know who my father is? Senator Ryan Sully. Ring any bells?"

"Is he at all relevant to this conversation?" I asked idly.

"I would think so," Sully said. "Considering he's on the committee that approves the budget for the FBI."

I bit the inside of my cheek to keep from snarling. *You spineless little weasel.*

"I would think your superior would find it highly concerning if I were to make a call to Senator Ryan Sully," he went on. "Maybe to cut the FBI budget by, say, a couple million?"

"You and I both know your father doesn't have that kind of power," I said.

"Are you sure?" Sully asked with a twisted smile. "Rather, how sure are you?"

"You're getting dangerously close to crossing the line," I said.

"That's politics, sweetheart," Sully said. He spun on his heels and slammed the bookstore door behind him. My fingers curled into tight fists, trembling in an effort to keep them from breaking something.

I saw movement from the corner of my eye.

"Here," Edgars said kindly, holding out a Band-Aid to me. I raised my eyebrows.

"You're bleeding," he said to my confused stare. His eyes slid down to one of my hands.

"Shit," I muttered, looking at where my nails had pierced the flesh of my palm.

"It happens," Edgars said with a calming smile, holding up the Band-Aid a little higher. I sighed, taking it.

"Thank you," I murmured.

"Anytime," he said, before chuckling. "You have a firm grip there."

"Only in the presence of . . . trying individuals." My eyes glowered at the door Mr. Sully had just left through.

Edgars nodded. "He tends to have that effect on people. It's a wonder this entire town hasn't gone mad."

"How was he elected in the first place?"

Edgars shrugged. "Connections. He knows the right people." He leaned over to tap the poster underneath the register for Sunny's Hotel and Spa. "Randall Niffler would be one of them. Owns most of the businesses in town. Whoever he backs in the town elections is who wins."

"Sounds like a powerful man," I said.

Edgars nodded. "A powerful man who wants the beaches to stay open," he muttered. "He can't make a profit from his hotels and restaurants if there aren't any tourists."

"I see . . ." I breathed. Nelson Edgars' face tightened when his cell phone buzzed on the counter. I glanced at it, reading the name.

"My brother," Nelson said before I had to ask.

"I thought you two didn't speak," I started, raising an eyebrow.

He sighed, his glasses slipping down his long nose. "Well, considering he's staying in my house, I suppose we don't have much of a choice these days."

I pursed my lips. "He came after all . . ."

Nelson nodded. "The last time I saw Peter, he was coming up with the name for this place. Bruce's Books was his idea." The man shook his head, putting *Jaws* onto the shelf behind him. "Who would have thought it would one day be so relevant."

25

ELLE

"She sounds like quite the character," Eric chuckled in my ear as I lounged on the thick carpet of my bedroom floor. I had to carve out a spot in between the large stacks of criminology books I had borrowed from the library, dead pens, and bits of scrap paper.

"That's putting it nicely," I huffed. "The woman's a nightmare."

"Maybe she'll loosen up after she gets to know you," Eric suggested.

"You said she's young, right?"

"Twenty-nine or something," I muttered.

"She's your peer then," Eric pointed out. "Only a few years older than you."

I scoffed. "*Roslyn Hunt* definitely doesn't see it that way."

"Because she's the boss," Eric reasoned. "I bet that's a lot of pressure."

"And because she's a raging bitc—"

"Easy," Eric laughed, his voice rumbling steadily in the speaker. I took a deep breath, trying to cool the angry flush that had taken over my face. I threw myself down on my back, wishing I could sink through the carpet.

"Not to mention that she totally hates me," I mumbled, more to myself than to Eric. I had never been *hated* before. I wasn't sure why it bothered me so much.

Except that it did.

"That can't be possible," Eric said. "You're the most positive person I know. It would be like hating sunshine."

"I bet she does."

"Just be patient," Eric assured me.

"That's not exactly my strong suit," I pointed out.

He hesitated, realizing he couldn't argue with that. "You've got plenty to keep yourself occupied," he said instead, before clearing his throat. "Speaking of . . . How's Andrew?"

"Oh. You know. Fine. He's . . . fine . . ." I said, shifting on the carpet. Suddenly I couldn't quite get comfortable.

"Good," Eric said, his voice sounding tighter than usual. "That's good."

"Yup."

26

ELLE

The next morning, I was determined to ease the tension between Hunt and myself. So, I did the only thing I could think of; I brought a box of the biggest, sugariest muffins into the station. Summoning my courage, I walked over to her.

"Muffin?" I asked sweetly.

Hunt barely spared the greasy box a glance. "Nothing about any of those resembles a muffin," she muttered, turning her nose up at them.

Sighing, I retreated back to my desk.

"Who hates dirt bombs?" I grumbled, taking a gigantic bite out of one.

Dalton chuckled next to me. "Bribery doesn't work on her."

"I was just trying to be nice," I huffed between mouthfuls of crumbs.

"Next time, go for something without a pound of powdered sugar," Dalton suggested.

"So, something without fun or happiness?" I clarified.

He laughed. "Something like that."

I looked back at Hunt. "Is she always this . . ." I paused, looking for the right word. A few came to mind: *Standoffish. Callous. Scary. Ruthless. Cold-blooded. Robotic. Mean. Heartless.*

"Intense?" Dalton offered.

I nodded. *Sure. Let's go with 'intense.'*

"She's always been like this," Dalton said. "For as long as I've known her at least. Come to think of it, she used to be worse."

I looked at him incredulously. "How is that possible?"

He chuckled. "Oh, you haven't seen anything yet. When she's pissed, it's downright terrifying."

"She seems permanently pissed."

"That's why it's that much scarier if she's *actually* mad," Dalton said.

"Why?" I asked sourly, shooting a glare in her direction.

Dalton only laughed. "Why don't ya go ahead and ask?"

I felt my heart start to race at the very thought of how that exchange would go. *Hey Agent Hunt, quick question, but why do you always act like you have a stick up your ass?*

"So, you don't know much about her either?" I asked the man next to me instead.

Dalton snorted. "She's not exactly a talker."

"Well, she's clearly got some kind of baggage," I muttered.

He shrugged. "Who knows?"

I watched Hunt. Her stone-like expression didn't even seem human. "I just don't understand her."

"Join the club," Dalton laughed. "I didn't know her first name for the first six months of working with her."

I shot him a quick look to see if he was serious. "No way."

Dalton nodded. "She's like a vault. Information goes in, but nothing comes out. It took forever to get her to even go out for drinks with us, but I finally won that battle."

I shook my head, growing more confused by the second.

Dalton leaned close to me, his voice low. "But seriously. Underneath all that, she's a phenomenal person. I know she's hard on you, but that's just how she is." He nudged my arm. "She'll warm up if you play your cards right."

"Okay. So, what do I do?" I asked him. "What's the trick?"

He smiled. "You can start with not wasting her time."

27

ELLE

"There wasn't any sign of Miles' camera at his foster house," Dalton reported as he walked through the room. Finally getting the warrant, he had been there most of the day searching through the place. "His new foster parents said they never saw one."

"There's, like, no cyber trail of him anywhere either," Bonnie said from behind her computer. "I can't retrieve anything."

"Sounds like he really is off the grid," Harold muttered.

"No kid is off the grid these days," Bonnie countered. "Not completely. I mean he has to be housing his pictures somewhere. Did you find anything on the family computer?"

Dalton shook his head. "Nothing."

"We need to go to his old foster house," Hunt said. "Maybe he left something there."

"His old foster parent was Rita Tumbler," Bonnie said, pulling up the file. "I've got the address. It's by the bridge to get into Cape August. Over an hour away with traffic."

"Not if you take back roads," I heard myself saying before I had thought it through. "It connects you to the main highway faster. It'll save you twenty minutes."

Hunt looked at me, her face tightening. "Fine," she said, resigned. "Let's go. You're driving."

"My car might not make it that far," I admitted. "The check engine light has been on for weeks, and this morning it started to make this—"

She held up her hand to silence me. "Just follow me."

Within minutes, I was driving the FBI's SUV. When Hunt had said we would take their car, I had assumed she would drive. For reasons that were beyond me, she had insisted I drive, leaving no room for argument. She still seemed reluctant to actually give me the keys.

We sped down the road in silence, and I couldn't stop fidgeting in my seat. In the back, Jasper had fallen asleep, his pointed ears twitching.

"Want to listen to some music?" I asked, searching desperately for something to do. I started flipping through channels, but with each one, Hunt made some snide remark about the 'quality' of the music, or rather lack thereof. While exasperating, it was hard to argue with her. I couldn't exactly say that Justin Bieber's 'Baby' was a masterpiece. Grumbling to myself, I finally hit the classical station. I saw Hunt visibly relax in her seat. She almost looked pleased.

"Do you know it?" I asked her, trying to make conversation.

She gave a small nod. "Dvorak's Symphony Number 9," she muttered, as though it were obvious.

"Oh, silly me. Of course, it is," I grumbled to myself.

Apparently, not low enough.

"It's one of the most popular symphonies of all time," she said pointedly. "Neil Armstrong took a tape of it on the Apollo 11 mission."

"Oh, duh," I said, not even bothering to hide my sarcasm. "Because everyone knows that."

Hunt sighed. "You'll recognize it if you stop talking for a second."

I opened my mouth to retort, then heard a few of the notes. "Oh!" I exclaimed. "I have heard this." A ghost of a smile swept across Hunt's features, but she didn't say anything. "I'm surprised I've only ever heard that part," I thought out loud.

"Not many people take the time to listen to symphonies in their entirety anymore."

"You listen to full symphonies?" I asked.

"Yes."

"Do you play an instrument?" I asked, eager to get in as many questions as she would allow with this new topic.

"Yes."

"Care to elaborate?" I pressed.

"Not particularly."

"Why?"

"Do you plan on interrogating me the entire time?" Hunt asked, exasperated.

"It wouldn't be an interrogation if you could have a normal conversation," I shot back.

"I can," she muttered. "I choose not to."

"I play the ukulele," I shared. "Not that you asked."

"Not that I cared," Hunt added in her dry tone.

I ignored her. For a minute.

"Why the ukulele, you ask?" I said airily.

"I didn't."

"Well, you see it all started . . ." I began a rambling and unnecessarily long story about the trials and tribulations of my adolescent musical endeavor, adding as much excruciating detail as possible. "And don't even get me started on the pros and cons of the group lessons—"

"Jesus Christ," Hunt muttered, pinching the bridge of her nose. "Don't you ever get tired of hearing your own voice?"

"Nope," I said. "I can go all day."

"Let's not test your endurance," she breathed.

Bickering proved to be the only way to ease the tension, and somewhere along the way, I could have sworn that Hunt began to enjoy it. Or at least not *hate* it.

It seemed like no time at all until we reached Mrs. Tumbler's house. Cottage might be a better word. It was small and homely looking. The grass was tall and unkempt, fighting with the weeds for control of the yard. A giant oak tree stood tall, thick limbs intertwining themselves above the little house in a mystical way.

It took a while before Rita Tumbler opened the thick wood door and longer still for her to actually get it open. After yanking it wide enough, her flushed face smiled. She was small, hunched, and weathered looking. Her pure white hair was thin and wispy, matching the white-stitched pattern on her worn blue sweater. Soon, we were sitting at an antique kitchen table with steaming cups of tea. Jasper stayed in the corner of the room, his dark eyes focused on Hunt as always.

"Cream and sugar?" Rita Tumbler asked as she hobbled into the room. Her wrinkled hands trembled under the weight of the sugar bowl and small cream pitcher.

"Thank you," I said, dumping three heaping spoonfuls of sugar into my cup.

"What can I do for you girls?" Rita asked with a smile as she plopped into a wooden chair.

"We wanted to talk to you about Miles Elliot," Hunt started.

Rita's aged face broke into a smile. "Oh, Miles. Such a sweet boy," she said. "I hated when they took him away."

"Why did they move him?" Hunt asked.

Rita sighed. "I can't drive anymore. Old eyes aren't what they used to be," she admitted. "So, I had to retire earlier than I expected. Income dropped a bit. I guess it was enough for DCF to worry though." She shook her head, taking a spoon to swirl her tea. "The poor boy. He was bounced from foster home to foster home. I wanted to be the one that stuck."

"So, you two got along well?"

"Very," Rita said. "Such an old soul, that one. I taught him everything I know about film photography. Lookie here." Rita turned her head, motioning to a wall of black-and-white photographs behind her. They were beautiful. Charismatic pictures of waves. Dark shadows casting dramatic lines in the dunes.

"Miles took those with an old camera I have. He's talented," Rita said proudly. "All developed in my darkroom downstairs. I'm just glad it was being used at all."

"You have a darkroom?" Hunt asked.

"My late husband was a photographer back in the day," Rita explained. She pointed to another wall where the pictures were older. Faded. "I hadn't been back in that room until Miles moved in. Couldn't bring myself to go in . . . Oh! That reminds me. Are you going to see him?" The old woman pushed herself to her feet and shuffled into another room as fast as her short legs could take her. "He left his new camera here the last time I saw him. Fancy digital one and everything. He seemed very distracted. I think he forgot to grab it."

"When was that?" Hunt called to the other room, her tone taking on an icier quality.

"Hmm . . ." Rita said, coming back with the camera. "I want to say maybe a month ago? Beginning of May? He was coming every week before that. Loved toying with old film and such. And he was always showing me pictures on his digital camera too. But he hasn't been here in a while now." Rita hunched slightly, her eyes suddenly glassy. She handed the camera to Hunt with shaky fingers. Hunt was quick to turn it on and look.

"There aren't any pictures on the SD card," Hunt noted.

"Really? Miles would take that thing everywhere," Rita said, confused. "Maybe he deleted some."

"Do you mind if we take this with us?" Hunt asked.

"Oh, please do! As long as you get it back to Miles," Rita said. "The Lord only knows how much it means to him. He would spend hours with Molly going out and taking pictures. Poor dears . . ."

"How would you describe his relationship with Molly?" Hunt asked.

"Two peas in a pod," Rita said. "Young love at its finest."

28

ELLE

I purposefully put on the classical station as we sped onto the highway. A new orchestra played, filling the car with sweeping cellos before a violin solo. I was just beginning to appreciate it when Jasper let out a low whine. Through the mirror, I could see that his entire demeanor had changed, his head low and his eyes anxious.

"Is he ok?" I asked Hunt.

"Yeah . . . He's fine," she replied, her expression guarded. She turned to look at the dog. "But we need to pull over."

"Does he have to go out?" I asked.

"Sort of . . ." Hunt's eyes flashed to the side of the road. She had that same tense look on her face as the other day.

"Are *you* ok?" I asked hesitantly.

"Fine," she said, but her rigid tone gave her away. "If there isn't a rest stop in the next few minutes, you'll have to pull up on the side . . ."

Wait, I thought frantically. *What?*

"Okay," I said, taking a careful look at her. She was clutching the door handle so tightly that her knuckles had turned an unsettling shade of white. We passed a sign for a rest area half a mile away.

Thank God. Careening into the empty parking lot, I lurched the SUV to a stop. Hunt's fingers trembled as she worked her buckle.

"Stay here," she told me, almost throwing herself out of the car.

Jasper jumped up to the front to get out too, staying by her side as she moved quickly toward the edge of the parking area. Ignoring what she had told me, I got out to follow. I had to jog to keep up.

In a small clearing lined with trees, Hunt stopped so suddenly that it made me freeze in my tracks too. I figured that she was about to turn around and scold me, but she didn't acknowledge my presence at all. Instead, her body was completely still. Rigid.

"Hunt?" I called out. A cold chill ran down my spine as Jasper's barks became frantic. I started toward them, faster than before. I was a couple of yards away when Hunt collapsed onto her back.

I broke into a sprint, diving onto the ground at her side. She lay unconscious, her face deathly pale and her body stiff as a board.

Oh my God.

I checked her pulse, and my body flooded with relief when I felt the rhythm underneath my fingers. But it was fast. I ran my hand over her cheek and called her name. Nothing. I bit my lip hard as panic tightened in my chest.

What do I do? I swallowed hard as my mind began to race. *Should I call 911?* I fished for my phone in my pocket. *Fuck.* It was still in the car. *Jesus Fucking Christ. Should I go get it?* But that would mean leaving her here. I looked around frantically. Was anyone else around? No.

Fuck.

It was then that I noticed Jasper. He had stopped barking, calmly positioning himself next to Hunt. She wasn't completely still anymore either. Her body was rigid, but her arms and fingers began to twitch and jerk.

Wait . . .

There was a bracelet on her left wrist. I turned over her hand, contorted myself to look at the underside of it. In clear letters was the explanation:

EPILEPTIC

I took a breath to steady myself. I'd read an article on this. As carefully as I could, I eased her onto her side. Then I ripped off my jacket and pushed it under her head.

I forced a breath through my nose, trying to stop my hands from shaking. I looked at Hunt. Her face was tense and looked almost pained as her body writhed. The movement of her limbs wasn't elaborate, especially compared to movie scenes of seizures, but each motion was still intense. Her arms hit the ground hard as she gave a violent thrash and I was sure she was going to be bruised tomorrow, but I didn't want to cause more damage by trying to restrain her either. Her breathing was uneven and labored. Her lips had lost all of their color. She looked so vulnerable, so unlike herself. I suddenly felt guilty, like I was intruding on something deeply personal. Realizing I had done everything I could almost made me feel worse. I stroked her shoulder gently, knowing that she probably couldn't even feel it.

I turned away to give her a shred of privacy.

It only lasted a minute or two, but it felt like forever. Her body finally relaxed, going limp against the ground. Her breathing evened out, bringing back some color to her cheeks. Jasper perked up, wagging his tail.

At last, Hunt's eyelids fluttered open.

"You had a seizure, but it's over now. You're ok," I murmured, unsure if she would remember what had happened.

Hunt took a shaky breath.

"All right. We . . . we sh-should . . . get going," she breathed, making moves to get up.

"Um . . . what are you doing?" I demanded. "Stop. Just stop. You need to give yourself a second." I put my hand on her shoulder to stop her, and she didn't have the energy to resist. It only proved that I was right.

She brought a shaky hand to her forehead and closed her eyes. "I'm sorry you saw that," she said.

I shook my head. "You have nothing to apologize for," I said, giving her arm a gentle squeeze. I half expected her to brush it off. She didn't.

"It must have scared you," Hunt muttered, sounding resigned. Tired. Jasper nuzzled into her side affectionately.

"It didn't scare me," I dismissed, although my voice was a little too high.

"Liar."

"Okay, fine. At first, I thought you might've dropped dead, which wouldn't have been ideal," I teased, just to break the oddness of the situation.

"Andrew Wells would've fallen deeper in love with you," Hunt said, "if you had managed to kill me off."

I gawped. "How do you—"

"I know everything."

A blush crept up my neck. "I'm not going to argue with you now. I just saw your entire life flash in front of my eyes."

Hunt scoffed, before making another move to get up. I instinctively offered my hand to help. I saw her glance at it as if to dismiss it, but she seemed to think better of it. I pulled her to her feet.

"Thanks for that," Hunt breathed, swallowing hard as she got her bearings.

"Of course," I said, hesitant to let go as she swayed. "Are you ok?"

"Yes," she muttered, but her voice was weak.

I kept hold of her arm as we started toward the car. It was slow, each step calm and calculated. Halfway, Hunt stopped, resting her hand on a tree trunk to steady herself.

"You ok?" I asked. It was hard to hide the worry from my voice. She was still so pale.

"Stop asking me that." She swallowed hard and looked like she was holding her breath. A moment later she lurched from my grasp, vomiting behind the tree.

When the moment passed, Hunt stumbled back from the tree. I didn't hesitate to grab a better hold of her arm.

"Sorry," she said.

"Stop apologizing."

It took another few minutes to inch to the car. Sliding back into the driver's seat, I realized the keys were still in the ignition . . . I decided not to mention it, hoping that it would go unnoticed.

"Were the keys left in the unlocked car the entire time?" Hunt asked. *Jesus, did she have to notice every little thing?*

"I guess," I said.

"You were the last one to leave the car," she pointed out.

"I was worried about you," I argued.

"Oh, nice. Blame the epileptic."

I froze before I could even put the car in drive, my mouth hanging agape at her.

"What?" she asked with mock innocence. She cracked open a water bottle and took a small sip.

"Nothing." The SUV lurched onto the freeway and silence fell over us. I could feel her watching me as if she wanted to say something, but it was a while before she actually did.

"Thank you . . . for before," she finally said, before adding reluctantly, "and I understand if you have . . . questions."

I shot her a quick look, convinced now that she must have hit her head when she fell.

"You're encouraging me to ask questions?" I asked, incredulous.

"*Encouraging* is a strong word," Hunt said, shifting in her seat.

I had been waiting for a moment like this, and now I had the chance to get to know the woman behind the mask. But, after thinking for a moment, I came up short.

"I actually don't think I have any," I replied.

She raised an eyebrow. "Seriously?"

"I mean, it certainly explains why you let me drive, and why you have Jasper," I started. I took a moment, before asking: "Isn't there medication for seizures though?"

A muscle in Hunt's jaw tightened. "Medication is great when it works."

"What do you mean?" I asked, confused.

"My prescription is being made generic, so there's been a pause in production," she admitted, her voice so low it was hard to hear.

"What have you been doing instead?"

"Looking for a temporary replacement," she said, pursing her lips with a strained smirk. "Clearly, it's working out wonderfully."

I smiled at the hint of humor, allowing silence to fall once again. In a weird way, it was an easy kind of silence this time. Gentle. Until a road sign told us that we were ten miles from town. From the corner of my eye, I saw Hunt stiffen.

"The rest of my team knows," she said, casting me a careful glance. "They weren't fully aware of what it could mean until recently, but they've always known."

"You don't owe me an explanation," I said, and I meant it.

"I know," she said. "I just want you to have the facts before you share the information with your friends at the station."

"What?" I asked. I must have misunderstood.

Hunt stared straight ahead. "It's a tough call, given the situation," she said. "So, I understand if you make a different decision than I have." Her expression darkened before adding: "But if I see this in your magazine—"

"I would never do that," I promised. "And I'm not going to tell anyone. You should be the only one who gets to decide who knows." A pang of guilt ran through me with my own statement. "I'm just sorry you didn't get that choice with me."

Her lips twitched as if she were deciding what to say before she said it. "It's. . . not terrible that you know . . ."

It was such a simple statement, but it meant so much more. She was trusting me at a deeper level than I thought she could. Definitely at a deeper level than either one of us had ever anticipated.

I smiled. "Want to hear the bright side?" I asked. "This makes you more human now."

She made a scoff that might have been a laugh. "Was I not before?"

"Not really, no," I admitted. "This whole thing almost puts you back on the same playing field as the rest of us. It keeps the balance."

"Ahhh," Hunt drawled. "So, my epilepsy helps keep the universe in order then?"

"Now we are finally on the same page, Agent Hunt," I said.

We shared an almost soft look. Almost human.

"Roslyn," she corrected.

"What?"

"I think we can be on a first-name basis at this point," she said, her tone still cool. Even so, I couldn't hold back the grin that burst onto my face.

"Okay, Roslyn," I beamed, savoring the casualness of the name. "But only if you call me Elle."

"We'll see."

A few minutes later, we pulled into the station parking lot.

"You sure you don't want me to just drive you back to your hotel? I can come up with something," I offered, already knowing the answer.

"No. I need to see if there was ever anything on that SD card," Roslyn said.

I kept half an eye on her as she opened up the back to let Jasper out. Her movements were a little sluggish, especially for her, but she looked stable. Walking into the station, Bonnie's voice carried all the way to the front door. In the back room, she was hunched at her desk, growling into the phone. The rest of the FBI team didn't seem to notice as she seethed.

Maybe they were used to it.

"Here's the thing, *sweetie* . . . I don't care if Uncle Joe or whoever the fuck told you not to talk to— No. Don't you dare put me on hold again! I know you don't have to help a customer! You never have any customers in your poor excuse of a bakery. Wanna know why? Because your food sucks. So, don't— Mother fucker!" she shouted, slamming the phone down.

"No luck?" Roslyn asked.

"Nada. Zilch. Nothing." Bonnie glowered at her computer screen, muttering something in Yiddish under her breath. "No one remembers seeing Felix Walker the morning he walked to that beach. Although no one will actually get on the damn phone to tell me that . . ."

"This might make you feel better." Roslyn held out the camera and blank SD.

"I fucking knew it! 'Lost' my ass!" Bonnie cried, snatching the card, and plugging it into her computer.

"Don't get too excited," Roslyn warned. "It's empty."

"We'll see about that," Bonnie said.

"Do you think you can recover anything?" Roslyn asked.

"I'll try. It might take a little while."

As Bonnie continued to type, Matilda pulled Roslyn aside. Her owl-like eyes were wide as she searched the blonde's face.

"Was it bad . . .?" Matilda asked in a hushed tone, looking carefully at me, and making sure not to give anything away. Except that I already knew.

Roslyn sighed, pinching the bridge of her nose. "I forgot you could do that."

"You have a look," Matilda answered simply. "So, on a scale of one to ten . . . ?" Concern filled Matilda's words.

"I'm fine," Roslyn said, ducking the question. "Ms. Wolfe was extremely helpful."

Matilda's big eyes snapped to me as I became the center of attention.

"So . . . she knows?"

"She does now," Roslyn said wryly.

Matilda studied my face, before deeming me worthy of the information.

"You should be resting though," Matilda scolded. "It takes a lot out of you."

Roslyn waved her off and began to walk away.

"You're at least going to go back to the hotel tonight," Matilda called after her.

"Hmm," Roslyn hummed noncommittally. She'd spent the previous eight nights in a row at the station, sleeping at her desk and using her jacket as a make-shift pillow.

Time flew by and before long the sun began to sink in the sky. After the Cape August officers had trickled out of the office, Matilda went to force Roslyn to the hotel. At first, she tried to gently coax Roslyn away from her desk. When that didn't work, she resorted to other methods which included threatening to physically throw Roslyn over her shoulder and carry her out. That would have been especially interesting to watch, considering Roslyn was much taller . . . But somehow, I knew she was serious.

Despite Matilda's elaborate threats, Roslyn continued to read through documents. I could, however, see a vein in her forehead begin to pulse with frustration.

"They balance each other out," Dalton mused, at a volume so that only I could hear. "They've known each other for a while."

"Really?" I asked.

"They went through training together," Dalton explained. "I think that's where they became close. They ended up taking different jobs in the beginning. Roslyn started working in this division first, back when Harold was the head honcho."

"Harold was the unit chief before Roslyn?"

"Yeah. For fifteen years actually. He hired Roslyn and offered her his own job shortly after," Dalton said. "When another spot on the team opened up, Roslyn recommended Matilda for it."

"Where was Matilda working first?" I asked.

Dalton's demeanor became more serious. "The Witness Protection Program."

"*Matilda* worked for the Witness Protection Program?" I whipped my head around so fast I almost made myself dizzy. It was difficult to imagine Matilda keeping a low profile. One look at Dalton's face told me that he wasn't joking.

"She rose to the occasion," Dalton said with a tight smile. "She was good at it too from what I hear, which makes sense. She connects with people, sees the best in them, helps them see it for themselves."

I found myself nodding in agreement. Even though I hadn't known her for very long, I could see Matilda had a way of making you feel comfortable and accepted in the most genuine way possible. She probably would've been great at Oliver's liaison job too.

"The Witness Protection Program is tough though. It doesn't always go well." Dalton's tone grew somber and my body tensed in response. "I don't know the details but one of the guys she had orders to protect . . . Well, let's just say he wasn't one of Boston's finest." His eyes darkened. "There was an incident . . . and I think it really messed with her head. She wasn't going to leave her post though. She's not one to quit. Her sense of loyalty is too great. I think Roslyn knew what was going on. They were close even when they didn't work together. So, when a spot opened up with us, Roslyn really fought for her. She knew that the only way Matilda would leave the job she already had would be if she saw the new one as equally important."

"The fact that she would be working with Roslyn was a key selling point too, I'm sure," he continued, his tone brightening. "They're like sisters, always looking out for each other. When people give Roslyn a hard time, Matilda goes nuts. It's terrifying, actually." Dalton laughed lightly before continuing.

"It sounds cliché, but we really are like a family, in some ways, even closer. Family is something you're born into, not something you constantly work to create like this is. We have to rely on each other completely. Have total trust in one another. There isn't anything I wouldn't do for my ladies, or Mr. Pops and Oliver Twist over there." He jutted his thumb in the direction of Harold and Oliver. Oliver was talking on the phone in a hushed tone while Harold stared at the whiteboard, muttering to himself.

"And I know that they would do the same for me," Dalton continued. "That's why this works, and that's what makes it special."

29

String theory. It was something Harrison needed to understand by the end of summer if he was ever going to have any chance with Nancy Haywood. She was so gloriously smart. Too smart, many said. But to Harrison, it was one of the many wonderful things about her.

He flipped through the pages of the book quickly, as if he might see something that resembled English. Anything he might recognize. But considering nothing in there was about making the perfect lemon sorbet, he supposed it was pointless.

He sighed, closing his hands around the book, and putting it gently on the sand next to him. He had been out here for hours, hoping the ocean would provide some sort of magic to make it all click. But the water just continued to churn.

"Yeah," Harrison grumbled at the waves, running his fingers through his dark, curly hair. "I know. I know. I'm just taking a break. Stop nagging."

He looked out over the water, bringing his knees up to his chest and nestling his head between them. His skin was still warm from the sun that had begun to sink in the sky.

Shhhzzt.

Like a soft thud of someone stepping on sand. It made Harrison turn, his eyes looking toward the dune behind him.

He saw nothing but the wisps of dry grass shuddering in the wind.

He shook his head. All this string theory was making his mind play tricks on him. He chuckled, wondering if Nancy Haywood ever had one of these moments if she studied too hard. It was brain-scrambling stuff.

From a distance, a seal popped its head up over the water, casting Harrison a singular glance before ducking back down. Harrison smiled at the rippling spot, hoping the seal might surface one more time.

Shhhzzt.

The sound was louder this time. Closer. Harrison froze. Something about it made the hair on the back of his neck stand up.

He turned toward that sound. The same direction it had been the last time.

Right behind that same dune . . .

"Hello?" he called, trying in vain to keep his voice casual. It was probably just a seagull. Or an abandoned flip flop stuck in the sand and flapping in the wind.

Except that somewhere in the back of Harrison's mind, he knew it sounded far bigger than either one of those. More careful. Purposefully stepping just so.

Harrison's chest tightened, his fingers trembling as he reached for the 25th-anniversary edition of *Superstring Theory.* It was 609 pages and heavy. Enough for a black eye at the very least.

Shhhzzt.

Closer. More to the left. Harrison's grip tightened around the lightly used cover.

SHHZZT. SHHZZZT

The steps quickened, throwing secrecy to the wind. Harrison reeled back, ready to let the book fly.

"Argh!" Harrison yelled, using the book to shield his head as something launched itself at him. But the impact never came. It took Harrison a second to recover before his eyes focused on a girl rolling on the sand, laughing hysterically.

"Y-you should h-have seen y-your face!" she cackled, pointing at him.

"What the *hell,* Sasha?"

"Hey, you can't swear! That'll be one nickel please," Sasha said, holding out her palm.

"Don't sneak up on me like that," Harrison said with a scowl.

"Don't be a big nerdy baby," Sasha said, rolling her eyes. She looked at the book in his

hands. "What were you planning on doing with that?"

Harrison paused. "Defense," he admitted with a mumble.

"Like, read a page so that I kill myself?" Sasha laughed.

"Would that work?" Harrison asked, sarcastically eager.

"More likely that than getting a girl to go out with you," Sasha said, a wicked grin on her lips. "Even Nancy Haywood."

Harrison ducked his head. "You know about that?"

"Mom told me," Sasha said, eyes skimming over the book fast, without really reading the cover. "And if making her that cake didn't work, learning about yarn really won't."

"First of all, it was a soufflé, not a cake," Harrison corrected. "And second of all, this book is about physics. Not yarn."

"Even worse," Sasha shuddered. "You're going to die a virgin."

"What are you even doing here?" Harrison asked, burying his face in his hands.

"Mom wanted me to tell you that dinner will be ready in an hour," Sasha said. "Made me walk all the way here to tell you that."

"'All the way here?' It's a two-minute walk from the house," Harrison pointed out.

"Still, you owe me," Sasha said, getting up and brushing sand off her clothes. "You coming?"

"You go. I want as much distance between us as possible," Harrison grumbled, opening up the book again.

Sasha grinned. "Love you too, big brother!"

Despite himself, Harrison couldn't help but smile back. He chuckled, looking back at the first page of the book.

He sighed. "This really does make a person want to kill themselves," he muttered dryly to the ocean. He just hoped it would all be worth it.

30

Leslie Greene used to like cleaning. Well, maybe not *like* per se. But she didn't mind it. Not in the beginning. And even during the off-season, she could honestly say that there were moments cleaning Ms. Tulip's house that she legitimately enjoyed. The woman might be senile, always picking up stray cats and calling them Mr. Snuggles, but she was also quite darling. She would even offer Leslie a glass of homemade lemonade after the job, although, these days, Leslie noticed that Ms. Tulip couldn't tell the difference between salt and sugar . . . Even so, it was always a pleasant afternoon.

Not like cleaning the shithole rentals these jerks left in the summer. Especially the ones closest to the beach. She picked up the third used condom and grimaced. It was on the stairs for God's sake. *College kids*, she thought to herself.

Bracing herself, she didn't waste another moment. She had another house to do after this and it was already three-thirty. It took a whole three hours before the house was respectable enough to leave. Dragging the trash out to the dumpster on the corner took all of her determination and quite a few breaks to catch her breath. It was only at times like this that she thought about quitting her smoking habit. Then again, she'd smoked a pack a day for the last fifteen years and she wasn't dead yet.

Wiping her forehead with the back of her hand, Leslie looked at the beach through the cracks between the dumpsters. The sun had just sunk behind the horizon, bathing the beach in a glow that radiated off the water. A light, salty spray drifted to Leslie's nose, helping to mask the smell of tourist trash. She smiled, cracking through the two-day-old makeup that she was always too exhausted to take off properly. She didn't get to go to the beach. She didn't have the luxury of time. Hell, she hadn't had a day off in . . . well, who knows how long.

Sometimes, there were moments after a long day of cleaning houses, as she microwaved her freezer-burnt *Lean Cuisine* and read another page of a book she would never finish, that Leslie Greene would even forget that the ocean was pounding just a mile away.

So, it was little moments like these—simple, easy, forgiving—that she remembered how much she loved it. That she could savor that spray and be reminded of the novelty of this town where she had chosen to raise her boy.

A seagull called, flapping just above the water. The bird drifted down, hopping onto the beach to avoid the foamy backwash.

Landing close to someone laying on the beach.

That poor sucker better get a move on, Leslie thought. *Tide's comin' up. He'll be wet real soon.*

But whoever it was didn't move.

Leslie wasn't a curious person. Not as a child. Not as a mother. And certainly not now. And yet Leslie found herself moving around the line of dumpsters for a better look. There was something just . . . off.

Wrong.

"Hey there," she called out, thinking the boy might be asleep. "You'll be soaked if you don't giddyup."

Still, the young man stayed motionless.

A cold dread invaded Leslie. Something she had only felt one other time. And even that paled in comparison to the icy feeling that crawled up her body now. She continued forward, her bad foot cramping awkwardly as she hit the sand. Next to the young man, the seagull cocked its pale head to one side.

Leslie hobbled on, step by step.

"Are you all right?" she asked, worry coloring her gravelly voice.

The closer she got, the younger the man looked. More like a boy. Not even of college-age.

The seagull hopped onto his chest, poking at his orange Scholastic T-shirt.

Leslie craned her neck, her skin straining as she tried to look at his face. Another wave crashed, soaking the boy's pant leg. Not that it mattered.

He would never feel it.

The roar of the waves couldn't drown out the terrified scream of Leslie Greene before she clapped a hand to her mouth in horror. Overwhelmed with fear and desperation, Leslie whirled around and sprinted in the direction of her car. She had never run so fast. Not ever. Especially with her bad foot.

Behind her, the waves continued to nibble at the sand, slowly inching with the tide. Within twenty minutes, the ocean would swallow the last bit of the beach, finally washing away the blood that slowly streamed toward the water. It would be then, as police and members of the FBI examined the body, that Officer Jay Kama would see something tumbling in the whitewash. The cover would almost disintegrate when the book was finally fished out . . .

With the explanation of string theory hidden somewhere in the soaked pages.

31

ELLE

I was next to Roslyn when she got the call. Her entire body tensed for a fraction of a second before she was barking out orders. The rest of the team rushed around, some taking off to evaluate the scene, others getting on the phone. Bonnie typed away so hard that I was certain she might break the keyboard.

But if that was organized chaos, then the rest of the station was a madhouse. Cops sprinted from one end of the station to the other, grabbing crime scene tape, stray files that were left in the coffee room, or just trying to figure out what they should do.

It made the silent car ride with Roslyn a relief. I drummed my fingers on the steering wheel as we pulled up to the tattered apartment complex with the faded awnings and the trail of cigarette butts leading toward the door. The place looked no better than it did the last time I was here when I had insisted on going trick-or-treating in the area. My seven-year-old thinking had been that the close configuration of apartments would make it an amazingly efficient way to maximize my 'candy-per-hour' rate. I soon learned that my calculations had been way off, walking away from the building with a broken razor head and a lint-covered multivitamin in place of candy.

"The last time I saw her, Leslie still had her cat," I said to Roslyn, casting a glance at Jasper before adding, "A cat that was never a fan of dogs . . ."

She sighed. "Then he'll have to stay in the car."

Jasper watched through the window as we walked toward the building. It took a few knocks before Leslie Greene opened the door with a creak. She looked like an older, more used-up version of the woman I had seen a couple of years ago. Her hair was an artificial black that was much too dark for her strawberry-blonde eyebrows, and streaks of grey snarled through the blunt, collarbone cut.

"You," she said, looking at Hunt uneasily. She pursed her uneven lips, a bare spot in the prune lipstick likely marking where her cigarettes rested. "I had a feeling one of you would show up."

"Ma'am, I'm Agent Hunt with the FBI—"

"I told the officer everything on the phone," Leslie said, making a move to close the door in her face.

Roslyn stuck her foot out, blocking it. "I promise, we'll make it quick," she said, shooting me a look. That was my cue.

"It's nice to see you again, Ms. Greene," I said, peeking through the crack Hunt had forcibly left open. "Remember me? Elle Wolfe? Tommy and I went to elementary school together."

Ms. Greene looked at me, recognition softening her features considerably.

"Little Ellie Wolfe, always in that striped, pink jumpsuit and the pigtails," she said, cracking a smile through the caked prune lipstick. "Haven't seen you in years."

"Since the town Christmas party at The Shack," I nodded. "Where Mrs. Tinker had a few too many cosmos."

Leslie chuckled, shaking her head. "That woman never could handle her liquor. Still can't." She paused, looking from me to Roslyn and back again. "Are you helping with the case?"

"Sort of," I said. "As a consultant."

Leslie eyed Roslyn suspiciously. "Really?"

"Indeed," Roslyn said, before flashing her eyes toward the inside of Leslie's apartment. With a sigh, Leslie opened the door wide and motioned for us to come in.

The place was tight, with a scraped-up oak floor that even the large, worn-out, orange rug couldn't hide. The walls were a yellow-tinted eggshell that appeared to have taken to soaking up the cigarette smoke that floated in the air. The door led straight into the living room, where hand-me-down, mismatched furniture sagged. Along every surface, pictures of Tommy and Leslie brightened the dark space, one with him as a boy holding a striped bass proudly, and another of mother and son with wide smiles. Each frame was lovingly spotless.

We followed Leslie the two-and-a-half strides into the kitchen, where I almost tripped on a spot missing a large tile.

"I've been meaning to get that fixed," Leslie noted, catching my flustered recovery. "But Pip got himself whacked by a tricycle. The scrapper needed surgery to set his paw straight." Hearing his name, the black-and-white cat limped up from his spot under the small wooden table. One of his front paws was wrapped in a heavy, bright-blue cast. I bent down and gave him a pat.

"Can I get either o' you somethin' to drink?" Leslie asked, shuffling to the fridge. "I don't got much. Water, milk, Diet Coke . . . oh." Leslie reached inside and turned around with a smile.

"You still have that sweet tooth from when you were little?" she asked, holding out a can of Dr. Pepper.

I chuckled. "My mom waited for me to outgrow that phase. She's still waiting."

Leslie shook her head as she handed me the can.

She turned to Roslyn. "What about you, Grace Kelly?" she said with a smirk.

Roslyn ignored the nickname as she pulled out a notebook. "I'm quite all right. Thank you."

"You sure? I've got harder stuff too," Leslie offered. "It's after five somewhere." I could have sworn Roslyn seemed to consider it.

"I'm on the clock," she said regardless.

"Well, I hope you don't judge me for doing it then," Leslie sighed before grabbing the whisky bottle next to the dented toaster. "But I think I'm gonna need it."

"Understandable," I agreed, popping open the Dr. Pepper with a *ftzz*.

"This is Tommy's stash," Leslie said as she smirked at me, pouring a healthy dose into a chipped, red mug. "So, this is officially our little secret."

"What's Tommy doing these days, anyway?" I asked before I could help myself. I winced when Roslyn shot me a look. She had given me a specific warning in the car . . . No 'chit chat.'

Oops.

"Workin' at Brody's Cafe," Leslie said. "Makes the fish tacos himself now. Way better than when that Greg made 'em. They were always too . . ." She paused, as if not wanting to say the blasphemy out loud.

"*Greasy*," I finished for her.

"You said it, not me."

We both laughed.

"Well, I'll have to try Tommy's," I said. "If they're half as good as the juice pops he made in third grade, I know I'm in for a treat."

Lesli's eyes shone with pride. "It was the hint of Fanta that made those things really sing."

"I tried to recreate them, but I could never get it quite right."

"He never woulda told you," Leslie chuckled. "It was his secret ingredient."

"Oh, just like—" I stopped short when something hard stepped on my toes. I winced, looking to see Hunt's sharp heel pinning my foot to the broken-tiled floor. I cleared my throat and looked sheepishly at her.

"Ms. Greene," Hunt started, taking control of the room within an instant. "Do you remember seeing anyone else on the beach?"

Leslie sighed, swirling the whisky in her mug. "Nope. But that's normal. It's a small beach. Private access, mostly. Surrounded by rentals. The only people who go there are the ones renting those houses or people that know about the path."

"What path?"

"Small little trail. Ya have to know it's there."

"Would other tourists know about it?"

"Not unless they got lucky," Leslie muttered, knocking back the contents of her mug. She looked at me, then Roslyn. "And between me and you girls, who the Hell is that lucky these days?" She shook her head. "Not that Scott boy . . ."

32

ROSLYN

Elle Wolfe fidgeted uncomfortably as we pulled into the morgue parking lot.

"Stay in the car," I said, leaving no room for any argument. "I'll be back in a—" I cut myself off, looking at the front door of the building. "What the fuck ..." I got out quickly, walking with smooth steps toward the door and the two people in front of it. Before I could get close, the man hurried toward me, leaving the woman behind him alone.

"FBI?" he asked. His lips were thick and dry, matching his crusty, balding head. I nodded once.

"Gary Bunt," he said. "Medical examiner. If you'll come with me—"

"What is she doing here?" I asked, looking around him at the woman. Her eyes were bloodshot and raw around the edges. I already knew who she had to be.

"The boy's mother," the medical examiner whispered in my ear. The man's breath was hot and smelled intensely of fish chowder.

I made sure not to react, directing my attention toward the woman.

"Mrs ..."

"Scott," the woman finished for me as she approached. Her voice was scratchy. Hoarse. "Michaela Scott. I'm Harrison's mom."

"Has someone from the station spoken to you yet?" I asked. My orders couldn't have been more clear.

"Y-yes," Mrs. Scott nodded. "They told us to come in for more questioning. I sent my husband to go with our daughter, b-but . . ." Her brown eyes shot behind her, watering when they focused on the building. "H-he's just lying there. How am I supposed to leave him?"

I bit the inside of my cheek, weighing my words. "How about we give you an escort?" I offered. "I just need to go in there for a few minutes." I didn't like the idea of leaving her here unsupervised, but my options were increasingly limited.

Mrs. Scott gave a tentative nod, shuffling back to sit on the sidewalk. I was about to head inside . . .

Until I saw Elle Wolfe jogging toward me.

I sighed. "I thought I told you to—"

"I know," she said, holding up her hands. "I was just going to sit with her if that's okay." She glanced at Mrs. Scott before gazing up at me imploringly.

My eyes narrowed. "This is hardly the time for you to be asking her questions for your articles."

Wolfe shook her head hard. "Of course not," she said. "I just know I wouldn't want to be alone. If it were me."

My reflex was to say no. But there was pureness in Wolfe's eyes. A softness.

"Fine," I heard myself say, before turning to follow Dr. Bunt inside. I turned to see Elle Wolfe approached Harrison's mother gingerly, kneeling beside her. She took Mrs. Scott's hand, enveloping it in both of hers.

The closing metal door blocked the two from view.

"I'm putting the time of death at around 18:30," Bunt said, lurching down the hallway. He had an awkward gait. Hip replacement, most likely.

Inside, the lighting was bright and artificial. A strong smell of antiseptic seemed to emanate from the bare walls, burning my nose. It almost masked the musky smell of death.

Almost.

"Slash to the throat, just like the others," Bunt said, opening the door to a side room. A gust of cold air hit me hard in the chest as soon as we crossed the threshold.

"I keep it extra chilly in here," Bunt noted, perhaps seeing the look on my face. He motioned to the middle of the room. "Keeps everything fresh."

My mouth set into a thin line as I looked at the table only feet from the door. There, cold and still, lay the Scott boy. His body was straight. Every finger neatly arranged on the metal table. Not a toe out of place. Literally. Even with his eyes closed, he looked too sterile to be mistaken for someone asleep. Too stiff. Lifeless.

I studied the gaping gash along his throat.

"One stroke?" I asked, lowering my face in line with the body.

Bunt grunted the affirmative. "By the looks of it, he never saw it coming."

"How do you know?"

"The muscles weren't tensed," Bunt said. "Whoever killed him must have caught him by surprise. He didn't have time to seize up."

"How fast did it kill him?"

"Within seconds."

I nodded, easing closer. I looked at it clinically. Separating myself from the reality that this husk of a thing was once alive. Was once a son. A child. A human being. Death sucked out all of that. Whatever lay on the table now was just a lump of flesh and bones.

It made it easy to compartmentalize.

Mrs. Scott followed us back to the station in the family-sized minivan. A fresh Connecticut College sticker was pressed onto the back window. Harrison was going to apply there this coming year. Early decision.

It had been his number one choice.

Elle Wolfe was uncharacteristically quiet as she drove. She gripped the steering wheel tight, probably in an attempt to keep her hands from continuing to shake. Every emotion was clearly written on her face. She seemed to have soaked up grief from the mourning mother. A sympathetic kind of pain that made her lips tremble and her gray eyes glisten with unshed tears. She didn't hide it, or rather if she was trying, she wasn't succeeding.

"You helped her, you know," I found myself saying before I could think better of it. "By being there."

Wolfe shook her head, her shoulders slumping. "I just sat there."

"Exactly," I insisted quietly. "You didn't dig into their personal lives like law enforcement has to. You didn't push a camera in her face. You were just there." My gaze softened on her, unsure why I felt the need to comfort her at all. And yet . . . "Trust me. You doing nothing was what she needed most."

33

ELLE

I spent the rest of the night in the station with the FBI team. Ever since the unexpected turn of events coming back from Mrs. Tumbler's house, Roslyn's attitude toward me had warmed considerably. Nothing like seeing someone have a seizure to break down barriers, I guess.

Who woulda thought.

Exhausted, but not wanting to go home, I pushed two chairs together for a makeshift bed while a few of the others passed out sitting up. Roslyn had skipped sleep altogether, and I woke up to find her pacing with Jasper, just like she had been doing hours before. The first beams of sunlight shone in through the blinds. The rest of the team was already up as I rubbed the sleep from my eyes.

"Hey, um, Agent Hunt?" Benjie said, peaking his boyish face into the room.

"Officer Hara," Roslyn replied politely. He blushed, fumbling with something behind him before revealing a paper coffee cup. Based on the logo, it was from the bakery in the opposite direction of his commute to work. They were supposed to make the best coffee in town, which naturally meant that they charged three times more than anywhere else on Cape August.

"I . . . erm . . . the coffee isn't great here at the station . . ." he started shyly. "So . . ." He thrust the cup forward, almost throwing it at her. Roslyn stared as Benjie began to tremble.

"Oh, thank you," Roslyn said, before carefully taking the cup. "How much was it? I have some cash—"

"No!" Benjie yelped, making everyone jump. "Sorry, I just . . . Don't worry about it. My treat. I . . . yeah! Thanks!" He ducked his head, careening out of the room before anyone could say anything more. Roslyn's eyes were wide as she blinked after the young man.

"I think Benjie has a little crush," Dalton noted, shooting Roslyn a wink. "You always have them falling at your feet."

"He's . . . sweet," Roslyn offered, looking at the coffee in her hands.

"Too bad the poor guy doesn't stand a chance, eh?" Dalton chuckled.

Ouch. I winched at Dalton's words. Roslyn raised her eyebrows.

"More than you ever did," she shot back at him.

Dalton feigned pain, putting a hand over his heart dramatically. "You hurt me," Dalton pretended to wince. "And my manhood."

"Well, your manhood would be one of her issues," Bonnie pointed out from behind her computer. I cocked my head at Bonnie and saw that she was sharing a smirk with Roslyn before continuing. "Although, maybe not the *biggest* issue . . ." Bonnie lazily let her eyes wander toward the area between Dalton's legs. He yelped, turning his chair away as Bonnie laughed.

"Maybe I should follow your lead and switch teams too," Bonnie went on to Roslyn.

Wait, what? A voice in the back of my head did a quick double-take. I fought the urge to look at Roslyn.

"Saying I switched teams would imply that I ever entertained playing on yours," Roslyn muttered, eyeing Dalton and Bonnie in turn. Did that mean it was true? Was Roslyn a lesbian? I felt my eyes widen as the realization dawned on me. I had just assumed . . .

I mentally scolded myself. She'd given me no reason to assume her sexuality was one way or the other, not that it mattered. What was more confusing was the fact that she, of all people, was so open about it, especially given how she reacted to *everything* else. Roslyn was always cryptic. Vague. Evading personal questions like the plague. And yet...

"That part of herself has never been a secret," Oliver whispered to me, understanding in his eyes at my personal epiphany. "She's always been open about it, even if she isn't open about anything else."

I nodded slowly, looking back at Roslyn.

"How's it going with your current lady anyway?" Dalton asked Roslyn.

"I'm sure you're not asking about my personal life," she warned. "Because that would be highly unprofessional."

"Oh, come on," Dalton argued. "We're friends too."

"We're not friends at work," Roslyn clarified.

"We've been here all night. I think we can take a break from being co-workers," he pointed out. "Spill."

"We are not having this conversation."

"Her name is Emily, right? She picked you up after work once."

"I didn't even realize you were still seeing her," Bonnie piped up. "You must be setting a new record for yourself."

Roslyn shot her a piercing glare. "*Seeing* is a strong term," Roslyn growled, more to herself than anyone in the room.

Dalton seized the opportunity. "Would you prefer fu—"

"Finish that sentence and see what happens," Roslyn said, bristling. "I hope you're feeling especially brave."

He laughed. "I'm always feeling brave, Boss. Are you two exclusive?"

"I'm sorry, Dalton, but I think you have one too many appendages for her," Roslyn deadpanned.

Bonnie let out a loud '*Ha,*' pointing at Dalton.

"Not where I was going with that, but I'm sure I could rock her world," Dalton teased, shooting a playful glare at Bonnie.

"Many men have tried and failed," Roslyn coolly countered. From behind her, Harold fought a chuckle as he tried to actively stay out of the conversation.

"So, not exclusive?" Dalton pressed. Roslyn just pursed her lips, attempting to ignore him.

"Let's get the journalist's opinion about relationships," he suggested. "It's her job to be unbiased."

"And Elle's the only one here that has a truly uncomplicated situation," Bonnie pointed out. I looked at her questioningly. I hadn't mentioned anything about my engagement to Eric. "This station is teeming with gossip if you know how to listen," she said with a shrug to my silent question.

"A secret? I love secrets! Oooh, tell!" Matilda chattered, grabbing the side of my chair, and shaking it with enthusiasm.

"It's not a secret, it just didn't seem relevant . . ." I trailed off, glancing at Roslyn. She was looking at me with the mask she always wore, but there was a hint of curiosity in her eyes.

For reasons I couldn't understand, it only made the words harder to choke out.

"Welll . . .?" Matilda urged, shaking my chair with extra vigor.

"I'm engaged," I said, plastering a smile on my face.

"TO BE MARRIED?" Matilda leaped up from her chair, sending it toppling behind her.

"That would be the kind, yes," I laughed.

Matilda tackled me into a hug. For someone so small, she was surprisingly strong. "What's his name? Is he handsome? Handsome to you is all that matters! Is he smart? Mostly smart? Almost smart? What's his favorite color? Astrological sign? Number of toes? Spirit animal—" Matilda didn't even stop to take a breath.

"Why don't you ask for his social security number while you're at it?" Bonnie muttered.

"She can't answer you if you're crushing her," Dalton pointed out.

"It's a crush of love!" Matilda cried, giving me one last squeeze before releasing me. She retrieved her chair before dragging it as close to me as possible.

"His name is Eric Diakos and he's a mechanical engineer," I said.

"When's the big day?" Bonnie asked.

"October nineteenth."

"Oh wow! That's so soon!" Matilda cried.

It was.

"Congratulations," a smooth voice said. It forced me to look up into the bright blue-green eyes I had actively been avoiding. I found Roslyn smiling. It was small but kind. With the tiniest hint of something else.

"Thank you," I murmured. I held her gaze until the blush inching up my neck forced me to look away.

"If you need an escape plan, just call me," Bonnie piped up. "In my experience, you might need it."

34

ROSLYN

"Hunt," I said, picking up the phone on the second ring. I had just spent the morning using Elle Wolfe as a personal driver to each of the crime scenes. She seemed hellbent on filling each and every moment of silence with fast-paced conversation . . . More so than usual.

"Hey," Bonnie's voice cut in quickly. "I just got a call from a Mr. Alexander over at the cemetery. He said you told him to call if he noticed anyone hanging around."

"Yes," I said, already motioning for Wolfe to turn the car round.

"Well, someone's hanging around," Bonnie continued. "I figured you would be the closest."

"I'm headed there now."

We were at the cemetery within five minutes. Sure enough, even from the parking lot, I could see the figure of a man standing next to Molly Edgars' fresh grave.

"Stay here," I told Wolfe before getting out. I didn't look to see the pout that I knew would be on her face.

Approaching the man, I saw that he was tall and thin, with the same slightly hunched shoulders as someone else in town.

"Paying your respects," I said quietly, moving next to him with Jasper by my side. He jumped, pushing an eerily familiar pair of square glasses back onto his face.

"Oh! Y-yes. She was my niece," the man said. He had narrow features, with thick eyebrows. He was a little shorter than Nelson but virtually identical in every other way.

"Peter Edgars, I presume?" I asked.

The man looked surprised but nodded. "Have we met?"

"No," I said, taking out my badge. "SSA Roslyn Hunt with the FBI." I watched him. His dark eyes widened as he shifted his weight from foot to foot.

"Oh, you must be working the case then?" Peter Edgars asked.

"Indeed."

"Any leads?"

"It's an ongoing investigation," I said, glancing at the flowers on his niece's grave. "It's a shame you missed the funeral."

"Yeah," he said, shifting his weight again. "I was in Italy. I came as soon as I heard."

"Italy?" I repeated. "Your brother didn't mention that."

"Probably because he didn't know," Peter Edgars mumbled. "We don't exactly stay in touch."

"I'm aware," I noted. Peter shot me a questioning look, but I didn't expand on the statement. "Why were you in Italy?" I asked.

"I lead a summer program there," Peter said. "I'm a professor at Williams College."

"Teaching?"

"The origin of words, rather."

"That's very specific."

"I teach linguistics too," he shrugged. "That's usually a more popular class."

"Italy seems like a logical place to go then," I agreed. "Is that why we couldn't get a hold of you?"

"Pardon?" Peter asked quickly.

"We tried to reach you," I clarified.

"For any particular reason?" he asked, a nervous twinge in his voice.

I shrugged noncommittally. "Well, your niece was found with her throat slit." From the corner of my eye, I saw him fiddle with his hands. "How long are you in town?" I asked.

"Erm . . . A few days. I wasn't planning on staying," he said.

"Would you mind coming into the station?"

"Why?"

"Standard protocol."

"Oh."

"Is that a yes?"

"Well . . ."

"Wonderful," I said. "After you. We can take my car."

"I don't think—"

"Nonsense," I said with a smile. "I even have someone to drive us."

35

ROSLYN

Peter Edgars rubbed the back of his left hand nervously as he sat in the investigation room. I watched, unseen on the other side of the one-way glass. He had been in there for over thirty minutes.

I had spent every one of those minutes watching.

"Aren't you going to go in?" Elle Wolfe asked.

"Yes."

But I didn't move.

"Like . . . now?" she asked, tugging on her fingers. It was a nervous tick.

"No."

"Why?"

I fought the urge to sigh. "Because."

I could feel her eyes watching me. She was practically vibrating with the questions I knew she wanted to ask.

"Boss," Dalton said, coming into the room to hand me a file. "Bonnie found this."

I flip through it, my eyes flashing over each page. I nod to myself, slap the file shut, and head into the room.

"I apologize for the wait," I said, but I didn't bother trying to sound genuine. "We were just running background checks. You know how it is."

"Of course, of course," Peter Edgars said. The back of his left hand was red from the incessant rubbing.

"It took us a little extra time to find the record of your flight back to the States," I noted.

"Well, the university pays for the flights of the program," he said.

"Of course," I said with a smile. "Except, you left before the program even started. Last-minute too. That must have cost more."

He shrugged. "A little bit more."

"How much more exactly?" I asked.

"I'm not entirely sure . . ."

"Well, you must have some idea," I said. "Especially considering you paid in cash."

His eyes shifted around the room, looking anywhere but at me. "It was easier," he said, rubbing the back of his left hand again. "I had it on me."

"You had an extra 478 dollars in your pocket?" I asked, raising an eyebrow.

"Umm, yeah. I guess."

I let silence fall over the small room. Edgars fidgeted.

I let him wait.

"Here's the thing," I started, my voice quiet but sharp. I took the seat across from him. "We have footage of you checking into a motel on the outskirts of Cape August the day before your niece was found dead. Weeks before you said you were even back in the country."

Peter Edgars' face paled, but I didn't stop.

"Now, I think what you were trying to do was to pay for everything in cash so that we wouldn't be able to prove that," I went on. "But airport security still had a record of you. Maybe that thought hadn't crossed your mind."

I leaned closer to him. He flinched back.

"What I'm trying to understand is why you didn't come to Molly's funeral if you were back in town already," I wondered out loud. "Or, why you rushed back here from Italy before she died unless you knew something."

"I . . ." He trailed off.

"Take your time," I drawled. "I can wait."

He shook his head. "She was having a hard time," he finally said.

"What kind of a hard time?"

He shrugged. "Classic teenager stuff."

"Enough for you to fly all the way back here?" I asked.

"She was a tender-hearted girl. I wanted to be there for her."

"How *there* for her were you?" I asked, a cold chill creeping into my tone.

His eyes snapped up to look at me. "What are you—"

"She was pretty," I went on, getting up to walk around him. Circle him. "Sure, she was your niece, but she wasn't a little girl anymore. She was developing into a fine young woman."

"What the hell are you implying?" he asked, anger creeping into his weak tone.

"You tell me, Edgars," I said, my voice rising. "Why did you come back into town? Was she going to tell someone something . . ."

"No! I told you," he yelped. "She was having some trouble. I was worried, so I came back."

"Without even telling your brother?"

"I . . . It's complicated."

"Uncomplicate it then," I said. Edgars fell silent, rubbing the back of his hand again. I threw his file onto the table in front of him. The *slap* made him jump.

"We found a sealed record in your file," I said. "What can you tell me about that?"

"That was a long time ago," Peter said quickly.

"So, you should have no problem telling me what it was about," I said. "Otherwise, I can find out for myself."

He opened and closed his mouth a few times but said nothing.

Minutes ticked by. I didn't sit back down. I loomed over him. I'd wait all night if I had to.

Finally, he took a slow, steadying breath, looked me right in the eye, and said the only words that made me shiver.

"I want a lawyer."

36

ELLE

The room was especially tense after Peter Edgars' lawyer showed up. I could have sworn fire was about to shoot out of Roslyn's eyes. Twenty-four hours later, Peter was free to go. There wasn't enough evidence to charge him with anything, and with his lawyer present, Peter Edgars didn't say anything else.

We all watched as Peter left the station. Roslyn clenched his file so hard in her hands that her knuckles had turned a scary shade of white. She ordered her team every which way to dig up more information about Peter. Once everyone was gone, she began to pace the room.

Back and forth. Again and again.

I was desperate to break the restless energy, even for a moment.

"Twizzler?" I offered, holding up the bag of long red candy. It made her pause, even if only to roll her eyes.

"Do you ever eat anything that resembles real food?" she asked.

"Do you ever eat anything that resembles fun?" I retorted, bouncing the bag of candy in front of her. She wrinkled her nose at it.

"There is nothing fun about early-onset diabetes," she muttered.

"That would have already happened by now," I said with a shrug, taking a big bite of one. "Besides, it's brain food. Come on. You need a break."

"It probably rots your brain through your teeth."

"I'll have you know that I take great care of my teeth," I said, pointing the half-eaten Twizzler at her.

"You say as you continue to gnaw on solidified, artificially colored corn syrup."

Failing to come up with an adequate comeback, I took the Twizzler and hurled it at her.

She dodged it lazily. "And now it has you resorting to violence," she said sarcastically.

Fighting a smile, I took another strip and aimed it at her head. I was about to let it fly when Matilda and Dalton walked in.

"Are we playing a game?" Matilda asked, failing to hide a hint of excitement.

"No. Ms. Wolfe is busy playing with herself," Roslyn deadpanned. My mouth dropped open while Matilda barely held back a giggle.

"I just got off the phone with some of the police departments in Western Mass.," Dalton said, "and something sounded familiar. Did you ever hear about that case from ages ago? The guy who killed twelve women in under two years?"

"They called him the Berkshire Killer," Roslyn recalled. "They caught him fifteen years ago."

"Yeah," Dalton agreed. "But I noticed a lot of similarities between the cases. The way the victims are hunted on sand here is like how they were hunted in the woods there. The way they are killed with a single slash to the throat . . . The victimology is completely different, of course . . . But, what if we are dealing with a copycat?"

"Peter Edgars went to Williams College before becoming a professor there," Harold said as he walked in. "Maybe there's a connection."

"I checked the timelines," Dalton added. "He was at Williams shortly after the case was solved. He would have heard about the murders. Maybe something made him snap here on Cape August, and he chose to mimic that."

Roslyn nodded slowly. "I want you to find out everything you can about that case," she ordered. "Compare the details and see if Edgars or anyone else has had any correspondence with the Berkshire Killer."

"Should we go talk to the Berkshire Killer?" Matilda offered. "He might know how to catch our guy if this really is the work of a copycat."

"Umm . . . That might be a problem," Bonnie muttered from behind her laptop. "Bobby Michaels, AKA the Berkshire Killer, hung himself in his prison cell six years ago . . ."

Roslyn swore under her breath. "Fine," she said. "But we can still talk to the prison guards and maybe his cellmate. Matilda, call Williams College and see what you can find. Harold, try to get in touch with Michaels' family and see if any of them have been in this area. The rest of you, keep digging. I also want an officer on Edgars at all times."

Roslyn stalked back to the whiteboard with Jasper in tow, staring at the pictures. She didn't say another word for the rest of the night.

37

ELLE

"Oh, come on, Elle," Dalton teased. "What did I tell you? Fists up!"

"They *are* up," I grumbled, sweat beading down my face. Everything in my body hurt. Why on earth did I wake up at five o'clock for this?

"You call that up? Come on! Up, up, up!" Dalton grinned as he barked orders at me.

Maybe if I could get one good swipe at him, it could all be worth it. I lunged for what felt like the hundredth time, throwing punches at the empty air as he stepped away. I stumbled, trying to regain my footing as I sucked in as much air as my lungs could manage.

"Are you trying to kill our personal publicist?" a voice called. The way the room was shaped, it sounded as if it was coming through the walls.

"Roslyn. Help," I begged dramatically as I circled around trying to find her.

"What are you doing here? I thought you trained last night?" Dalton asked the voice as he looked for her too. Finally, he stopped and I followed his eyes. She approached the mats from the back door of the gym. Her hair was braided back and she was wearing a light workout jacket with skin-tight leggings.

"Well, that's the thing about training, Jason. You have to keep doing it in order to maintain the results," she said.

"That sounds like a challenge," Dalton said eagerly.

Roslyn smirked, before nodding back to me. "Finish up with Wolfe first. I didn't mean to interrupt."

"No. Please interrupt," I panted. "I need a breather." I was also dying to see them in action.

"You heard the lady," Dalton announced. "Let's go, Boss."

As Roslyn approached, she shrugged off her jacket. Underneath, she wore a workout tank that showed off her lean arms and toned shoulders. I caught myself staring and rushed to look away. I moved to join Jasper at the edge of the mat. The dog almost looked pleased to see me. I swear I almost saw him *think* about wagging his tail.

Seeing Dalton and Roslyn next to one another in their skin-tight attire, I realized how much bigger he was. He easily had seventy pounds over her and I could only imagine what kind of damage one of his fists could do. While built of lean muscle herself, Roslyn was still thin with a willowy figure. She simply wouldn't have the padding to cushion the impact of a hit if it connected in the wrong place. I bit my thumb to hold back a protest. They knew what they were doing.

They started to spar, and after a couple of seconds, I realized my worries were unnecessary. What Roslyn lacked in size, she made up for in speed and agility. Every time Dalton struck, Roslyn danced just out of reach with smooth, elegant movements. She was light on her feet, barely touching the ground before pushing off again.

The pair were so polished, it almost seemed like the entire thing was choreographed ahead of time. It was like watching a kind of performance; beautiful and precise.

"You've been practicing," Roslyn praised as she twirled to avoid Dalton's fist.

"One of these days it'll pay off," Dalton said. He threw another punch that Roslyn dodged with ease. She was playing defensively, avoiding blow after blow, but never throwing her own.

"You never know. Miracles can happen," Roslyn said, side-stepping a well-aimed kick.

"Come on, when are you gonna give me something?" Dalton taunted as he advanced, noting her defensive moves.

"It would be over too quickly," Roslyn said. "I wouldn't want to crush your newfound confidence." She moved with a refinement that was impossible to teach.

"You seem awfully confident for someone who hasn't even thrown a punch yet," Dalton teased, although his brow was furrowed with concentration. A singular bead of sweat had begun to slide down his forehead.

"I just want you to believe you are doing well," Roslyn said. She wasn't even out of breath.

"Or maybe you've lost your touch," Dalton challenged.

She feigned a sigh. "Have it your way, then."

In an instant, Roslyn's tactics changed. She switched to the offensive, jabbing at Dalton with speed and dexterity. Dalton was ready for it, bobbing and weaving through her advances. I found myself fighting the need to blink, fearing I would miss something even in that split second.

While they seemed evenly matched to my untrained eye, it was their facial expressions that hinted at the true nature of how the fight was going. Dalton's mouth was tense with pure concentration, while Roslyn looked relaxed. I could swear I even saw a smile growing on her face, and I soon saw why. Dalton threw another punch, and Roslyn, instead of pivoting right like she normally had, pivoted left. It was the extra millisecond that Dalton needed to recalibrate that presented Roslyn with her opportunity. She dropped to the ground and swept out her foot, knocking Dalton's legs out from underneath him. With a startled grunt, he landed hard on his back.

Roslyn sprang back up and brushed off her hands.

"Fuck," Dalton groaned, more from frustration than pain.

I released a breath I hadn't realized I had been holding.

Roslyn offered an elegant curtsy before helping him to his feet.

"You get me with that every time," Dalton complained, shoving her playfully.

Roslyn cocked an eyebrow. "Which would make one wonder why it always works."

"Maybe I let you win," Dalton countered. "Wouldn't want you to look bad in front of our audience." Dalton winked in my direction.

"Would you like to go again, then?" Roslyn asked innocently.

"Uhh . . . I'll let you take a break," Dalton said, rubbing a spot on his back that had hit the ground the hardest. "Just remember that not all of us used to do MMA."

"Wait," I started. "What?"

Roslyn rolled her eyes. "For the hundredth time, it wasn't MMA." She sighed. "It was a self-defense club in college."

"What kind of self-defense, then?" Dalton asked knowingly.

"Muay Thai," Roslyn said as if it were just another workout class.

I looked to Dalton for more of an explanation when it became clear she wouldn't elaborate.

"It's a kind of martial art. Based out of Thailand," Dalton explained. "Which only proves my point."

"Hardly MMA, which is barbaric and classless," Roslyn said, turning up her nose.

"Yes, and you're very classy," Dalton mocked. "Does that stem from your days of ballet? I guess old habits die hard."

Roslyn's eyes narrowed. "And to think you had your ass handed to you by a former *ballerina*," Roslyn noted.

Dalton grimaced.

"You used to dance?" I asked. "For how long?"

"Fourteen years," Roslyn answered, her tone suddenly careful.

"Was on her way to going pro before she chose this instead," Dalton said, nudging Roslyn with his elbow.

I started to chuckle at the joke, before catching the sharp look she gave him. He wasn't kidding. My eyes widened. It made sense. She had the right build, the athletics, the poise, and the natural elegance. The attitude. Even when she sparred with Dalton, her movements resembled dance.

"You gave it up?" I asked. Roslyn's body stiffened and her mouth became a hard line.

"Yes." Her answer was short and final, leaving no room for further questions. She began to retreat off the mats.

"Well, as lovely as this has been," she said, "I have some work to do." She collected Jasper before angling toward the punching bags. "I'll see you both at the station."

"I'm gonna grab some breakfast," Dalton said, looking at me. "You coming?"

"Actually, I think I'll do a cool down in the pool," I said, stretching my aching arms. "I'll catch up with you."

"Okay," Dalton said with a smile. "Text me if either of you wants me to bring you back anything."

Soon I was in the pool, working the stiffness out of my limbs. Before I knew it, an hour had passed. I cursed as I rushed out of the pool. I didn't want to miss anything at the station. Careening into the locker room, I reeled back, grabbing hold of the corner of a locker to keep from smashing into someone.

"Woah. Where's the fire?"

Naturally, it was Roslyn. Because that's how my life goes . . .

I realized with a heavy blush that she had just gotten out of the shower. Her hair was wet, her cheeks tinted pink from the heat of the water, and she was just putting on her underwear.

"Sorry," I stuttered, averting my eyes quickly, but not before seeing that every part of her was tight and lean. She didn't have an ounce of body fat.

I gulped.

"Relax. There's nothing here you haven't seen before," Roslyn said with what sounded like a smirk. "Or have you never been in a locker room?"

I rolled my eyes, fighting the heat crawling up my neck. "I played ultimate frisbee in college. You just surprised me."

Roslyn scoffed. "Ultimate frisbee? Is that even considered a sport?"

"Rude," I shot back, chancing a look at her face and *only* her face. "Ultimate is actually quite physical."

"Oh, I'm sure," she said sarcastically. "Quite physical."

My mouth felt oddly dry. I swallowed hard. "It's not Mu Thi, but it's still intense."

"It's *Muay Thai*," Roslyn corrected as she pulled out pants from her bag.

"That's what I said."

"You butchered it."

"Why'd you choose Muay Thai anyway?" I asked.

"It was practical," Roslyn said, slipping pants over her hips.

What happened to only looking at her face?

"Odd transition from ballet to something like that," I pressed, forcing my voice to be even.

Roslyn shrugged. "The themes are the same," she reasoned. "A need for patience. Control. Restraint."

"Sounds like you should have tried fencing," I teased.

"The fencing club only met once a week," Roslyn murmured.

I blinked, trying to figure her out. "You fenced too?"

"I dabbled."

I shook my head. "Was there anything you didn't do?"

"Ultimate frisbee." Roslyn smiled, wrinkling her nose in mock disgust.

"Hey," I said, pointing a finger at her. "I'm not making fun of you for dancing."

"I'd like to see you try," she said.

"Do you ever miss ballet?"

She hesitated before answering, but when she did, her voice was soft. "Every day."

"Why did you stop doing it then?" I asked.

Her eyes darkened. "It . . . became irrelevant."

I waited for her to elaborate but realized she never would. I used the time to search for a towel. When I looked back, Roslyn was fully dressed.

I took a deep breath and started to relax.

"So, want a ride back to the station?" I asked.

She gave me a small, rare smile as she grabbed her bag. "Sure."

38

ROSLYN

I could hear the yells from outside of the station. I rushed in just as a giant man slammed into me. Jasper jumped back, barking ferociously.

"What—"

The man shoved me aside, hurling himself toward the door. I reacted without thinking and grabbed him. He lashed out, scratching my arm, and snapping the cuff of my shirt. I yanked him back into the station by the scruff of the neck. Within an instant, four cops were on him, locking his hands behind his back.

"What the hell?" I huffed, chest heaving with the sudden exertion and surprise. "Who the fuck is this?"

"Our guy!" Benjie Yin cried from behind the scuffle.

I looked at the large man who was being dragged to his feet in handcuffs. He was tall and thick, with a scruffy, uneven beard. His shirt was covered in white powder. Flour, judging by the consistency.

"That's Joe Campbell," Elle Wolfe said, rushing next to me. Her eyes were wide as she watched the scene. "He's the baker at the French bistro in town."

"Some of the other officers saw him hanging around one of the beaches late at night," Benjie Hara added, scurrying around the chaos toward us.

My jaw clenched. "Is that the only reason why they think he's responsible for the murders?" I asked, trying to keep my voice calm. *I leave this place for an hour. . . One. Hour.*

"Uhm," Benjie Hara started, looking at me nervously.

I'll take that as a yes.

"And this is how everyone thought to handle it," I growled under my breath, watching as Joe Campbell was led away. *Stupid, impulsive, careless—*

My hand went to roll up my torn sleeve, and I noticed my suddenly bare wrist. The wrist that was never bare.

My chest tightened as I forced myself to calmly look at the floor.

Only to see that it was too late.

39

ELLE

"What the hell is that?"

I turned and saw with horror that Andrew was looking down at a silver bracelet lying on the ground. My chest clenched, not daring to look at Roslyn. Andrew picked it up, turning it over in his hands.

"Whose is this?" he asked, fury seeping into his normally mild tone.

I risked scanning the room and saw that everyone had frozen to their spots with various forms of panic in their eyes. Those who didn't know what was going on—all of the Station Boys—were taken aback by Andrew's sudden change in demeanor. He was normally so level-headed. The FBI team looked horrified for a different reason. They knew exactly what was happening.

One person in the room looked eerily calm.

"That would be mine," Roslyn said. Her expression was composed and relaxed. Andrew on the other hand ...

"You're fucking epileptic." Andrew didn't phrase it as a question.

"I am," Roslyn confirmed, facing Andrew directly. He glared at her with an intensity I didn't know he could manage.

"Andrew—" I hadn't realized I had moved until I was right next to him. I started to reach up to his shoulder, but he jerked away.

"Are you fucking kidding me?" Andrew started, shaking the bracelet at Roslyn. From the corner of my eye, I saw Dalton take a step closer, angling his body so that he could be ready to physically block Roslyn if necessary. Harold muttered something to him, but I couldn't make out what it was. Hopper's face was tense and serious underneath the gray beard.

"I'm not kidding," Roslyn said to Andrew. "However, I am happy to answer any questions you might have."

Andrew chuckled darkly, and the hairs on the back of my neck stood up. I made a move toward him again, but strong fingers closed around my wrist to stop me. I glanced back and saw that it was Jay.

"Oh . . . I have questions," Andrew hissed at Roslyn. "I think all of us have plenty of fucking questions."

"Why don't we all just calm down . . .?" Harold warned, but Andrew ignored him.

"Were you ever going to mention this?" Andrew demanded. "Were you ever going to say a fucking thing?"

"It wasn't relevant," Roslyn said coolly.

"Not fucking relevant?" Andrew asked. "You have no business carrying a fucking gun!"

"I can assure you all that I have my condition under control."

"You expect me to believe that?" Andrew snarled. "Figures that the one time they send the feds, they send us the *defect*."

Roslyn's face twitched at the word, but the rest of her remained composed. Meanwhile, fury flushed my cheeks and made my entire body feel hot.

I wasn't the only one.

"Say that again," Dalton growled, taking a step toward him, "and I will break your jaw."

"Stop," Roslyn ordered, forcing Dalton to a halt. She looked at Andrew. "Lieutenant Wells. We can discuss everything once you've had the chance to cool off."

"Andrew, man, let's just go outside," Benjie tried, having finally found his voice. He carefully reached out a shaking hand to his superior.

"Don't fucking touch me," Andrew hissed. Benjie recoiled. A scowl twisted Andrew's face and he spat in Roslyn's direction.

Rage flared in Dalton's eyes and he moved toward Andrew.

"Dalton," Roslyn ordered.

He stopped inches short of Andrew, tendons popping out of his neck as his fists trembled at his side.

"Your master's calling you—" Andrew sneered at Dalton, having to look up slightly to face the man in front of him.

"—and you better hope I listen to her," Dalton warned.

"Why do you want to defend her so badly, huh?" Andrew asked. "Do you have a little crush?"

"Shut your mouth," Dalton bristled. "Everyone can see what you're trying to compensate for." Dalton's eyes flickered down in disgust toward Andrew's groin. "I guess poor Elle had to find that out the hard way—"

Andrew yelled in rage, taking a swing toward Dalton's face. It took everyone by surprise.

Everyone except Dalton.

Dalton was ready, turning his head so that Andrew's fist only skimmed the surface of his cheek. He grabbed Andrew's arm and threw him to the ground. Andrew lunged at Dalton's waist, bringing him down to the floor too. Bonnie yelled. I strained forward but Jay had me in a death grip.

A bone-crunching crack echoed in through the shocked office as Dalton punched Andrew hard in the face.

"ENOUGH." That one word was enough to make even the brawling men freeze for a moment.

Which was all Roslyn needed.

She shoved Dalton away from Andrew with surprising force. The three of them formed a lopsided triangle.

"Are you insane?" Roslyn snarled at Dalton. "Make another move toward him and I'll ship you home in a crate." Her voice was low and dangerous. Dalton's chest heaved as he glowered at Andrew. "Get out of here. Now." Roslyn commanded Dalton. He finally made eye contact with her and saw the murderous look on her face. Fists trembling, he spun on his heels toward the door.

No sooner was his back turned than Andrew lunged for him.

Roslyn stepped in between before he had the chance to connect. I had never seen a human move so fast. She slammed Andrew into the wall, knocking the wind out of him.

Dalton turned around with the commotion and stared dumbly at the new development. The entire station watched in shocked silence.

"How dare you go after him when his back is turned," Roslyn seethed through bared teeth. Her face was inches from Andrew's and her voice was low with barely controlled rage. "The next time you have a problem, come at me directly. I shouldn't be too intimidating for you . . . considering I'm *defective*." She shoved him harder against the wall before sending him sprawling to the ground.

Roslyn spun around and pointed at two of the closest Station Boys. They flinched. "Pick up your lieutenant and get him out of here," she commanded. They hurried to pull Andrew up off the floor and out the door. He didn't protest.

Roslyn looked at Dalton, who was still rooted to the spot.

"You. What did I say before? Get to the hotel and stay there until I say otherwise. Now." Dalton left in a few quick strides but Roslyn's gaze continued after him.

"Bonnie," Roslyn started, her voice a little softer. "Go with him. He listens to you."

Bonnie nodded and left without a word.

Roslyn looked around at the remaining crowd, shoulders back and head high with authority.

"Would anyone else like to voice their concerns?" she asked. No one spoke. "No? Good. Now, get back to work."

The officers hurried to their desks as Roslyn swept toward the back room with Jasper. I made a move to follow but Jay still had me trapped next to him.

"Let her have some space," Jay said.

"I need to make sure she's okay," I said.

His hold became gentle, but still firm. "What she needs right now is to be alone."

I was going to argue until I felt something wet on my cheeks. I was crying.

40

ROSLYN

I needed to get away. To put physical distance between everyone and myself.

I had had confrontations before, but they had never been as eventful. In my head, I berated myself for not shutting it down faster. I wanted to defuse the situation quietly, but I had underestimated Andrew Wells' resolve and allowed myself to make mistakes in the process.

Mistakes that started from the very beginning; my bracelet should never have been on the ground in the first place.

I stalked toward the whiteboard. I couldn't afford to make mistakes. They were careless and avoidable. And yet here I was. The person to blame wasn't Andrew Wells. He had acted out of emotion. He couldn't stop himself even if he'd wanted to.

But I knew better.

Behind me, I heard the unmistakable creak of the door opening and someone shuffling inside. I didn't turn. Maybe if I ignored them, they would go away.

Except, I recognized the footsteps. They were heavier than most on my team and hinted at age with the way they hit the floor. Hopper. I should have anticipated that he would search me out.

He sighed. "Do you wanna talk or would you like me to?"

I stayed silent, continuing to stare at the whiteboard.

"All right. Me then." He paused to take a long, purposeful breath. From the corner of my eye, I could see him lean up against the desk second closest to me, allowing me space.

"Do you know why I gave you this job?" he asked after a moment.

"Because your wife was going to leave you if you didn't," I muttered, and internally winced. It was true that his wife had given him an ultimatum; he could either cut back his hours or she was going to file for a divorce. They'd compromised, and soon he relinquished the unit chief position to stay on the team and work under me.

But just because it was true didn't give me the right to rub his nose in it . . . Thankfully, I heard him chuckle.

"That's why I *gave up* the job, but it doesn't explain why I would give it to *you,* smart ass," he said. "And I wasn't talking about the promotion. I was talking about your first job with this unit."

He cleared his throat when I didn't respond and continued. "You know, there were over a dozen reasons I shouldn't have," Harold mused, and started counting on his fingers. "I mean, for one, you were hard to relate to. Never talked about your personal life. Rarely smiled. You were young. Ten years younger than me before I got the job. You were too thin. Too surly." He chuckled, shaking his head.

He had forgotten one.

"Are you saving the best for last?" I asked, turning to face him. I wasn't going to shy away from it. When he said it, he was going to have to look at me. I waited.

He gazed straight into my face, clasping his hands in front of him. "There were plenty of reasons why I shouldn't have given you the job," he repeated. "But not one of them was because of your medical history."

A lump formed in my throat and I tried to swallow. He was full of shit.

"So, what? Are you going to tell me that it was actually why you gave me the position? 'Overcoming the odds' and whatnot?" I asked sarcastically.

He snorted. "This isn't a Nicholas Sparks saga."

I gave him a look.

"My wife reads them," Harold said by way of explanation. "And . . . I dabble." He shrugged.

The corners of my mouth twitched, but I didn't smile.

"When you first applied, I didn't know how you had even gotten that far," he continued. I could feel my expression harden again. "I thought that they must have loosened up the requirements for you. I mean, I just didn't see how you could have passed the physical tests and evaluations. I thought it might be one of those, umm whadda they call 'em. . .?" Harold waved his hand in the air, searching for the word. "Oh. A 'diversity hire' type of thing."

Ouch.

"Which, honestly, really chapped my hide," he went on, "because there shouldn't be any shortcuts in the FBI. Especially in our particular department. People can die with one wrong move. I remember thinking, 'are they seriously willing to put people's lives at risk for some good PR?'"

I kept my face neutral, but my arms crossed over my chest. In the early days, I had battled those thoughts myself. It had taken a long time for me to overcome them in my own head. Hearing them resurface, especially from Harold Hopper of all people, made it that much worse.

"So, I wanted to have an interview with you. I wanted to see for myself just how much they were willing to let slide for the sake of publicity. The way I saw it, you were likely going to work at some desk behind the scenes as a paper pusher regardless. So, I met with you. Do you remember that interview?"

"Vaguely," I said, pleased that my voice sounded stronger than I felt. I took a moment to look out the window at nothing in particular. The light shining in was a deep orange as the sun slipped in the sky.

"Yeah, well I remember all of it," Harold said, his voice more intense than it was before. "I was ready to drill you. Give you a little tough love. Tell you the things everyone else seemed too afraid to. But you know what? I forgot."

My eyes snapped back to him. He held my gaze.

"I forgot all about it," he admitted. "You came into my office and started right in, listing references and past job experiences. You had this force about you. This desire to do something. Be someone." He smiled.

"You never mentioned your condition directly and I forgot that it was even an issue in the first place." He shrugged. "At the end of it, I wanted you with us. I hired you right on the spot, remember? It was you that hesitated. Maybe because you hadn't forgotten."

"I never let myself forget," I breathed. I didn't have that luxury.

Harold nodded.

"I remember what you said when I offered you the job," he recalled. "You said, 'Are you sure you don't want to compare your notes with my file?' It was the first time during the entire interview that you sounded unsure. Do you remember what I told you?" He chuckled at the memory. "I said 'you have sixty seconds to decide before I give the job to someone who wants it.'"

His smile grew, clearly still pleased with himself for that.

"I continued to forget," he went on. "And one day, I woke up and realized it never mattered in the first place."

There was a warmth in his face that he rarely allowed. My chest tightened.

"This fact about you doesn't define who you are. It isn't what makes you a good agent, and it isn't what holds you back. You have other qualities that do both of those things," he stated pointedly, but his expression remained soft. "It was never a factor. You didn't let it become one."

"And you've never lost that force. That intensity," he continued. "It makes you work to be better, to push harder, and it demands everyone surrounding you to do the same. It's a force worth following. Hell, I was even willing to follow it myself."

He let his words hang in the air for a moment. I felt tears burn in my eyes but refused to let them fall. Instead, I held his gaze, just like I always had. Like I always would.

"Now, why don't you buck up and I'll buy you a steak from that place right on the edge of town," Harold said with a smile.

I almost laughed. This was a tradition of ours, trying a steak from every town or city a case brought us to. The places had, of course, ranged in quality depending on the area, from a five-star dining experience to a gray piece of meat from a questionable diner. It helped to provide a distraction from everything we might have had to deal with during a case.

He had been talking about this particular place for weeks.

"I thought your wife was trying to get you to lower your cholesterol intake?" I questioned.

He waved me off. "Don't be a buzzkill. You want the steak or not?"

"Fine, but I'm paying this time," I said, grabbing my coat.

"That would defeat the purpose of me 'buying you the steak.'" He wagged his finger at me knowingly.

I didn't have the energy to argue.

41

ELLE

I didn't realize I was heading to his house until I was standing outside the door. I looked at the wood panels, the inches of separation between me and the man I had once loved.

It was tempting to just let myself in. I knew it wasn't locked (what was it with cops not locking their front door?). I used to be able to just open the door. Before.

Maybe that was why it felt even more important to use the doorbell now. To put distance between the way we were then, and the way we had to be now. Back then, letting myself in represented a closeness, a comfort level . . .

I rang the bell again and again, insistent. I decided to give him exactly four seconds before busting through the barrier regardless. I heard shuffling behind the door as I got to three.

With a creak of the worn wood, Andrew pulled open the door. He was still wearing his beat-up uniform. The right sleeve was ripped, and he was covered in dust from rolling around the station floor. His eyes were bloodshot, and the skin around his left was already turning purple. Blood from his split lip had crusted over.

He looked at me wearily, shoulders hunched. "Didn't expect to see you," he said. His voice was hoarse.

"Ta da," I muttered.

He motioned for me to come in, and I brushed past him without a word. In the kitchen, a small hand towel lay on the counter with fresh blood stains. I stopped, staring at it. I felt him behind me, but I didn't say anything.

I wondered how long we stood there in silence. The tension was thick and tangible, but I didn't care.

I realized I was waiting for him to speak first. As if he might have some explanation. As if that would make it better.

Finally, he broke the silence.

"Did you know?" His voice was quiet, but his tone made it sound more like an accusation than a question.

I turned to face him. "Yes," I said. I saw a hint of surprise in his face as if he hadn't really believed that that would actually be my answer.

A muscle in his jaw tightened. "And you didn't tell me." The air in the room felt heavy with the statement. He looked at me like I had betrayed some trust, some vow I hadn't been aware of making. I almost laughed at the irony.

"After how you reacted, I don't see how you can blame me," I said.

"I had a right to know," Andrew all but growled.

Something in his words made me snap. "You had a right to nothing," I hissed, pointing my finger at him. "You. Had. No. Right—"

"No. *You* have no right." He squared his shoulders as if daring me to challenge him. "You come into our station asking for a favor, and then you have the nerve to pal around with *them*? Does loyalty mean nothing to you?" I heard his voice break just a little. "You find *this* out, this thing that could affect the safety of all the people you claim to care about, and you do nothing? Instead of protecting us, of protecting your family, you protect *them*? Protect *her*?"

I blinked, stunned at the accusation.

"*We* are the ones who agreed to help you," he went on. "*I* am the one who agreed to help you." He jabbed a thumb into his chest for emphasis, hurt filling his eyes. "I was the one who was there for you, Elle. Me. I got everyone to agree to letting you hang around. I did that. Not any of your new FBI friends. I was there. I've always been there. But, then you do this? Lie to me? Go behind my back—"

"I never lied to you," I cut him off, forcing my voice to remain calm.

"I never went behind your back. I did what someone had to do. I bridged the gap, instead of shutting out the people who are here to help. I made a choice. A choice I would have made for you too, by the way."

He sneered. "I've never needed anyone to lie for me, thank you very much."

"This was none of your business," I said. "It's none of anyone's business other than Roslyn's." His eyes widened as he heard me use her first name. But I didn't care. "This was personal information that you had no right to announce to everyone, let alone exploit." Roslyn's face flashed through my head for a moment. I could only imagine what she must have felt. "How could you do that? How can you show so little regard for someone? What the hell is wrong with you?" I realized I was screaming.

"Me? What the hell is wrong with you?" Andrew bellowed. "You stand here and defend *her* when she could have gotten us all killed!"

"What do you—" I started, but he cut me off.

"What would happen if she has a fit during a gunfight, huh? What if we have our heads blown off because we have to cover her ass?"

"She has ways to handle it," I shot back. "That's clearly enough for the FBI, so why isn't that enough for you?"

"Sometimes the FBI cares more about who they can showboat than they do about actual credentials," he mumbled.

I stared at him before something clicked. "Is . . . Is that what this is about?" I asked. He froze, his eyes widening as he realized his slip.

"Because the FBI didn't hire you . . ." I started, my voice dangerously low, ". . . you're taking it out on her."

He opened his mouth to retort, but his eyes confirmed my words.

"You son of a bitch," I breathed, feeling like I wanted to laugh at the absurdity of it all, slap him, or just start crying.

"You don't know what you're talking about," he started, but he had lost his momentum.

"This must've really stung, huh?" I whispered, my voice just audible enough for him to hear the fake pity dripping from it. My fists were clenched so tight that my knuckles hurt. "Finding out she had a disability must have been really hard for you. Must've made the fact that they rejected you hurt just a little bit more."

He started toward me. "Don't you dare imply that I—"

"Am I wrong?" I yelled, taking a step toward him too.

"Of course, you are!" he screamed back, but his eyes wouldn't meet mine. "This has nothing to do with—"

"Then why can't you look at me when you say it?" I snapped, taking another step toward him. We were a foot apart now. I could smell the sweat, blood, and dirt on his clothes. My eyes never left his face, daring him to look at me.

He couldn't. My nose wrinkled in disgust.

"How did I not see this before?" I whispered, mostly to myself. "All those years of being with you, of missing you, when this is the kind of person you are."

"You don't get to judge me," he said, traces of something that looked like shame swirling in his eyes. "You lost that the moment you left."

"Oh, I see . . . Your moral and emotional shortcomings must be my fault," I said sarcastically through clenched teeth.

"You know what I mean," he said. "You left and you didn't look back. Moved on to bigger and better things and left us all behind to rot. Left me behind . . ."

I shook my head. "This has nothing to do with any of that."

"Of course, it does!" he yelled. His voice cracked with emotion. It took me by surprise. "I lost everything when you left!" Tears glistened in his eyes, and despite myself, I felt a lump form in the back of my throat.

"The bureau was the last thing I had. The thing that was going to get me out of here. The thing that was going to give me . . . something! It's what I held onto when you drove off. It was the only thing that kept me from falling apart. It didn't matter you were leaving because soon, I would be too. I would be too caught up with my job to miss you. Too busy to think about how I let you slip through my fingers. It was the only thing that kept me from hating myself. Hating that I had let you walk away. I needed that job, Elle." His face contorted with raw emotion and my chest tightened.

But it didn't excuse what he had done.

"Don't turn all this around. Take some fucking responsibility," I said. "You didn't have to stay here, no one had a gun to your head." Part of me registered the poor choice of words. "What was I supposed to do? Put my life on hold? Stop everything so that you had time to catch up?" As the full extent of my anger hit the open air, Andrew flinched like I had physically struck him. I winced, feeling guilt rise in the back of my throat like bile. I looked away.

"Sorry," I muttered.

"No. Don't hold back. Tell me how you really feel," he said, before sighing. His shoulders slumped, all of the anger fading away. "It's not like I don't know . . . I know."

Silence sucked the fight from the room.

"You were always destined for more," he breathed, a small, sad smile forming on his lips. "I'm sorry I couldn't give that to you."

I wondered what kind of more he was referring to. Was he talking about my career? Who I was with?

"There was nothing more you could have given me, Andrew," I said, my voice hushed. "Not here. I needed to see what else was out there. I needed to see what more I could be, what more I could do. I had to leave this place . . . and you . . ." I hesitated. "You didn't follow me." There was no malice in my words. It was just the truth.

We locked eyes.

"I didn't know you wanted me to," he admitted.

"Of course, I did," I whispered. I thought back to the day I left for my first real job. Andrew and I had stood by my car, avoiding eye contact. As if that alone would make us fall apart. I remembered hoping that he would offer to come with me. To tell me that he could transfer to another station in Providence. I wouldn't ask him. If he had wanted to come with me, I figured he would have done it on his own.

I remembered hoping that he would chase after the car as I pulled out of the driveway. Hoping he wouldn't let me leave without him.

And I remembered sobbing on the freeway when he never tried.

I quickly wiped away a stray tear as it fell down my face. Andrew took a deep breath, trying to collect himself.

"I never got over you, you know," he said. I hadn't realized how close we had moved to each other during the fight. He was close enough to touch. There was something in his eyes that I hadn't seen in years. A look that I was once able to return.

"Andrew . . ." I said, starting to shake my head. I needed to stop him before he said or did something he shouldn't. Something that would destroy the rocky friendship we had.

"Elle." He said my name with a firm softness.

"Don't," I almost begged.

"Why?"

"Because that was a long time ago," I said.

"That's what you're resting your case on?" he asked.

What did he—?

Oh.

"—and I'm engaged!" I rushed, trying to make up for the fact that that wasn't the first thing on my mind. *I'm so sorry, Eric.*

"Sure you are," Andrew chuckled.

"I am," I said, having to crane my neck to glare up at him.

"Who are you trying to convince?" he said with a growing smirk. I didn't find it funny. Heat spread to my cheeks and I opened my mouth to retort but thought better of it.

I turned my head away.

"Do you still love me?" Andrew asked. The question was so abrupt that it took me by surprise.

"What?" I stuttered.

"You heard me."

I could feel his gaze boring a hole through the side of my head.

"No," I said, forcing myself to look right into his eyes as I said it.

"Really? Not at all?" he said, raising an eyebrow. Goading me.

"No." I looked away again.

"Well, now I know you're lying."

"I'm not! I'm sorry, but I don't. Not anymore."

"Elle." He cut me off, putting his hands on my shoulders and turning me to face him. I was startled by the contact. He stared at me, deep into me, and he was getting closer. My pulse raced and I couldn't tell if it was with anticipation or dread.

"Look at me and tell me you don't feel anything," he whispered, his breath washing over my face in a pleasant warmth. This time I really looked at him. I let myself remember the way he made me feel when he lifted me up and swung me around. The way he held me when I was upset, his strong arms wrapped around me, protecting me from the world. The way he could tell the worst joke in the world and I would still feel a thrill when he got to the punchline. The way he would point out punch buggies, only to let me punch him first. The way he was always there for me after all these years, even when I had smashed his heart into pieces . . .

"You know I do," I sighed, and I saw the hope flash in his eyes. My heart clenched. "But not like that."

Just as quickly, the light in his face faded.

"I love you, and a part of me always will, but I've moved on," I urged quietly. "It's not the same anymore. You know that. Too much has happened. I'm not the same person I was then."

"You're still you," he vowed, his hand cupping my cheek and forcing me to look at him again.

I hadn't even realized I'd looked away.

"So, this fiancé then. Do you love him?" Andrew's gaze intensified as he said it, reading my face as if it would give him an insight into what I was thinking.

I paused.

"Yes. I do."

"You hesitated," he argued. I thought about fighting that, but he wasn't wrong.

"I was thinking about it," I reasoned, pulling away from his touch.

"You had to think about whether you love the man you plan to marry?" he pressed.

Fuck.

"N-no. I was just . . . thinking about . . . everything." I said, hoping he didn't catch the stumble. He did and snorted a chuckle.

"If you don't even know if you're in love with your fiancé, how can you know whether you love me in the 'right way'?" he asked, a knowing smile spreading across his face as if he knew he had me cornered. I opened my mouth, hoping something brilliant would come out.

Nothing did.

Andrew cocked his head to one side as if studying something

interesting while I struggled to collect my thoughts into something that made sense. He was right. I loved Eric, but was I in love with him? If I was being honest with myself, I would probably realize that I wasn't. When I was in love with Andrew, I knew it. With Eric . . . I'd never gotten to that point, but maybe I would eventually?

A part of me knew I was lying.

But it had always been easy with Eric. We never fought, we never argued . . . There was never a need to. It was as easy as breathing with him, from our first date to moving in together, to even saying yes to his proposal. But there was always something missing. While I was attracted to him, it wasn't the kind of attraction that gave you a jolt when your eyes met from across the room. A blush that crept up your neck. I never shivered when he brushed against me or forgot to breathe when he smiled at me in a certain way. I had only felt that with Andrew.

I felt my face grow hot.

Huh?

I shook my head trying to clear it. *This is not the time to be thinking about this,* a voice in my head warned, but it was too late.

The evidence was right there in front of me, and it took this moment of comparison to see the irrefutable facts.

The feelings I once had for Andrew, I was starting to have for Roslyn.

It's because she's completely unattainable, the voice in the back of my mind tried to reason.

But I knew the voice was lying. That wasn't why.

Okay . . . So, maybe you have an infatuation. But that's all it is.

Except it was more than that.

"I have to go," I said hurriedly. I had the sudden urge to flee.

As if you can run from this, the voice taunted.

"Watch me," I growled.

"Watch you what? Leave?" Andrew asked, confused. Yup, I was truly losing it.

"Sorry, I just . . . I have to lie down," I said.

It wasn't exactly a lie. I felt nauseous.

"Elle, I'm sorry. I didn't mean to—" he started, clearly concerned. My face must have looked as distraught as I felt.

"No no, you didn't do anything wrong," I said. It was ironic that I had literally come here for the sole purpose of telling him how much he had done wrong. But I could deal with the moral implications of that later.

I rushed to the door and wrenched it open. Andrew was there in an instant.

"Elle, wait. I didn't mean to upset you. Just come back inside and we can talk about this."

"I can't. I'm sorry. It's not you," I said. Realizing the truth of that statement only added to the guilt I was already feeling. "I just have to go."

I couldn't look back as I sprinted to my car. Within seconds I was on the road, headed for Zoey's place.

42

ELLE

"So, let me get this straight," Zoey said slowly, holding up her hands to cradle the sides of her face. The pressure was squishing her cheeks together. "Your ex, from a billion years ago, just publicly humiliated himself, got himself beaten to a pulp, exposed your bitchy FBI friend's biggest secret, and confessed his undying love for you. Which was when you realized that you might actually have feelings for the bitchy FBI friend that you think are strong enough for you to call off your entire wedding, lose the security deposit on it, ditch Prince Charming, become essentially homeless, get into a custody battle over your cat, and have to come out as gay to your entire family, which includes, in case you've forgotten, your very traditional grandmother with the heart condition . . ." She risked glancing up at me, clearly hoping I would correct her.

"Well, it sounds bad when you put it that way," I mumbled.

She smashed her cheeks even harder. "No, it sounds insane!" Zoey squeaked.

"I know!" I shouted back, practically hysterical. I had come out as bi to Zoey years ago and she had been more than accepting, so I knew that wasn't the issue. The issue was . . . well, everything else.

Zoey looked up at me desperately. "I mean . . . maybe this is just pre-wedding jitters. That's a thing," she tried.

"It's not that," I mumbled.

"Okay so . . . maybe you actually are attracted to this chick for real. Who cares? She's hot and you're human. Honestly, I would be more concerned if you *weren't* attracted to her. I saw her the other day. I'd bang her and I'm straight."

"*And* in a relationship!" Travis yelped from the kitchen. Zoey ignored him and continued.

"You'd have to be blind not to be into her," she went on. "She has that sexy, brooding thing going on . . ." She cleared her throat when she realized she was no longer helping. "So what?" she continued with newfound enthusiasm. "I'm attracted to plenty of other people. It doesn't mean anything."

"*What*?" Travis shrieked, whipping his head around the corner from the kitchen. He was cooking some sort of pasta-shrimp thing.

Zoey waved her hand at him, dismissively. "Oh, relax. Like you didn't have a thing for Darleen Maxwell."

Travis' face paled and he ducked back around the corner.

"Exactly," Zoey turned back to me, grinning as if she had just made her point. "It's no biggie."

"I'm not just attracted to her," I muttered.

Zoey looked at me, confused. "What do you mean?"

I bit my lip.

"Wait . . . You . . . You're not in love with her, are you?" she asked.

"No!" I said quickly, shaking my head hard and fast. "No. No. No. We aren't even seeing each other, and we've only known each other for like a month. Come on . . ." I trailed off, not looking Zoey in the eye.

"But . . ." she pushed.

"But . . ." I started slowly. "Given the chance . . . Who knows . . ." I looked up to see Zoey staring at me, her eyes as wide as saucers.

"Well, what am I supposed to do with that?" She threw her hands up in the air.

"You're supposed to be supportive, Z," Travis called from the kitchen.

"I *am*!" Zoey shouted back, before looking at me seriously. "Really. I am. All I want is for you to grow old and stupid-happy with the love of your life. I just don't want you to risk everything that has already made you happy, for something you don't even know will work."

"In fact, it's much more likely it won't work at all," I laughed, but it wasn't funny.

"You're only making my point for me," Zoey said.

I sighed, trying to organize my thoughts.

"Hey," Zoey said. "You don't need to make any decisions tonight. It's been a long day. Sleep on it. We can talk more about it tomorrow."

I nodded. Maybe all I needed was some sleep.

But later that night as I lay in bed, sleep seemed impossible. I continued to toss and turn for hours until I gave up. I decided to head to the station, figuring that I could occupy my brain with real problems.

In hindsight, I should have realized that Roslyn would be there, even if I did have to disable the security system myself (Andrew had told me the code weeks ago so I could stay late). I walked into the conference room to find Roslyn curled up in an office chair with her jacket tucked under her head, fast asleep. I froze as soon as I saw her.

As I stood motionless in the doorway, I couldn't help but wonder how she was able to sleep in that particular position. She had somehow managed to contort herself into the chair, her entire body twisted in a way so she wouldn't fall. Her arms were wrapped around herself tightly as if she were cold, and her face looked tense. I felt an urge to shrug off my own jacket to put over her but worried that would wake her up.

It was as if my thoughts alone caused a disruption in the room, and she began to stir. Frozen to the spot, I watched her eyes open and instantly focus on me. I offered a shy, apologetic smile. She uncoiled herself, stretching her limbs like a cat after a nap.

"What are you doing here?" she murmured, her voice soft with sleep.

"I just wanted to get a head start today," I said. "I'm sorry. I didn't mean to wake you."

"Don't apologize. I'm the one who dozed off."

As she rolled up her sleeves, I saw that the silver bracelet was back on her wrist. It forced the memories of the previous day back to the surface. I gulped as I considered bringing it up. *Bad idea,* my internal monologue warned. *That would be a very, very bad idea. Do not. Don't even think about—*

"Roslyn," I started, unable to help myself. "I'm so sorry for yesterday. I-I had no idea Andrew would do that."

She stiffened, and I wished I could suck the words back.

"What happened yesterday was in no way your fault," Roslyn said, moving about the room to collect files. I think it was just an excuse to do something.

"But—"

"Do not apologize on behalf of others. That is not your responsibility."

She was so forceful, I realized arguing was pointless.

"I'm sorry it happened," I whispered instead.

She looked up.

"I am too," she admitted, her voice so hushed that if I hadn't seen her mouth move, I might not have believed that she had said anything.

We stood there in silence for a moment, looking at one another.

"Anyway . . ." Roslyn said as a way of moving on.

It was another hour before I ventured into the break room. From the corner of my eye, I saw Andrew slip past. I pretended not to see him, despite feeling his gaze.

Chief Ramos flung his office door open. I could just make out the tired sound of an old CD before it was drowned out by his voice. "I just fucking heard," Ramos shouted at Andrew, jabbing his thumb back toward his office. "Get in here."

Ramos slammed the door after them, but it wasn't up to the job of blocking out the sound from within.

"Verbally attacking an FBI unit chief, assaulting an agent . . ." Ramos' voice shook through the office.

If Andrew responded, I couldn't make it out. I felt someone beside me and turned my head to see Benjie. He was watching the scene through the shades at the office windows. You could just make out the dramatic hand gestures Ramos was making.

"I ratted on him," Benjie murmured to me. He looked as if he had aged five years in the last twenty-four hours. "Someone had to. So . . . I did." Despite his soft voice, his eyes were determined.

"You did the right thing," I said.

With a bang, Ramos slammed his hand against the glass, rattling the shades and making them quiver and shake. Benjie and I jumped. Andrew walked out of the room wide-eyed and shocked.

Before making a beeline for Benjie.

"You told him," he growled. It wasn't a question.

I looked at Benjie, surprised to find him calm and collected, even under the harsh stare of his superior.

"Yeah." The young man nodded. "It was me."

"What the fuck?" Andrew breathed, sounding more hurt with betrayal than furious.

"It wasn't right, Andrew," Benjie said, his voice quiet but firm. Gone was the frightened boy of yesterday, and in his place stood a man who was sure of himself. He was still gentle, but there was a confidence that had been missing. "What you did . . . It wasn't right."

I saw Andrew's eyes soften as he looked at the young cop, a range of emotions fighting for control of his features. There was a softness underneath the hurt. A pride that shone as he looked at the boy he had trained. It had taken courage for Benjie to go against him. After years of encouragement and mentorship, the young cop was doing what Andrew would have wanted him to, even if it was against him.

Andrew stood there for another few moments, before turning and walking out the door.

Benjie sighed, putting his hands deep into his pockets. "This whole thing is kind of a shit show, isn't it?" he muttered.

"That's putting it lightly," I said.

"It . . . can't get worse . . . right?" Benjie asked.

"I don't see how," I muttered. From inside Ramos' office, I could just hear the gravelly voice of the CD as it played on. It was a playlist of old sea shanty tunes. I caught some of the lyrics:

> *Farewell and adieu, to you fair Spanish ladies,*
> *Farewell and adieu, to you ladies of Spain . . .*

43

ROSLYN

A knock on the door made me turn.

"Agent Hunt," Ramos said, peering in.

"Chief Ramos," I greeted, motioning for him to come into his own meeting room.

He moved stiffly, clearly agitated.

"I was informed about the events of yesterday," he began. He watched me, his dark eyes gauging my expression. "I just wanted to apologize on behalf of my lieutenant. I assure you, disciplinary action will be taken."

I pursed my lips, debating how best to play this. Andrew Wells wasn't the only one who could lose his job after yesterday.

Dalton could too.

"I can look past it if you can," I said. "We need to focus on the task at hand."

Chief Ramos nodded as he walked further into the room. "I can agree to that," he said. His eyes trailed over the crime scene pictures. "Any other leads?" he asked, his gaze fastened on the pictures. Unblinking.

I sighed. "Nothing concrete."

Ramos didn't say anything as he continued to stare at the pictures, his expression blank and impossible to read. Finally, his eyes snapped back to me.

"One day at a time. Right?" he said, a tired smile warming his face. He eased out of the room, freshly polished handcuffs swinging from his belt.

I focused back on the whiteboard. After another hour, the fluorescent light overhead started to make my head pound. I closed my eyes for a moment.

"Long morning?" someone said behind me. The voice was gentle. Caring.

I chuckled dryly. "You could say that," I allowed, opening my eyes to the blinding fluorescent light again.

"Well, if you're trying to get some sleep, I would suggest at least going back to your chair," Elle Wolfe teased as she walked through the doorway. She was wearing her hair back in a messy ponytail, locks of her thick hair slipping out of it.

The look suited her.

"Unless you can sleep standing up too," she grinned. "Which wouldn't surprise me."

I let out a breathy laugh, but it sounded more strained than I anticipated. Her smile faded into a look of concern. She opened her mouth to say something, but I shot her a look of warning.

"How'd the talk go with Ramos?" she pivoted instead.

"We didn't talk about the specifics of your boyfriend's job if that's what you were wondering," I replied curtly. I winced at the bite in my tone when I saw her flinch at the words. I sighed, pinching the bridge of my nose. "That wasn't fair," I muttered by way of an apology.

"It's okay," Wolfe said brightly, bouncing back fast. "You've had a hard twenty-four hours. You're allowed to be a little snippy." She smirked. "It doesn't explain the other ninety-eight percent of the time. But right now, you get a pass."

I decided to ignore the comment. "Did you need something?"

"Oh, right," she exclaimed, looking down at the brown bag in her hand. "I went to grab myself something and brought you a muffin. A boring one this time. Lemon poppyseed."

I smiled at the gesture. It was simple, but thoughtful, nonetheless.

"Thank you."

"Any time," she said, warmth flooding out of her expression as I accepted the bag. Our eyes locked for a moment and she held my gaze. There was something curious in her expression.

Something that made me hesitate.

A nudge of a body between us broke the stare.

"Jasper," I breathed as he butted his head into me, his eyes on the bag. "I think he thinks it's for him."

"I'll make sure to get some dog treats later," Wolfe laughed, kneeling down to scratch him under the chin. The dog gave a content grumble, leaning into her hand shamelessly.

"Don't encourage him," I tried and failed to scold.

"How could you not? Look at him," Wolfe cooed. "He's so stinkin' cute."

Jasper, as if to prove her right, let his tongue loll out to give Wolfe a lick.

"You should be honored. He usually doesn't like people," I said. Police canines weren't happy idiots like others of their kind.

"I wonder where he got that from?" Wolfe teased, shooting me a look from her spot on the ground.

I shrugged. "Blame the breeding."

I was about to turn back to work when I heard her voice again.

"I . . . actually wanted to suggest something too," she offered slowly. "If you're up for it."

I arched an eyebrow. My reflex was to brush her off, but she was looking at me with such hope in her eyes that it made it more difficult than it should have been. I gave a nod, allowing her to continue . . .

Within the hour, we had Benjie Hara and Jay Kama in the back room with the rest of my team. They looked uncomfortable, to say the least, but over the course of the day, they seemed to loosen up.

Wolfe had coaxed them into what had apparently been dubbed 'FBI Territory.' According to her, these two cops were the most willing to set their differences aside. By the end of the day, it seemed that a United Nations between the FBI and the Cape August cops had been formed. We compared notes, exchanged theories, and helped one another think things through.

Whether it would last would remain to be seen.

"You're staying the night again?" Wolfe asked as she packed up for the day.

I glanced at the clock. It was already 10:28 p.m. I rubbed the back of my neck, trying to work out the stiffness before nodding.

"You're going to collapse," she warned, before realizing her words. "From exhaustion! I didn't mean it as a dig for your epilepsy. I swear."

I could barely suppress an eye roll. "You do realize that every little thing is not tied to that?"

She looked sheepish. "I know. Sorry. I just don't want to offend you or say the wrong thing."

"You won't offend me," I muttered. "But you will annoy the living hell out of me if you keep tiptoeing around it."

"So, all that PC stuff just isn't for you then, huh?" she chuckled, her gray eyes brightening.

I twitched a smile. "Goodnight, Wolfe."

She sighed dramatically at the use of her last name.

"Goodnight, *Hunt*," she mimicked, before heading toward the door. From the corner of my eye, I saw her hesitate.

"Yes?" I asked, wondering what else she could possibly want.

"Uhh . . ." She sounded nervous. I felt my expression soften despite myself.

"Just, don't stay too late," Wolfe said, offering a small, shy smile. "Even a robot needs time to reboot."

"I'll send that message to the motherboard," I said.

"That wasn't funny," she snorted, light dancing in her eyes.

"Noted."

44

ROSLYN

I went to the hotel not long after Elle Wolfe left, walking down the long, artificially lit hall until I reached number 23. I wrapped my knuckles twice and Dalton opened the door quickly, as if not wanting to give me another reason to reprimand him.

"So . . ." he started, inviting me in. His eyes darted from me to the floor and back to me again. It was the first time we'd seen each other since the brawl.

"What the hell were you thinking?" I tried to keep my tone calm. Composed.

"I couldn't let him talk to you like that," Dalton mumbled.

"You're lucky," I said, anger coiling in my stomach. "I talked to Ramos this morning and we've agreed to look past this whole thing."

"What?" Dalton demanded, his tone forceful and angry. "What does that mean about Wells?"

"We made a trade," I said. "I don't go after him and he doesn't go after you."

"So, you're not going to do anything?" Dalton asked, his voice rising.

"You should be thanking me," I said. "They could just as easily be reporting you for the shit you pulled."

"He swung first—"

"You antagonized him," I said, my eyes flashing a warning.

He began pacing the room, agitated. "The things he was saying—"

"—were none of your concern." My voice was calm, final.

"Are you kidding?"

"Hardly," I said, fighting back a low snarl as I went for the jugular. "In fact, I seem to recall a time when you shared the lieutenant's opinion."

It was as if I had smacked him across the face.

"You know how sorry I am for that," Dalton whispered, sounding ashamed.

"I don't need you to be sorry, and I sure as hell don't need you defending me."

"So, what, I was supposed to just stand there?" Dalton argued. "While you just allowed him to—"

"Yes," I cut him off. "You stand there. You be a fucking adult, instead of throwing a tantrum." I dug my nails into the tender part of my palms. It kept me grounded. "You seem to forget that you don't just represent yourself. You represent the entire FBI. What you do reflects on everyone. You could have lost your job today, and for what? One good punch? If the director heard about this, he'd take your badge. Do you understand that? There would be nothing I could do." I fought the lump that was forming in my throat at the thought. If he had gotten fired because of me . . .

I rolled my shoulders back, my resolve stronger than ever.

"As it stands," I started, pleased that my voice sounded cold and detached, "you're out of the station for a week."

"A week?" Dalton choked. "When there's a fucking psycho on the loose? We need all the time we can—"

"Which is why your timing is so unfortunate," I said icily.

"Roz, don't—"

"That's *ma'am* to you," I snapped. "And you *will* be working. Just not in the station. You'll stay in this hotel and you won't leave under any circumstances. I don't care if the place is about to burst into flames." I took a step toward him, my chest aching with the effort it took to keep my voice level. "And, if you ever pull something like this again, you're done. I'll write the report and throw you out of the bureau myself. Is that clear?"

We stared at each other, and I saw the hurt in his eyes. I kept my mask in place. He needed me to be this firm. He'd forgotten his place because I'd let him.

Dalton glowered. "Yes, *ma'am*."

Turning on my heel, I swept from the room, unwilling and unable to look at him for another moment. To stare at the purple bruise on the side of his cheek that so clearly represented my own failure. I didn't need the reminder. I already knew that the events of yesterday were my fault.

And it didn't even have anything to do with the silver bracelet cuffed around my wrist . . .

I fought the tremble of self-contempt as I heard the door shut roughly behind me. I'd gone soft, and that was why Dalton had crossed the line. He hadn't just reacted out of loyalty for his boss, but out of devotion to protect a friend.

The deeper I stalked through the empty hallway, the harder my emotions fought against my weakened resolve to keep them at bay. With each step, they pushed against my crumbling mask of composure. These phantoms of guilt and shame knew my game. They were no match for me when I had appearances to uphold. I was too practiced. Too disciplined. But they were patient.

Alone, I was vulnerable to them.

It was at times like this that these voices fought from the deepest corners of my subconscious, clawing their way to the surface. Their screams of self-loathing rose in volume the deeper I went into isolation. Shrieking things that dwarfed the words of Andrew Wells, or anyone else for that matter. My internal demons were the harshest of critics and they knew exactly where and when to strike.

They swirled in my skull, yowling of my weakness. My inadequacy. My *defects*. Not one of which included epilepsy.

Ironic.

45

ELLE

Dalton's absence in the station was noticed, as was Andrew's limited appearance, but no one discussed the incident again. Benjie and Jay now entered the conference room every day, working hard to bridge the gap between the locals and Roslyn's team. When Dalton finally returned to the station, he didn't acknowledge their presence. Instead, he went right back to work as though nothing had happened, although he and Roslyn were noticeably stiffer toward one another.

As the FBI team discussed theories, I could feel the chill in the room.

"Hunt—" Oliver began but was drowned out by Dalton's tense voice.

"We know Peter Edgars is hiding something," he said, shooting a dagger-filled glare at Roslyn. "So, why can't we just bring him back here?"

"For the *third* time, we need to find something concrete," Roslyn muttered, her jaw tight with agitation.

"Hunt. I think you might—" Oliver started, a little louder. He was staring out the window.

"We can try a different questioning tactic," Dalton argued, crossing his arms over his chest. "He's bound to break eventually."

A snarl twitched Roslyn's face. "I already told you, no. If I need to say it one more time—"

"Roslyn!" Oliver squeaked. Everyone looked at him with surprise, stunned by the quiet man's outburst.

"Yes?" Roslyn asked.

"I think someone is here to see you." Oliver seemed even more flustered than usual.

Roslyn shot him a puzzled glance. "Were we expecting someone to come in?"

"No . . ." Oliver said, casting a nervous glance out the window again.

"Then, how do you know someone is here to see *me*?" Roslyn pushed.

"Call it a lucky guess . . ." Oliver mumbled. Dalton, who was closest to him, walked over and took a look out the window for himself. He started to chuckle, some of the rigidness melting away despite himself.

"*Ma'am* . . . You're in for it," Dalton said, his eyes training on something or someone outside. "Brace yourself."

"What are you—" Roslyn started, before the station door creaked open. She backed up a couple of steps to take a look.

She raised her eyebrows in shock.

"Rozie," a voice said. It was a high voice with an accent that I couldn't quite identify and was accompanied by the quick sound of heels. A pale, porcelain-like woman swept into the room. She was tall, probably close to six feet, with auburn hair that fell slightly above her shoulders. Her eyes were an annoyingly dazzling blue and were framed by eyelashes so long they almost looked fake.

The stranger threw her arms around Roslyn and went in for a kiss, but Roslyn dodged her lips and quickly held her at arm's length. While the woman clearly looked disappointed, she settled for clinging to Roslyn's arm like it was some sort of lifeline.

I instantly hated her.

"Emily." Roslyn greeted her with a conservative smile. "You remember the team."

"Of course, of course." Emily beamed at them. "It's so good to see you all again."

Her voice is too cheerful. I thought to myself. *And the way she's hanging on to Roslyn . . . It makes me just want to—*

"And this is our local consultant, Elle Wolfe." Roslyn's voice brought me back to reality and I saw that all eyes were on me.

"A pleasure to meet you, Elle," Emily said, gracing me with a huge smile.

"The pleasure is all mine," I said, sounding as nice as I could. Sickly sweet. I smiled, but it felt more like a grimace.

"What are you doing here?" Roslyn muttered.

That's what we all want to know, I thought.

"I have to go to Martha's Vineyard for work, and this wasn't far out of the way," Emily said brightly. "I wanted to see how you were doing. Are you still working tonight?"

"We are still wrapping up," Roslyn said.

"Well, I can wait out there. Maybe then I can buy you dinner?" Emily asked.

Roslyn hesitated. "That . . . sounds nice."

"Brilliant! We need to put some meat on those bones," Emily said playfully.

"You're one to talk," Bonnie muttered under her breath, too low for anyone else to hear.

"See you in a minute," Roslyn said as she redirected Emily to the break room.

After Emily was gone, there was a moment of silence. All eyes were on Roslyn.

"What?" Roslyn demanded.

"She's *so* nice!" Matilda chirped happily.

"—and ohhh so hot," Dalton said with a wink, apparently getting over whatever bitterness he had toward Roslyn. For a second, I thought Roslyn's expression toward him softened.

"Enough," she said regardless.

"You must have done something pretty great in a past life, Boss," Dalton teased. "Or maybe you're just really good in be—"

"Finish that sentence and I swear you'll never make it back to Boston."

Dalton beamed, pretending to zip his mouth shut. I caught half a smile as Roslyn shook her head.

After another hour, Roslyn began to reluctantly pack her stuff.

"Is everyone all right for the night?" she asked.

"I think we all can manage one night without you," Dalton said with a devilish grin as he walked up to her, totally comfortable again. He lowered his voice. "This is probably the first time you didn't outlast us, Boss. I guess you'll have to make up for it by trying to outlast Emily in—"

Dalton cut himself off with an *oof* as Roslyn's sharp elbow jabbed into his side.

"I think the rest of us are going to use this as an excuse to head out ourselves," Harold interrupted.

"Yes, please," Bonnie muttered, rubbing her face with her hands. "I think I'm going to go cross-eyed if I trawl through any more records."

Within a few minutes, the entire team was outside in the cool night air.

"I'm parked over here," Emily said, pulling on Roslyn's arm to guide her away from the group.

"Hey, Em, just make sure she can walk tomorrow. That's all we ask," Dalton called as he backed toward the SUV.

Roslyn's hand twitched a certain finger.

I felt glued to the spot, watching Emily's hand linger on Roslyn's hip as they walked away. My mouth went dry as I came to a very important decision.

I needed a drink. A strong one.

46

ELLE

It wasn't long before I had a margarita and a half in my system.

"Take it easy," Dalton laughed. "I think the glass is bigger than you."

"Yeah, yeah," I waved him off. "Leave me alone."

"Yeeahhh. Leev 'er 'lone," Bonnie slurred. She had gone straight for the vodka.

"I think it's time for you to go home," Oliver suggested, gently poking at Bonnie's shoulder.

She grumbled something unintelligible as she slumped in her chair.

"Is she okay?" I asked Dalton. He just chuckled, tousling his hair for the fourth time. The more he drank, the more frequently he did it.

"She's fine," he said. "Just a long day."

"Lung munth," Bonnie corrected.

I stayed silent, swirling the straw in my drink. Dalton an eyebrow at me.

"What's up with you? You've been acting weird all night," he noted.

I blushed, before glancing at Matilda who swayed alone in the middle of the bar with no music at all.

She'd only had a Virgin Mary.

"Have you seen the people you hang out with?" I challenged, refusing to meet his gaze.

Dalton laughed into his scotch. "You fit right in."

"That's the nicest thing you've ever said to me," I swooned, putting a hand on my heart.

"Don't get used to it," he warned with a grin.

"Ya. He's a bug softy underneath it ull," Bonnie slurred, poking at the yellowing bruise on Dalton's face. "Ask Roselun."

Dalton rolled his eyes as he looked at his watch. "All right. Party's over," he said. "Time to go."

"Fivvee mur minutess," Bonnie whined.

"Nope. You gotta sleep it off," Dalton said, getting up to pry Bonnie off the bar counter. She tried to use her dead weight as a way to resist his efforts . . . Or maybe she just couldn't stand.

Dalton threw her over his shoulder regardless.

"Do you want a ride home?" he asked me.

I shook my head. "I'm going to go back to the precinct and get some more writing done."

"If you say so."

Walking into the empty station, a blast of frigid air made me shiver. I spent over twenty minutes trying to turn down the AC, accidentally breaking off a panel. Soon, I found myself knee-deep in office supplies, breaking into a cold sweat and searching for tape to fix it.

"Where is it . . ." I muttered to myself.

Then . . .

"I just think we should talk . . ." a high-pitched voice carried through the station, making my hand freeze in mid-air.

"I don't know what there is to talk about," Roslyn snapped back, her voice tense. They had just entered the station.

Run, my brain screamed. But my legs wouldn't move.

"I deserve a bloody answer, Roslyn," Emily pressed. She sounded angry and hurt. A deadly combination.

I practically flung myself toward the open door of the closet as I heard footsteps approaching. Instinct took over and I crouched to the ground, wrenching the closet door closed as quickly and as quietly as possible. I had already heard more than I should have. I couldn't expose myself now. My heart raced as my eyes fought to adjust to the darkness. The only source of light seeped in through the grates in the lower half of the door.

"What do you want me to say?" Roslyn's voice sounded exasperated as I heard the pair enter the room.

Unable to resist, I contorted myself to peer through the grates.

"I want you to tell me the truth. What am I to you?" Emily pushed. I could see their legs and feet now. Roslyn was ahead of Emily (I recognized the black heels), facing away from her.

"Am I an easy hook-up? Or some pet that you don't mind keeping around?" Emily asked, taking a defiant step in her bright red pumps.

Roslyn spun around with an indignant gasp. "What? No! You know that's not how I see you," she argued defensively.

"How would I know that?" Emily sounded like she was on the verge of tears. "You don't answer the phone when I call, I barely see you when you're home, and then when I come here it seems like you're not even happy to see me!"

"I have a job. An important one. It takes a lot of my time. You know that," Roslyn retorted sharply. "I don't know why you came here and expected something different."

"So, you're saying I shouldn't have come," Emily said, her voice quivering.

"I didn't say that," Roslyn muttered.

"No, but that's what you wanted to say, isn't it?"

"Fine. You shouldn't have come," Roslyn stated, her voice suddenly cold. "I'm working. I can't be distracted when lives are literally relying on me to do my fucking job."

"I just missed you," Emily's voice broke, "and I thought that maybe, if I missed you, that you might have missed me too. And maybe I thought that since you have so much pressure on you, with these lives *literally* resting in your hands, that you might need someone who's there just for you. Even for a second." The red heels stepped closer to Roslyn. "Because that's what I would need. The reminder that someone's there for me . . . That . . . That someone loves me."

I heard the hesitation in Emily's voice and realized, probably around the same time Roslyn realized it judging by the way her legs tensed, what the woman had just said.

"Because I do, Rozie. I-I love you," Emily admitted, her voice sounding carefully hopeful.

"Emily—" Roslyn started. There was an edge of panic.

"You don't need to say it back," Emily interrupted. "You don't need to say anything at all." Her voice was so hushed that I had to strain to hear. "I just want you to think about it," Emily whispered. "I know it scares you. Letting people in. But I'm here. I'll always be right here." I heard Emily take a shaky breath before clearing her throat. "Anyway, I should be off. I'm supposed to be on the Vineyard first thing in the morning . . . Just promise me you'll mull it over?"

"I will," Roslyn murmured. There was a moment of silence. A long, agonizing moment when I could only imagine what was happening beyond my view before the red heels slowly backed away and clicked out the door.

I watched Roslyn's feet stand frozen to the spot for a long while. There wasn't a single sound and, if I hadn't been staring at her, I would have sworn that Roslyn had left the room too. I couldn't even hear her breathe.

After what felt like an eternity, there was an exasperated huff and the black heels began to pace. They would click in and out of view in fast, agitated movements.

I shifted, accidentally brushing a box of office supplies. I froze at the muffled clanking, looking down as if a glare alone could shut them up. Ironically, the tape I was looking for was right on top.

The universe had a cruel sense of irony.

I glanced at the black heels. They had stopped their pacing and were facing right at the door.

She's gonna kill me, I thought to myself. *Honestly though, I kind of deserve it.*

One long moment after another passed while Roslyn's feet remained fastened to the same tile on the floor. I didn't dare move. Maybe if she hadn't opened the door by now, maybe she would just leave and—

"You can come out now, Elle."

I felt all the blood drain from my face. Slowly, I rose from my spot on the floor and took one final breath before opening the closet door.

There was Roslyn, leaning against the desk with her arms folded as she faced me. She was wearing a dress that hugged her body perfectly, ending above the knee to show off her long, toned legs without flaunting them.

I looked sheepishly at her face, expecting her to be angry at me for eavesdropping. Instead, she just looked tired, which somehow made me feel worse.

"I'm so sorry," I blurted. "I didn't mean to hear any of that. I wanted to keep working on this article and . . . well, then . . . I . . . tape!" I yelped, grabbing the roll with sweaty fingers to show her.

Roslyn continued staring at my face. Then she sighed. "I'm sorry if any of that made you feel uncomfortable."

"What?" I stuttered, truly stunned by her reaction. "You . . . aren't angry?"

"Of course not," Roslyn said. "I was having a personal conversation that I chose to bring to the workplace. That's on me." Roslyn brought a finger to her temple. "I shouldn't have subjected you to any of that. It was unprofessional. I apologize."

"Oh," I murmured, not sure how to respond. I would have bet all of my savings on her having a vastly different reaction. I wracked my brain for something to say.

"More unprofessional than hiding in a closet?" I finally offered.

She chuckled and I felt myself smile.

"How did you even know it was me in there?" I asked.

"That's your mug," Roslyn said, eying the polka-dot coffee mug, freshly brewed coffee still steaming. It was an ugly little thing, covered in blotchy colors that didn't go together, but Stevie had made it for me when he was forced to take an art class.

"And that's why you get paid the big bucks," I teased. "Why did you come back here, anyway?" It was a risky question to ask her, but I figured I might as well push my luck.

"I wanted to get some more work done," Roslyn muttered. "Emily offered to drive me on her way out." At the mention of Emily, I saw her tense again. "But honestly, now that I'm here, I don't think I can look at files right now."

"Oh," I muttered. I didn't want to overstep, but I was just so curious. "How are you feeling about everything?"

She looked at me pointedly and I was certain she was about to scold me for my boldness.

Instead, she just laughed. "That's the question of the day now, isn't it?"

"Well . . ." I started, feeling suddenly brave. "Do you love her?"

Roslyn let out a low breath through a minuscule opening in her mouth. She was quiet for a moment, and I assumed she wasn't going to answer.

Until she did.

"No." Her voice was quiet but firm. "I don't."

I was about to respond but realized I couldn't. What was I supposed to say to that? *That's okay. Actually, I'm relieved to hear you say that. Why, you ask? Well, it's a funny story . . .*

"It would be easier if I did," Roslyn continued, breaking me out of my thoughts. She stared at the wall, her eyes glazed over. "The next step would be clear. Easy. Uncomplicated . . ." She trailed off. I could almost hear her mind running through the different scenarios.

"Except maybe the next step *is* clear," she said, her gaze coming up to look at me. Her eyes were piercing and intense. I stared, feeling like it had just gotten a thousand degrees hotter in the room. Maybe it was because of the now broken AC fan.

"Anyway, enough of that," Roslyn said, pushing off from the desk. "I'm in desperate need of a drink. Care to join me?"

47

ELLE

It was a surreal experience walking into a bar with Roslyn. She picked the same, worn-out bar where I had confronted her weeks ago. The place seemed too pedestrian for someone like her, especially with how she was dressed now, but I didn't question it.

The bartender shuffled his way over to us.

"May I have a gin on the rocks? Highclere Castle," Roslyn asked politely. I was surprised they even had that kind of gin here. The bartender smiled and bent down to get it from an obscure cabinet. Leave it to Roslyn to find the hacks no one else knew about.

"And an Old Fashioned for me, please," I ordered.

"An Old Fashioned?" Roslyn arched an eyebrow. "Again?"

"There's nothing wrong with going back to the basics," I shrugged, getting myself comfortable on my stool. I looked around. The red carpet was shabbier when you really looked at it, and the smell of fried wontons was stronger than before. "You do know there are other bars on Cape August . . ."

"There isn't anyone here to harangue me," Roslyn said. I couldn't fault her reasoning. This place was definitely off the beaten path, and the drunk fishermen were usually harmless.

"Well, this is a locals' joint," I noted.

"How long has it been since you were back home?" she asked.

"A while," I admitted, feeling a twinge of guilt saying it out loud. "What about you? Where is home?"

She hesitated. "I don't have a good answer," she said finally.

"Try me," I challenged.

"My family moved around a lot, but I was born in Alaska," she said.

"You're from Alaska?" I wasn't sure why I was surprised. I guess because Roslyn didn't look like someone from Alaska. Then again, what was I expecting? A mountain woman clad in bear furs?

"Technically. But we moved to New York City when I was seven years old," she went on.

New York made sense.

"An Alaskan raised in New York," I mused out loud, trying and failing to fight a smile.

"Something amusing about that?" she asked as our drinks appeared in front of us.

"It's just an odd combo," I admitted. "Although for you, I would say it fits."

"Did you just call me odd?" Roslyn asked, raising an eyebrow.

"Are you going to try and argue that point?" I rebutted.

She reached out to take a delicate sip from her drink. I took that as an admission of defeat.

"Do you miss it?" I asked.

"Which one?"

I shrugged. "Either one. Both."

"Sometimes. I miss the quiet of Alaska, but I miss the people of New York."

I scoffed. "No one misses the people in New York. They're all assholes."

"Precisely."

"See. That right there is why you're weird."

"You said 'odd' before. Calling someone 'weird' is just offensive."

"I bet people in New York wouldn't take offense," I deadpanned.

She laughed, putting a hand over her mouth in an attempt to stifle it. It softened her features, bringing a lightness to her that I hadn't seen before.

"They probably wouldn't," Roslyn admitted fondly.

"Is that where you started ballet?" I asked.

"I started in Alaska, but I began taking it seriously in New York," she said, although her tone sounded stiffer than before.

"Why did you stop?" I asked carefully. I could sense I was walking on seriously thin ice. Roslyn's fingers clenched around her glass. "Life got in the way," she murmured. There was a darkness creeping onto her face. I opened my mouth to change the subject, but this time she beat me to it.

"Why writing?" she asked. "I can't imagine it's a lucrative career."

"I always loved what it had the ability to do," I said. "Through words, you can connect people across the globe, share stories and create a universal understanding. Besides, I always loved to read."

"What's your favorite book, then?"

"Oh, that's a hard one," I said, taking a moment to weigh up this crucial decision. "I love anything Agatha Christie wrote."

"Murder mysteries, huh? That explains why you've been so interested in this investigation," Roslyn mused, before leaning forward slightly. "So tell me, if this whole thing was an Agatha Christie book, who would be the killer?" There was a glint of humor in her eyes as she gave a small, crooked smile.

"Hmm," I pretended to think about the question. "Well, it wouldn't be you. You'd be the main character."

"Is that so?" Roslyn smirked. "Why is that?"

"Because you're attractive and broody," I reasoned before I realized the words I had just said out loud.

Roslyn raised her eyebrows, laughter dancing in her eyes. "Oh, really?"

"That shouldn't be news to you," I said pointedly, hoping she wouldn't be able to see the blush on my face in the dim light of the bar. She shrugged, accepting the backhanded compliment.

"The killer would probably be Oliver," I redirected. "If this was an Agatha Christie story. He's the nice one no one would ever suspect."

"You know, I think you're onto something," Roslyn said sarcastically. "Really. I think all the pieces are finally coming together."

"Hey, you wanted to know what Agatha Christie would say," I said with a shrug. "What about you and your career? What drew you to it?" I leaned forward in my seat, wonder brimming in my voice.

"They offered me a very competitive benefits package," she said wryly, but a shadow crossed over her face.

"Well, sign me up," I chuckled. She smiled, but I could see that it was forced. Desperate, I reached for the nearest topic I could think of that wouldn't be too out of the blue.

"I bet the rest of your team joined for the same reason. Dental coverage can be hard to find. How else could Dalton have such perfect teeth?"

Roslyn made a sound that seemed like a sarcastic breath of air. "Don't tell him that. He already has a big head."

"You and Bonnie seem to try and keep him grounded, though," I said. "Much like he and Matilda try to get you to lighten up."

Roslyn arched an eyebrow at me. "Am I not light enough for you?"

I snorted. "Nothing about you is light."

"Ah. So, in the course of ten minutes you've managed to call me weird, broody, and now fat," Roslyn summarized sarcastically. "Am I forgetting anything?" She pretended to think. "Oh, and amazingly attractive."

I almost choked on my drink.

"I guess the last one makes up for it all," she mused.

"That's not what I said," I argued.

"I took some creative license."

"So, how did you and Matilda get so close?" I asked, trying to move the conversation toward something else.

"We were in training together," Roslyn said. "She's the one who decided we would be friends."

"How?"

"The second day of training, we had to pair up for an exercise. She came up to me and asked to be my partner. At the end of the drill, she looked at me and said, 'We're going to be best friends.' It wasn't a question. She said it like it was just going to be that way." Roslyn shook her head at the memory, a small smile playing on her lips. "Even after that, I tried to ignore her, but you've met Matilda. No matter how hard I tried, she just pushed harder. When I ignored her questions, she would fill in the silence. When I tried to walk away, she would follow me."

"Eventually, I stopped fighting it," she continued. "She was the first person in the force to ever accept me, for all of me." Her gaze flickered down to her silver medical bracelet. "Back then I was still working out some of the kinks with my medication. I made it through the first month and a half without an incident, but the nature of this condition . . . It's inherently unpredictable. You're fine until you're not. It ended up being a very public event. I knew it was overdue, but even so, the timing could have been better. Everyone in our class saw me seize. Including the trainers." Her tone was remarkably casual.

"Technically, they aren't supposed to treat you differently, but that goes against human nature. Most of the trainers saw my condition as a liability after that. They couldn't throw me out, so they wanted me to quit," she went on. "If I dropped out of the program on my own, they had plausible deniability that discrimination had anything to do with it. So, I was pushed harder than anyone else. The trainers would find reasons to give me extra laps and repeat drills. I didn't get breaks like the others, and I could forget about the luxury of getting a day off. I was training every second of every day as they attempted to wear me down." Roslyn chuckled as if amused by the idea.

"Everyone knew what was happening, but they kept their distance. Everyone except Matilda. When she realized what the instructors were doing, she didn't hesitate to start running the extra laps and drills with me." Roslyn smiled. "There wasn't one step that I had to take without her."

"They let her join you?" I asked, surprised that they wouldn't have stopped her.

"The Academy couldn't tell her not to train harder. That would have set a bad precedent," Roslyn reasoned. "Besides, I think many of the instructors hoped that she would drop out too. She was one of the first ones to get in after they took away the height requirement, and they were skeptical at best."

"The extra training had the opposite effect though," she said. "Instead of wearing us down, it made us stronger. Faster. We advanced more quickly than most of the others, which earned the respect of the majority of the trainers and trainees. Soon, we had a pack of people running the extra laps and completing the extra drills with us. They wanted to improve too. We became a real team. Supporting one another, making each other better. However, not everyone was enthusiastic about our success."

She sighed.

"During one sparring session, I was paired with Dave Hilcock. He was a misogynistic asshole on a good day," she said, rolling her eyes at the memory. "When I beat him, he was beside himself. He started shouting things that would make what Andrew Wells said sound like flattery." I felt my body tense, but to my surprise, Roslyn laughed.

"Before I even had the chance to respond, I just saw this little blur fly past me and careen into him," she continued. "Matilda had him pinned despite the fact that he probably had 100 pounds on her. Honestly, she looked deranged. Not even the instructor dared to get involved. She took Hilcock's face in her hand, squeezing his cheeks, and said, 'Say you're sorry! Say it! Say you're sorry!' He looked like he was going to either cry, shit himself, or both. No one there ever made a comment about my epilepsy again." She smiled knowingly. "And Matilda and I have been friends ever since."

I beamed. I was glad she had someone like Matilda. Someone who had her back so fiercely.

"You two are like sisters," I mused. "You certainly bicker like them."

"We have our moments." Her eyes clouded over for a moment and her fingers brushed over her bracelet. "She's my family. They all are." She said the words so quietly that I was certain they weren't meant for me to hear. Her expression was hard to read, with emotion after emotion flashing through her eyes while her face remained virtually unchanged.

Her words were reminiscent of the ones Dalton had said a couple of weeks ago, but they seemed to take on a new meaning when they came out of Roslyn's mouth. They seemed final. Finite. It made me wonder about Roslyn's real family. Did she talk to them? Did she even have one?

48

ELLE

Standing on the sandy beach, my eyes rotated between each of the three agents. Roslyn, Dalton, and Matilda all came to investigate where Jamie Kane was found. They were spread out along the expansive shore, but I wasn't sure what they hoped to find.

We had been to all of the murder sites this morning and it wasn't even eight o'clock yet.

I stood by the old wooden steps that looked over the beach. Next to me, an old woman sat cross-legged on a faded, torn sleeping bag. Her name was Crazy Anne, or that's what people called her at least. She had been homeless for as long as I could remember, but rumors said that she had been a physics teacher. When her husband died, she sold everything and wandered off. People thought she had died until she came hobbling back into town months later. She wasn't all there anymore, and the things she said rarely made sense, but she was always smiling. Always gentle and kind.

At the moment she was counting bottle caps and humming herself.

"The shores are all different," I heard Matilda say as the three agents walked back. "That means that low tide would have been at a different time at each location."

"We cross-referenced all of the fishermen, surfers, and

harbormasters. They're all the obvious people that would know about the tides," Dalton said. "They all came out clean."

"A tide book could tell someone all the information they need to know too," Roslyn sighed. "So, we're back to square one."

As the three continued to discuss, Crazy Anne began to sing:

> *Three blind mice. Three blind mice.*
> *See how they run. See how they run.*
> *They all ran after the farmer's wife,*
> *Who cut off their tails with a carving knife,*
> *Did you ever see such a sight in your life,*
> *As three blind mice.*

The agents gave her very little notice, except for Matilda who smiled at the nursery rhyme. It wasn't until Crazy Anne kept going that Roslyn looked over:

> *Three blind mice. Three blind mice.*
> *See how they go. See how they go.*
> *They all chase after the baker's guy,*
> *Who sliced through their necks and made us all cry,*
> *For did anyone see him, oh me oh my,*
> *Watch three blind mice.*

With the new words, Crazy Anne looked up and smiled toothlessly at them. She laughed to herself, before taking a long, bony finger and pointing at each of the three FBI agents to the beat of the song.

> *Three blind mice. Three blind mice.*

See how they hunt. See how they hunt.
They each search for the madman of death,
Who stole our wits and snuffed out the kids' breath,
Please hold on to your life, dear Lady Macbeth,
For three blind mice.

Dalton started to ask Anne to stop, but Roslyn held up her hand to him. Roslyn cocked her head inquisitively as if to watch the old woman from a different vantage point. Crazy Anne continued her song, bouncing slightly in her seat.

Three blind mice. Three blind mice
See how they're stumped. See how they're stumped.
This happened before, close by, no less,
I guess they thought they cleaned up that whole mess,
Now the monster's come back, with the same finesse,
Despite three blind mice.

Anne continued to hum the tune, swaying with the rhythm. Roslyn took a step toward her.

"Hunt," Dalton said, but she seemed completely absorbed, furrowing her brow as she moved her lips silently.

"Roz." Dalton raised his voice. Finally, she turned to look at him.

"We should bring her back to the station with us," she said.

49

ELLE

"What if it's not a copycat," Roslyn murmured, her voice low and thoughtful. It was just audible enough to be heard by the entire room.

"You mean, what if the guy who killed all those people in the Berkshires was our guy?" Bonnie asked, her voice rising an octave. Roslyn nodded slowly.

"But he's dead," Harold said.

"The person who went to jail for it is dead," Roslyn corrected. "But what if it wasn't him at all?"

"Seriously?" Dalton asked, his eyes widening. "The case against Bobby Michaels was solid. They had a witness, evidence . . . Hell, the guy even confessed."

"I know," Roslyn said. "But it doesn't necessarily mean that he did it. Law enforcement was getting desperate. In under two years, they had fourteen murders and no suitable suspects."

Roslyn paced.

"The timeline never made sense," she went on. "A fact that seemed to fall through the cracks at trial. And the witness they had was shaky at best."

Dalton opened his mouth to argue but thought better of it.

"Besides," Roslyn continued. "Look at the knife strokes." She held up two close-ups of the deadly slashes. One was from years ago. The other was only weeks old. They had matching deep red slices in blue-tinted skin. "Identical. Made with the same type of knife by the looks of it. Same depth. Angle. Same precision."

Harold nodded. "You're right."

"How would a copycat have been able to match it so perfectly?" Roslyn asked.

"But think back to the first murder here on Cape August. Molly Edgars," Dalton argued, walking up to the whiteboard and pointing at her slashed neck. It was a rough cut through delicate skin. Messy. "That was very different. There were hesitation marks. The angle was different. The cut was jagged, not smooth like the Berkshire Killer. No way was that the same person."

Roslyn paused, her eyes darting to all of the pictures. "Or maybe he was rusty."

Everyone fell silent, soaking in the information.

"So, I'm the Berkshire Killer," Harold said, waving his hand as he thought. "If I wasn't caught, what made me stop for fifteen years?"

"Maybe there was an accident?" Matilda tried.

"Or maybe they were getting close to catching him," Dalton said, playing along.

"If he was called in for questioning of any kind, he could have been spooked," Bonnie said.

"But the murders only stopped when Michaels was taken into custody," Dalton noted. "Why would that be the case if it was anyone but him?"

"Maybe it coincided with something else," Matilda said with a shrug.

"But then why change victimology this drastically?" Harold asked. "If this is the same guy, then he went from raping and killing eighteen-year-old brunette women to killing a much wider range."

"Maybe something happened in his life. Something that forced the change," Matilda said thoughtfully.

"If this is the same guy, it means that it can't be Miles Elliot," Harold added. "He would've been a toddler."

"It would make Peter Edgars more likely," Dalton said. "Even before he went to college in that area, he probably went to visit Nelson. He went to school there too."

"I don't think we should rule Miles out," Harold said. "Who knows? Maybe he studied up on the killings."

A muscle in Roslyn's jaw tightened.

"Let's find out."

50

ELLE

I had just walked into the house when I heard my phone ring. My heart tightened with dread. Had something else happened? I let out an audible sigh when I saw it was Eric, but then felt a whole different kind of foreboding . . .

"Hey!" I cried into the speaker. Watkins was so startled that he galloped into another room, fluffy tail, and everything.

"Hey, yourself," Eric chuckled through the phone. "How are you doing? Haven't heard from you in a while." I could hear the genuine concern coloring his voice. It made the guilt inside me threaten to bubble over.

"I'm fine," I squeaked, my voice rising a couple of octaves. "I'm sorry I haven't called. It's just been crazy here."

"I understand. I actually took a few days off so I can visit," Eric said.

I almost dropped the phone.

"Y-you what?" I choked.

"Don't try and talk me out of it," Eric said. His voice was steady. Sure.

"But," I started, trying to think of something quick. "It's a long trip just for a few days."

"You're worth it," Eric said.

Fuck me.

"Eric, you don't need to—"

"I want to be there for you when you're struggling."

I *was* struggling, but not for the reasons that would make the most sense.

"Eric—"

"I'll be there first thing in the morning," he insisted. There was no point in arguing.

"Okay," I breathed. I caught Watkins peering around the corner to see if it was safe.

"Okay," Eric said, and I could hear the gentle smile behind it. "I love you, and I'll see you soon."

I hung up and looked at Watkins. His golden eyes stared accusingly.

"Don't look at me like that," I muttered.

Eric came earlier than I expected, which meant that he met everyone at the station . . . And I mean *everyone*. All things considered, it went smoothly. He and Andrew bonded over their mutual love of grilling, and Roslyn gave a quick hello before ignoring him like she did everyone else.

Driving back to my parents' house with Eric, I couldn't help but fidget in my seat. Once we were in the house, I was almost able to shake the agitation when things started to feel normal. Like when he was cooking us dinner, or when we started to watch a movie on the plush, tan couch.

That shattered the moment we moved to my bedroom.

I gulped, sitting on the edge of the bed as Eric chuckled at the state of the place. Clothes were strewn haphazardly about the floor. Crumpled balls of paper that looked like they had dive-bombed from the ceiling were scattered among the worn-out erasers, dull pencils, and dead pens. Books were stacked in unsteady piles on the floor, making the now barren bookshelf look completely useless. In and amongst the clutter, there was an odd, body-sized clearing on the carpet, marking where I would fall asleep when I worked.

"Looks like you've been busy," he said, his warm eyes twinkling. I froze the moment he leaned in to kiss me but fought the urge to lean away. I kissed Eric back mechanically. He began to unbutton my shirt, and I let him, but only because I felt like I should. I felt no longing. No sudden need to be closer. No spark of passion or lust.

My mind began to wander dangerously to other things . . .

I forced myself back into the moment. He held me close, his hands caressing my body with such love and care that it made me feel nauseated because I couldn't return it. My fingers moved without feeling. Touched him without needing to.

I didn't feel the need to cringe away, but instead, I felt something that was arguably worse.

Indifference.

So, I played the role of someone else. Someone who had said yes to spending the rest of her life with him. But had that woman ever existed? The cold, hard truth was staring me in the face, and it took coming home to see it.

"I love you," Eric whispered in my ear. I flinched.

"I-I love you too," my voice said back. The voice of a liar. I felt tears in my eyes, but I forced them back.

He kissed me more urgently. More passionately. I hated that I didn't care.

I stared at the ceiling instead, but it looked empty. I couldn't take it. I closed my eyes instead, screwing them shut.

It felt like an eternity before it was over. His arms held me to him even after he fell asleep, and suddenly I felt like I was being strangled by his strong, steady embrace. I needed to get out, even if it was only for a few minutes.

I untangled myself from him and creaked across the floor toward the kitchen. I almost tripped over Watkins. The cat meowed angrily.

"I'm sorry," I whispered as he sulked away. I kneeled on the ground and tried to coax him over. He stayed near the stove, keeping his back to me as he flicked his tail in irritation.

"What? You can't even look at me?" I asked as his tail flopped against the ground. I sighed, looking at my reflection in the glass of the stove. I turned away.

"Yeah . . . Well, I can't look at me either."

51

ELLE

I stalled most of the next day, waiting for an ideal moment that never came. It wasn't until we were sitting on the couch the next evening that my body took matters into its own hands. When Eric went to kiss me, I couldn't help but pull back. The poor man almost fell off the couch.

"Are you okay?" he asked after he had recovered. Concern was written all over his face.

Fuck.

"Yeah," I lied, my voice much too high.

"Whatever it is, you can tell me," Eric said, folding my hands between both of his. I looked into his face. People said that we had the same eyes, but I had always known his were softer than mine. Kinder somehow.

I had to say it.

"Eric . . . I can't marry you," I murmured, fighting tears.

He blinked in surprise. "Did something happen?"

I gulped, shaking my head.

His eyes hardened. "Did something happen between you and him?"

"Who?" I asked. It took me a moment to realize what he was implying. "You mean Andrew?"

Eric gave a stiff nod.

"No," I said quickly. "Nothing. I promise."

If anything, Eric just looked more confused. "Then, why?"

"I don't love you the way I should," I whispered, giving life to the words that had been burning within me. "I want to. I thought I did. But I don't."

I looked into his face and I saw every emotion he was feeling as if it was flashing on a giant billboard. Hurt. Sadness. Anger. Betrayal.

I realized at that moment that he was the complete opposite of Roslyn. Eric clearly expressed his feelings, while trying to get a read of Roslyn's was like trying to break through stone. Eric was a happy person, infecting others with his joy, while Roslyn rarely smiled. Eric was easy, while everything about Roslyn was difficult. Eric would never hurt me, while Roslyn was not the type who could ever promise that. I knew Eric loved me, while Roslyn barely tolerated me.

But that didn't change what had to be done.

"When did you figure this out?" Eric asked. It wasn't meant to be accusatory, except that was exactly how it felt considering I knew the answer. *Well, Eric, now that you mention it . . .*

"I figured it out when I came here," I admitted, which was technically true. "It gave me time to really think about everything."

Eric nodded, taking my hand. He laced his fingers with mine and brought them to his lips, pressing a firm but gentle kiss on my knuckles. I felt my throat constrict with the simple gesture. It was tender. Loving.

And then, he left.

52

ELLE

Unable to bear the emptiness of my house and unwilling to relive the events of the day with Zoey, I headed to the station. Nothing like looking at blood and gore to forget about your relationship problems.

The station was dark and dismal without the warmth of human contact. I hunched over my computer, bathed in the blue light for over an hour.

"You're here late."

I whirled around.

"Woah, it's just me." Roslyn held up her hands. She was standing in the doorway, her hair in a loose braid. I hadn't seen her style it like that before. She probably deemed it too 'fun' for office hours.

I took a deep breath, heat rising to my cheeks.

"Sorry," I said, offering a shy smile. "I was just reading up on the Berkshire Killer case. I think it made me a little jumpy."

Roslyn waved off the apology as she and Jasper glided over.

"Which article?" she asked. I turned my computer toward her and she leaned over my shoulder to look at the screen. I felt heat rush down my neck with the close proximity. She smelled like fresh mint. Twisting my head sideways, I watched her mouth move silently as she read, murmuring the words to herself. Her blue-green eyes flashed over the screen, and this close I could clearly see the flecks of gold shimmering within them. They were mesmerizing.

"Yes," she hummed, her voice dragging me back to reality. "This was one of the first news articles after they made the arrest." She straightened, pulling away from the laptop.

Immediately, I missed the closeness.

"Do you really think it could be the same guy?" I asked, working to keep my voice even.

"Could be," she sighed. "There are a lot of similarities. In the Berkshires, the bodies were left in the woods where animals and the elements could distort evidence, not unlike how the killer here is using the tide . . ."

She pursed her lips, studying me. "So, what are you really doing here so late? Shouldn't you be with the fiancé?" Her tone showed interest and concern, without reflecting an ounce of nosiness. I knew that I could shoo off the question. She of all people would know to back off. But I felt oddly touched that she was giving me this opportunity to talk to her about something personal.

"Eric went back to Providence," I muttered. "I ended it."

Roslyn nodded, taking a seat next to me. "Are you okay?" she asked. Her voice was uncharacteristically soft. Caring, almost.

I chuckled. "Not really."

I deflated under the weight of that reality and almost jumped when I felt a touch on my shoulder. I looked to see Roslyn's hand. She looked a little uncomfortable as if she was unsure whether she was doing it right, or if she questioned whether she should be doing it at all. But even if it was a little cold and detached, it meant the world that she was trying. We shared a small smile before she hastily pulled her hand back.

"So," Roslyn said, clearing her throat as she got up and walked over to another desk. "It just so happens that I know Oliver carries an emergency stash of bourbon." She began opening the draws of the desk that Oliver had been using. I figured she was kidding until she pulled out a brown paper bag with a black cap sticking out of the top. She looked quite pleased with herself as she pulled out the bottle.

"Why?" I asked, unable to hide my curiosity. Of all people to carry around an emergency bottle of hooch . . .

"It's mostly for family members," Roslyn explained. "If they need a little something to take the edge off. Or if one of us has had a particularly rough day . . . Which is why I feel completely justified in using it on you." She went to the water cooler to get two plastic cups.

"Won't he notice?" I asked.

She shook her head, pouring a generous amount of brown liquor before handing me a cup. "I'll replace it tomorrow," Roslyn assured, before smirking. "Or I won't. I'm the boss. I can do whatever I want."

I laughed. "Is that how that works?"

"There have to be some perks to being in charge." Roslyn shrugged as she poured her own glass.

"What is it with you and hard liquor anyway?" I asked.

She raised her eyebrows. "I'm waiting for the question."

"Do you ever drink wine or beer like a normal person?"

"I could. I choose not to."

'Hard-ass,' I muttered under my breath. She heard me anyway.

"Wimp," she breathed back.

"Excuse me if I don't drink plain gin, you monster."

"It's called sophistication," she said. "I'm not surprised you aren't familiar with it."

"There is nothing sophisticated about drinking straight paint-thinner."

"The brands I buy are hardly-paint thinner."

"Well, we pedestrians can't afford the good stuff, ya snob."

"People have different priorities," she shot back.

"How would you know? You're more of a robot than a person," I argued.

"I'll take that as a compliment."

"You're only proving my point," I said. "I bet you don't even need a gun. You can probably shoot bullets out of your eyes."

"That's not DOJ approved."

I looked at her questioningly.

"Department of Justice," Roslyn explained, before adding, "It was a joke."

"It's not funny if you have to explain it," I pointed out. I still had to fight a smirk. "You should stick with sarcasm. You're better at that."

She muttered something unintelligible into her cup.

"How do you use one of those anyway?" I asked, looking at the holstered weapon at her waist.

Roslyn scoffed. "I'm not going to show you."

"But—"

"No."

53

ROSLYN

With the new protocols and curfews along the beaches, there hadn't been a murder in over two weeks. Many, including the media, had chosen to believe it had everything to do with the arrest of the baker, Joe Campbell. He was in custody after all, and in their minds, the killer was caught. No one seemed to care about the fact that he was being held on charges that had nothing to do with the Cape August murders. That's what you get for smuggling drugs in cupcakes.

As each day passed, more and more tourists flooded the shores. With the holiday weekend hours away, thousands of people could be at risk. I decided to take matters into my own hands.

I pounded the stake deeper into the sand.

"What are you doing?" a flushed Mayor Sully cried, running toward me.

"Building a house," I muttered sarcastically, giving the sign a twist.

"It looks like you're closing the beach for the weekend," he squeaked.

"Very observant," I said, trying hard to keep my voice neutral despite the snark. "Hopefully beachgoers are all as clever as you."

"We talked about this," Sully hissed. "You can't close the beach. Especially over the fourth of July!"

"Oh, I can't?" I asked, feigning innocence as I glanced at the sign blocking the pathway to the water. "Huh. Well, looks like I already have."

I started to walk away when Sully grabbed my arm. It might have been meant to be intimidating, but his sweaty palm ruined it.

"Take them down, or I'll remove them myself," he said, before adding a rather half-assed, "Please."

I plastered a polite smile onto my face. "Take your hand off of my arm, or I remove all of your fingers *myself*," I threatened sweetly, before adding a sugary, "Please."

He pulled his hand away, gaping like a fish as he tried to form a response.

I didn't have the patience to see if he ever succeeded. I marched to another entry point on the beach and began pounding another sign. I heard frantic steps as the mayor caught up.

"You don't have the jurisdiction," he tried.

"Jurisdiction this," I said under my breath, whacking the sign hard.

"If you raise that hammer one more time," Sully huffed. "I will see to it that your entire team is removed from Cape August and stripped of their titles."

My mouth set into a hard line. I wanted to call his bluff, but whether I liked it or not, Sully's father had power. Or perceived power at the very least.

I lowered the hammer, giving him the deadliest glare I could manage behind the pretense of civility.

Sully cleared his throat, straightening the collar of his shirt.

"Look, I'm not a monster," he said. "Do what you need to do for this weekend. Police surveillance. Walkie-talkies. Whatever you want. But this is the busiest weekend of the entire summer, so come hell or high water, we will be open."

I saw red all the way back to the station.

"He's insane," Dalton said when I informed the team of the situation. "Certifiably insane."

"Could Sully be our guy?" Bonnie suggested. I shot her a look and she shrugged. "What? It was a legitimate suggestion. He's got 'psychopath' written all over him."

"It's not him," I said, although I would be lying if I hadn't thought about that possibility. I had already checked and his alibi was solid. Besides, it wouldn't make sense. He wanted to lure dumbasses to the beach, not scare them away.

I looked at our timeline written on the whiteboard.

"It's been two weeks since the last murder," I said. "That's way longer than he's gone before."

"Well, that's good, isn't it?" Elle Wolfe piped up, hope lighting up her expression. "Maybe that means what you're doing is working. Right?"

"Yes, and no," Harold said. "The guy we're looking for has a compulsion. He needs to kill to satisfy his urge. It's a high for him. An addiction." He drummed his knuckles on the desk. "We might have scared him, but it won't stop him."

"He's been without a hit for longer than before," Dalton said. "With the fourth-of-July crowds on the beaches, it'll be practically impossible for him to stay away."

Elle Wolfe's face paled. "So, that means . . ." she trailed off, looking at me for an answer. Trusting that I had one.

"It means that we need to be ready," I said, casting a look in the direction of the rest of the station. In the other room, I heard the low mumble of Cape August cops. "All of us."

Harold sighed, rubbing a hand over his face.

"With all those people, even if he is there, it'll be like trying to find a needle in a fucking haystack," he muttered. "He'll have plenty of cover."

"Maybe it'll rain this weekend?" Matilda offered. "That would at least keep people off the beach. Off his hunting grounds."

"Well, then pray for rain, people," Harold muttered. "Just pray for rain."

54

ROSLYN

Blue skies. Eighty degrees. July Fourth was already looking to be one of the top ten days of the year. Rays of sunlight reflected harshly off the surface of the water and I had to take special care not to look directly at it. Now would be among the worst times and places to have a seizure.

The Winslow Beach parking lot was filled by nine. From my earpiece, the voices of my team members reported the same at their locations. I had split them up throughout the town at all the most popular beaches, lakes, and events. Matilda had volunteered for the parade.

The town cops were with them too. It was one of the few things we all agreed upon. If we couldn't shut this place down, then it needed the most security possible.

Everyone was on high alert. Ready.

I still felt the itch to order every tourist home.

From the corner of my eye, I spotted the pale-pink button-down of Mayor Sully. He was probably here for the same reason I was; Winslow Beach was the most popular place in town on a nice day.

We made brief eye contact before I broke his gaze to look over the dunes. I had positioned myself on the highest hill, where I could see both the shoreline and the parking lot. For at least a mile, the sand was dotted with brightly colored towels and umbrellas. The wind carried the sound of gleeful chatter as children raced to the water's edge to wrestle for a constantly deflating football. There were easily a thousand people here. A thousand potential victims.

Jasper shifted at my side, sensing my agitation.

Let's corral a thousand people in a serial killer's hunting ground, I thought bitterly to myself. *That's a fucking brilliant idea. Oh, and let's not listen to anything the FBI says. They couldn't possibly have a point.*

A headache prickled behind my eyes. It had been exactly fifteen days since the last murder. With the clear presence of the FBI, along with the extra security measures I had forced, we had made it much more difficult for him to get anyone alone. But today, with all the chaotic crowds, it was a lot harder to see what was going on. Any one individual was pretty much invisible.

"How are things looking?" I asked into my earpiece, keeping my voice low as a family of four walked by.

A chorus of 'all clears' echoed in my ear.

"It's so crowded," Matilda said.

"Yeah, it's like no one cares that five people were murdered," Dalton's voice muttered.

"Easy to ignore that when a tan is on the line," Bonnie chirped sarcastically.

"Good thing mine is built-in," Dalton said with an audible smirk.

"Yes, you're very special," Bonnie said. I could hear the eye roll behind it.

"Want to hear the other perks? My family is also known to have huge—"

"Enough," I said, silencing them all. "Have you all been in touch with the officers in your area?"

There was a pause on the other end of my earpiece.

"I want that line of communication open at all times," I instructed for what felt like the tenth time. "Check in with them every twenty minutes. You don't have to like it. Just do it."

After a few lukewarm 'yeses,' the voices in my ear fell silent.

I looked back over the overcrowded beach, hearing the distant argument about someone forgetting to put the mustard in the cooler.

I adjusted my sunglasses, wishing they could block out the glare reflecting off the rolling waves entirely. I rolled up my sleeves with neat folds as a way to accomplish something.

"I might have something," Harold's voice crackled in my ear. Everything in my body tensed.

"What is it?" I asked, keeping my voice cool and collected. People were all around me. I had to be calm until proven otherwise.

"A skittish white male, six feet, alone, fiddling with something in his pocket."

Fuck.

"Where is he?" I asked. "Do we have eyes on him?"

There was a second of silence. Blood pounded behind my ears. I forgot to breathe.

Then . . .

"False alarm," Harold said. "He was just messing with an engagement ring."

"Aww!" Matilda cooed loudly in my ear. "That's adorable! See if the person says yes—"

"Do *not* do that," I snapped, mostly to Matilda over Harold. "Stay focused."

Turning back to my sandy perch, I grimaced when I saw Sully waving at me.

"Miss Hunt! Looking beautiful, as always," Mayor Sully called, flashing me what I knew he thought was a dazzling smile. "How are you this fine morning?"

I muttered an unintelligible snide remark as the man approached.

"You should take a break," Sully said. "Go for a swim. Relax."

"Do you even understand the *concept* of my job?" I asked. The man chuckled, running a hand through his perfectly moussed hair.

"You're still worried," he said. "But it's been two whole weeks. Your guy has probably moved on from Cape August." He said the idea so flippantly, it made me want to throttle him.

"Oh, yes. And having him somewhere else killing people would solve the problem altogether," I said sarcastically. He ignored the comment, stretching out his arms in the sun.

"You know what your problem is?" he asked, beaming.

"A low tolerance for stupidity?" I tried.

"You're too uptight," he corrected. "Always wanting to do things by the book. But look!" He waved out across the sea of people clamoring to claim a spot. "You wanted to deny all these people a day in the sun, and for what? No reason at all."

"Tell that to the families of the first five victims," I hissed.

"You'll see," Sully said. "Mark my words. By the end of today, you'll be the one getting your tan on."

"Only if Hell freezes over first," I muttered to myself.

"Exactly!" Sully said excitedly, clearly hearing only some, or none, of the words.

It was a relief when he sauntered away.

I pinched the bridge of my nose as if it would help release the pressure building behind my eyes, before grabbing the walkie-talkie from my hip. The cops in my location were on a different channel than my team. It helped limit the confusion.

"How's everyone doing?" I asked.

"All clear at my end," said Jay Kama.

"Mmm-hmm," Phil Gregory agreed, mixing with static.

"Looks good to me," Elle Wolfe said with a hint of uncertainty. I sighed. I wasn't sure how useful she would really be with the surveillance. She didn't know what signs to look out for, or what to do if something came up. But she had insisted on helping, and at least she was an extra pair of eyes.

My gaze skimmed over the sea of people, oiling themselves up to lay face down and fry in the scorching sun until their skin blistered. I never understood how that could ever be considered enjoyable.

Jasper let out an exasperated huff.

"I know," I muttered to him. "I know."

55

Victor Taylor had saved up for months for this vacation. He had been fixing elevators for the last twenty years and while it wasn't the most glamorous job in the world, he liked it, even if it didn't allow for much time off. Five days on the beach was a special treat for some father-daughter bonding with Melanie. And yet it was still like pulling teeth trying to get her head out of that goddamn book.

Some Shakespeare shit.

"Mel, come on," Victor groaned, running sunscreen over his balding head. "It's the Fourth of July for God's sake. Try and have some fun."

The girl next to him murmured a quiet 'uh huh' between flipping the page and adjusting her round eyeglasses. Victor snatched the book from her lap.

"Hey!" Melanie yelped.

"We didn't come all the way here for you to do the same thing you do at home," Victor said. "You can get this back after you dip one toe in the ocean."

Melanie grumbled something that Victor couldn't quite make out as she glanced at the water.

She swallowed hard. "D-do I have to?" she asked quietly, toying with the end of her black ponytail. It was too crowded. Too loud.

Melanie chewed on her bottom lip as she thought about having to take off her long-sleeve shirt and jeans. She was wearing a bathing suit, but no one had ever seen it but her. She would prefer to keep it that way.

"Yes," Victor said. "You need to get over this 'being shy' business. Think of this as step one."

He saw the worry on her face and pursed his lips in thought.

"I'll make you a deal," he started. "You go into the water with me now, and later I'll watch any boring movie you want."

Melanie looked at him quickly. "Really?" she asked, starting to smile.

"Cross my heart," Victor said, running a finger over his hairy chest.

The girl nodded so fast that her glasses threatened to fly off her face and was even faster to take off her clothes down to the one-piece bathing suit she wore underneath. "I've really wanted to see *The King's Speech* again," Melanie chattered, as she walked down to the water's edge with Victor. She barely noticed the swarms of people running around them. Victor just nodded along as his daughter talked about the movie's historical accuracy.

They got about ankle-deep in the water before Melanie paused again.

"I-I think I'm fine here," she said, crossing her arms over her chest. Victor nodded. He had pushed her enough.

"I'll be right back," he called, heading deeper. The sun was so goddamn hot, he needed a quick dunk. Especially if he was going to be expected to watch a two-hour movie about a guy with a stutter.

Again.

56

ROSLYN

It happened fast. One second, everything was calm. The next, the entire beach had erupted into a disorganized mass of yells and screams.

I sprinted to the heart of the crowd, Jasper right next to me.

The girl was lying on the beach, gasping as blood poured from her neck. I jumped on top of her, desperate to stop the bleeding.

"Fuck," I hissed, forcing my hand harder against the gushing stream. The girl's eyes widened in horror behind her blood-sprayed spectacles. She opened her mouth as if to scream, but nothing came out. She tried to wiggle free of my grasp. I pinned her harder into the sand.

"Stay still," I demanded in a growl. Realizing how harsh my voice sounded, I tried again. "Just look at me. Okay? Just look at me and try to keep st—"

"Melanie!" a man cried as he rushed from the water. He had the same nose as the bleeding girl. He was probably her father.

Just fucking fantastic.

"Sir, I need you to stand back," I said, but no sooner had the words left my mouth than I saw him lunge at me. I braced for impact, hunching my shoulders in the hopes of somehow knocking him off and maintaining the pressure on Melanie's bleeding neck.

Luckily, I didn't have to.

"Sir, don't!" Jay Kama said, restraining him. "She's trying to help her!"

A crowd formed around us. Under my hands, the girl trembled. Tears streamed down her face, mixing with the blood.

Despite myself, I felt my chest clench.

"You're going to be okay," I whispered, a tenderness sneaking into the lie. "Just look at me. Don't think about anything else."

I kept repeating the words. Over and over again. Until they turned into a kind of mantra. And slowly, the world around us began to slip away. Drifting into a kind of fog, before evaporating into nothing. The people on the beach, with their wide and curiously horrified expressions. The cries of the terrified father. The distant scream of sirens. The blood. The fear.

Even the beach under us.

Slowly, it was only the two of us. She looked at me with a strange calm, taking a shuddered breath, as her pulse continued to thump in my blood-soaked hands.

57

ELLE

It was a mess getting to the hospital as we navigated through the summer traffic. Even the ER was flooded with people who had burned themselves on grills or scratched themselves up after falling from rental bikes. Roslyn stalked the brightly lit hallway, trying to see if she could talk to Melanie Taylor, the girl who had been attacked. She was still alive, and very well could have seen something. But as she was rushed in for surgery, the chance of talking to the girl slipped away.

"You." The girl's father, Victor Taylor, stalked toward Roslyn. "You were in charge on that beach?"

"Yes, sir," Roslyn said, a resigned look in her eyes.

"What the fuck happened?" he demanded, an angry flush rushing up his neck and purpling his cheeks. "I thought you had a handle on this fucking shit!"

"Mr. Taylor—"

"No. NO!" he yelled, pointing a finger. "You said these beaches were safe!"

I stepped forward, shaking my head. "She was never the one—"

Roslyn pushed me back. "Don't."

"A psycho attacks my kid in broad fucking daylight," Victor went on, his voice rising. "And then I have all your people questioning me like they figured this shit was gonna happen again? Like you fucking knew it would? What, were you just waiting for it?"

Roslyn's face remained calm. Neutral almost. But it looked like she was biting the inside of her cheek.

"This is your fault!" Victor bellowed, and for a second I thought for sure he might hit her. "And if my daughter dies, that's on you!"

He took a forceful lurch back, spitting in Roslyn's general direction before stomping away.

"Why didn't you say anything?" I asked Roslyn incredulously after he left. "You tried to get the beaches closed—"

"That doesn't matter," Roslyn said. She brought her fingers to her temple.

"Of course, it does," I said. "He was wrong—"

"He's scared," Roslyn said, cutting me off again. "His daughter is circling the drain after being attacked by a man we knew was still out there. If Mr. Taylor wants to yell at me, that's fine. I can handle it." She paused before adding: "And to be honest, he's not wrong."

"What do you mean?" I asked, confused.

Roslyn looked at me from the corner of her eye.

"I was waiting for this to happen again," she admitted. "A murder was long overdue and with that many people to choose from on the beaches today, it was too tempting. We were practically baiting him."

"You *tried* to close the beaches," I insisted. "And Mayor Sully wouldn't let you."

To my surprise, Roslyn just laughed. It was a humorless laugh. Tense.

"That's precisely the problem, isn't it?" she seethed, her laugh turning into a kind of snarl. "I allowed him to stop me."

A determined glint flashed in her eyes before she turned on her heels without another word. Jasper hurried after her.

"Where are you going?" I asked, making a move to follow.

"Stay here and keep the media away from Mr. Taylor," Roslyn called, without slowing a single step. "We don't need him beating the shit out of one of them."

"But—" I started, but before I could finish, she was gone.

58

ROSLYN

Not even the receptionist was staffing the mayor's office today, but the building was open regardless. Seemed like quite the security problem, especially in the current climate. Then again, no one asked for my opinion. Blinding sun came in through the large windows, unsympathetic to the events of an hour ago. It was the only source of light with the ceiling lamps turned off, but it still led clearly to the mayor's office.

The door was open a crack, revealing a stressed and sweaty Keith Sully hunched over his desk. His eyes were wide as he stared at nothing in particular, and his lips were ghostly pale to match the rest of his face. His mouth hung open as if he had given up on trying to close it altogether.

He didn't hear me come into the room. I slammed the door. Hard.

The bang made Sully yelp and cower. It was oddly less satisfying than I would have hoped. He just looked pathetic. His eyes found mine, and the panic eased into the gentle throb of guilt.

"Bad day?" I asked, not even bothering to sugarcoat my bitterness.

Sully looked at me as if he had seen a ghost. "Is she dead?"

"No," I said. "Although the knife was a millimeter from nicking her carotid. She's in surgery now."

"J-Jesus," he stuttered, wringing his hands. "The media is going to have a fucking field day with this. Wait. Where's Elle Wolfe? Maybe she can—"

"Enough." I snarled.

He looked up at me fast, as if he had misheard. We stared at each other for a moment, until he couldn't stand it any longer and looked down at the floor. It was another couple of seconds before he was brave enough to speak. Or maybe he just couldn't help himself.

"I didn't think this would happen," Sully whispered. He licked his lips and ran a hand through his deflated hair. "I swear. I just thought . . ." He trailed off as if realizing that the truth was that he hadn't actually *thought* of anything.

"You think I'm awful," he continued, gnawing on his bottom lip. "I know. I think I'm awful too. It's just . . . I thought I was doing the right thing." He looked up at me, his eyes begging for understanding. Acceptance. I gave him neither. He hung his head.

"My sister was on that beach today," he murmured, his eyes glistening with thick tears. "She has three kids. She even asked me . . ." He hesitated, scrunching up his face. "I thought . . . I thought it was safe. I thought—"

"No."

He froze, a limp noodle of hair flopping in front of his face. His shocked expression made it look like he didn't understand the meaning of the word.

"What?" he croaked.

"No," I repeated. Cold. Harsh. Unforgiving. "Just. No."

Trembling, he finally nodded and fell silent. My lips hardened into a thin line as I looked at the helpless man. He was a pitiful sight, with his wrinkled shirt and dust-covered face. Both of his boat shoes were untied.

But I felt nothing for him.

"You're not going to get my sympathy," I said bluntly. "Or my respect. As far as I'm concerned, you lost both of those the day you wanted to label these as shark attacks." My fingers iced over into fists.

The man hugged himself as if trying to keep warm from the chill of my tone.

I took out the neatly folded paper in my back pocket. "This is an order to close the beach," I said, handing him a black pen to go with it. He looked at me with wide eyes. My own narrowed with warning. "You are going to sign it. Right now. Not tomorrow. Not 'after you call Daddy.' Now." My voice was low and calm, but I knew he could hear the danger creeping into it with every word. "Then, you're going to clean yourself up, and head back out there to be the leader your town should have had from the very beginning."

I forced the pen into his hand.

From behind me, I felt Jasper's silent presence. Always there. Always watching.

I rolled my shoulders back and waited. I wasn't going to leave until every letter of Keith Sully's name was curled onto that page. I'd had enough with the games. Enough with the less than subtle threats.

Enough.

Sully didn't even bother reading the document, although signing took him longer than it should have. His hand was shaking terribly.

He had barely finished the curl of the 'y' before I snatched the document from him. I went for the door, before stopping short.

"And if you ever threaten me, my job, or my team again," I said, not even bothering to look at him while I spoke, "I will ensure that you never hold another position of office inside or outside this town. I don't care who you're related to."

I was almost outside when my phone buzzed.

"What is it?" I snapped.

Dalton's voice was grave in my ear. "We've got another problem."

59

ELLE

"A four-year-old child went missing over an hour ago, and I'm only hearing about it *now*?" Roslyn seethed, the tendons popping out of her neck.

"Mia Roberts was playing in the sand and, in all the chaos, her babysitter thought that she got lost in the crowd," Dalton explained. "We called you as soon as we heard."

"Jesus fuck," Roslyn breathed, pacing the floor of the precinct.

"Do we even know whether it's our guy?" Bonnie piped up.

"Another predator wouldn't have chosen that moment to abduct a girl," Matilda said. "They would have been too spooked after the attack. Not to mention the clear police presence."

"And Mia was standing just feet from the scene," Dalton said. "I bet she saw something. Our guy must've panicked and grabbed her."

"Well, the good news is that if we haven't found her body, she is probably still alive," Harold muttered. "For now."

"We need to go back to the beginning," Roslyn muttered.

"We've gone through Molly Edgars' timeline fifteen times," Dalton sighed. "She went to school. Came back. And then ended up dead on the beach that night. No one saw her in between."

Roslyn tapped her foot, agitated. "Wait, that's not entirely true,"

Roslyn started. "She takes the bus, so the driver would be the last person to see Molly before she was killed."

"I'm on it," Bonnie called, typing fast. "Dimitri Ivanov has been driving that route for the last thirteen years. Second-generation immigrant out of Russia. Clean record. Lives on 65 West Elm Street."

"I know him," I piped up. He would always buy a box of Thin Mints when I sold Girl Scout cookies. "I don't know if he'll remember me, but I can try and make the introduction."

He remembered me all right. As soon as he peeked out the window and saw me, the big man burst through the door and pulled me into a gigantic bear hug. He smelled like he hadn't showered in a few days.

"Wolfe Girl," Dimitri chuckled. "I was wondering when you'd stop by." His smile strained when he saw Roslyn. "You brought a friend . . ." he said wearily.

"Roslyn Hunt," she said politely, extending her hand. Dimitri just stared at it.

Roslyn slowly pulled back her hand. "We came to ask you a few questions about Molly Edgars."

"Barely knew her," Dimitri said, turning his back on us.

"But you were the last one to see her alive," Roslyn called.

Dimitri hesitated.

"It won't take long," I added. "We promise."

Dimitri looked back, his gaze shifting between Roslyn and Jasper, before settling on me.

"The dog stays out here," he said gruffly, jerking his head to the Doberman mix that was peeking out of his window. "Lola doesn't play well with others."

While reluctant, Roslyn put Jasper back in the car.

The house was rough and grimy, smelling of dog food and dirty laundry. The walls were thin and the paint was peeling. In the living room, a TV blared with a baseball game. Red Sox versus Giants. Dimitri didn't bother turning it off as he led us in.

The Doberman lowered her head and growled at Roslyn. From the corner of my eye, I saw her finger twitch toward her gun.

"She's harmless," Dimitri chuckled, scratching the dog behind her pointed ears. Seeing Roslyn's apprehension though, he begrudgingly dragged the dog to her crate in another room. Roslyn took the opportunity to scan the living room, sweeping over the race car posters and faded photographs.

"So, what do you want to know?" Dimitri asked, picking at a stain on his shirt as he came back into the living room.

"You would pick up Molly Edgars every day, correct?" Roslyn asked, continuing to walk about the room.

Dimitri nodded. "Yeah. Sweet girl. Didn't deserve what she got." He went to a half-broken armchair and sat down heavily. He grabbed the remote and turned up the TV a few notches. Roslyn pursed her lips but didn't ask him to turn it down.

"Did you notice anyone hanging around near her?" Roslyn asked instead, raising her voice to be heard. "Anyone that shouldn't have been there?"

"Can't say I did," Dimitri said, watching the screen.

"How did she seem that Friday?" Roslyn asked, continuing to walk around the room.

Dimitri shrugged. "Eh. Hard to remember. All the days blend together after a while."

"Was she always your last stop?"

"Yeah. Woah!" Dimitri cheered, watching a home run. "Woohoo! Look at him go!"

Roslyn's gaze hesitated on a tattered picture taped to the wall. Her eyes narrowed as she glanced back at Dimitri, but he was fully absorbed with the game. She pulled it off the wall and turned it over. On the back was a little note written in a language that looked like Russian, but I couldn't be sure.

Roslyn's entire body stiffened.

Dimitri was too engaged with the game to pay any attention. Slowly, almost imperceptibly, Roslyn began to reach for the gun at her belt holster. She stopped right before she reached it though, her eyes flashing at me before retracting her hand. Her gaze held a clear warning: danger.

My heart began to race. What should I do? What did *she* want me to do?

"Hey, Elle, do you think you can go check on Jasper outside? He probably needs to be let out," Roslyn said casually.

She was trying to get me out of the way. I swallowed the lump in my throat that seemed to be growing in size, threatening to choke me.

"Yeah, of course," I replied as calmly as I could, easing toward the door.

"Leaving?" Dimitri asked, getting up from the chair with a huff. I froze, my mind going blank.

"Just checking on the dog," Roslyn answered for me. Her voice was calm. Easy. "He's not used to being cooped up."

"I was going to grab a beer. Want one?" Dimitri asked me, about to slip into the kitchen.

"I'm okay," I said with a little laugh, moving toward the front door. I just had to make it five steps. How hard could that be?

What could possibly go wrong in the time it takes to walk five steps?

Apparently, everything.

I was about halfway across the room when I heard a muffled cry coming from underneath the floorboards. I paused. It was too loud to pretend that I hadn't heard it.

Before I could think of how I should react, I heard two distinct clicks in the same instant. One of them was from the gun that Roslyn held at Dimitri while the other click was from where Dimitri was standing behind me. I turned my head slowly, to see that Dimitri was pointing a gun right at my skull.

I couldn't breathe. My eyes snapped to Roslyn.

"Don't," she said to Dimitri. Her mouth was pressed into a thin line, her body rigid.

I bit my tongue to keep from crying.

"I'm going to count to three," he said, glowering at Roslyn. "And if you haven't dropped your gun, I'm pulling the trigger."

"Let's just take a breath," Roslyn said, her tone measured.

"One."

As soon as Dimitri said the word, I felt my chest tighten, forcing the air out of my lungs. All I could do was stare at Roslyn. Tears gathered in my eyes.

"Listen to me," Roslyn warned through clenched teeth. "If you hurt her, you're dead. Do you really want to—"

"Two."

I shuddered. My limbs went numb. My head felt like it was going to explode, maybe because it actually could.

Roslyn growled, murderous rage contorting her features. "I swear—"

"Three."

I gasped.

"Okay!" Roslyn shouted at the man, dropping to the ground with the gun. "Okay." She slid the gun along the floor toward Dimitri.

Black spots danced across my vision and I forced myself to breathe.

"Good girl," Dimitri cooed to Roslyn. "Now, up against the wall."

I recoiled when Dimitri's arm wrapped around my throat. I could smell rancid peanuts and fish coming off of his breath. Anger and fear flashed across Roslyn's features in quick succession. I thought she was going to pounce on him when he pulled me closer.

"NOW!" Dimitri bellowed when Roslyn refused to move.

"What's your plan?" she asked, contempt burning in her eyes. "You know you can't kill us. My entire team knows we're here."

"I didn't say you could speak. Now back the fuck up."

Roslyn slowly retreated across the room. Dimitri's eyes slid over her body. He wet his lips with a thick coating of saliva.

"I bet people would pay good money for a fed," he murmured. "A pretty one too."

Roslyn's face was flat before she gave me an almost imploring look. It was as if she were trying to say something, but I wasn't sure what it could possibly be. Before I had time to think about it, Roslyn took a sharp breath, her eyes suddenly wide. A strangled gasp ripped through her as she stumbled, her limbs going rigid. The movements were reminiscent of . . .

"What the hell?" Dimitri yelled as Roslyn collapsed onto the ground, thrashing.

"Roslyn!" I screamed, straining to break free as Roslyn writhed. "Let me go! She needs help!"

"Tell me what the hell is going on!" he yelled, panic in his voice.

"She has epilepsy!" I shrieked. "Please, you have to let me help her!"

Roslyn let out a raspy gasp as she jerked.

"What?" Dimitri yelped. "You're fucking kidding—"

"That's what the dog is for, you dumb fuck!" I turned to face him in a wildly deranged state. "Check her wrist if you don't believe me. Her bracelet! It's a medical bracelet!" The look in his eyes was fearfully uncertain. He loosened his hold on me, lowering the gun as he glanced at the silver bracelet on Roslyn's wrist.

That was the opening Roslyn needed.

Everything happened so fast. Roslyn, magically recovered, kicked the gun out of Dimitri's hand.

"Down!" she said, and I dropped to the ground and out of his grasp.

Stunned, the large man froze. Roslyn threw herself at his waist, tackling him away from me. He fell hard, smashing the wooden coffee table into kindling under his gigantic body. He kicked at Roslyn's head, but she ducked and grabbed his leg.

Dimitri grunted as she forced his knee back. There was a pop that sounded painful and wrong. With a howl of pain, he tried to roll away, but Roslyn smashed his head into the floor with a sickening thud.

In the commotion, I scrambled for Dimitri's fallen gun.

Roslyn slammed Dimitri's face into the floor again and again, until he finally sank in submission. He whimpered in pain as she forced his hands behind his back. A stream of colorful language came hissing from her lips.

"Stay down, you useless piece of sh—"

I heard the footsteps a millisecond before another man rushed through the doorway. His eyes widened on us. He was small, pale, and greasy.

As soon as he realized what was happening, his eyes locked on Roslyn's discarded gun. It was right in front of him.

Roslyn and the man lunged for it at the same moment. I screamed. It didn't matter how fast Roslyn was. The man had only a foot to cover while she was across the room. There was a look in his eyes as he grabbed the weapon. A crazed, desperate glint as he pointed the barrel at Roslyn. I saw her tense as if preparing for the inevitable.

A shot rang out. Clear. Harsh. It cut through the commotion and silenced everything before the howl of pain made the floorboards quiver.

The greasy man dropped to the ground, Roslyn's gun slipping from his hands as he clutched his thigh. Blood seeped between his fingers, staining the mahogany floor.

I stared, hands shaking as I continued to aim at him.

At the man I had just shot.

Roslyn didn't hesitate. She snatched her gun back and pointed it at the wounded man's head.

"Hands behind your back," she commanded roughly.

"I-I'm bleeding! I'm going to die!" he yelped.

"Well, you should have thought about that before you tried to kill a federal officer," Roslyn said. "Now, hands behind your back, or I will make sure you bleed out."

His eyes widened. "You can't—"

"Want to find out?" Roslyn snapped, kicking the man onto his stomach. He whimpered as she restrained him.

Roslyn turned to look at me and began to approach slowly, her eyes flashing from my face to the weapon I still clutched.

"Elle," she started, her voice calm. Almost soothing. "You can put that down now."

I could barely hear her over the pounding in my ears. My hands were shaking so hard that it was difficult to keep the hunk of metal steady.

Roslyn eased closer, her hands outstretched in a submissive position. "I can take that," she murmured. I glanced at her face and I saw concern in her eyes, but there was something else too.

She held out the palm of her hand. Her fingers were covered in blood. I took a shuddering breath as I offered her the handle. She holstered the weapon with ease before taking hold of my arm with a soft squeeze. The gentle pressure centered me.

She didn't let go. Not even as she called the station.

It was another hour or so before Roslyn and I were back in the car together. After searching the house, a teenage girl from Boston had been found in the basement. Bonnie confirmed that the two men were part of a sex-trafficking ring. Girls taken from the city were held here before being sent out overseas.

But there was no sign of the missing four-year-old . . . Not even a trace. Roslyn said that it looked like she had never even been there, but that didn't mean Dimitri wasn't involved.

Andrew and some of the other cops stayed at the scene to continue poring through potential evidence, but Roslyn wanted to head to the station to question Dimitri. She invited me to come, mostly because I didn't think she loved the idea of me staying at the crime scene longer than I had to.

The car hummed as we drove back.

"Thank you," Roslyn murmured after a few minutes. "For having my back when we were in the house."

"Thanks for making sure I didn't get my brains blown out," I said.

A comfortable silence fell over us.

"It was a good hit, you know," Roslyn breathed eventually. "That shot."

"I was aiming for his face . . ."

Roslyn smirked. "Close enough."

"You put on quite the show. Pretending to have a seizure and all," I noted. "If all this FBI stuff doesn't pan out, you can head to LA and start an acting career."

"I'll keep that in mind."

"Have you ever done that before?" I asked.

She raised her eyebrows at me. "Faked a seizure when a gun was pointed at my head? No. I can't say that I have."

"What did you find, anyway?" I asked. "That made you suspect something was off?"

"That picture," Roslyn began. "It was signed by a man suspected to be involved in human trafficking years ago, but the FBI could never find him."

"Couldn't it have been a coincidence?" I asked.

"Men like that don't have casual friends," Roslyn said darkly. "Besides, I recognized his face from a case I heard about in Maine."

"How do you remember these kinds of details?" I asked. "Especially when it was never in your district?"

"It gets burned into your head," Roslyn muttered. "Names. Faces. The hard part isn't remembering. It's trying to forget."

60

ELLE

An hour later, my mouth hung open, completely indignant.

"Dimitri doesn't have anything to do with this?" I practically shouted. "At all?"

Roslyn shook her head, looking as irritated as I sounded. "No."

"So, they aren't responsible for any of the murders here?" I yelped, glaring at Dimitri through the one-way glass. He sat alone, handcuffed to his seat as Dalton continued to question him.

"Bonnie found solid alibis."

"What about the abduction of the little girl? Maybe he just never took her back to his house. Maybe he—"

"They weren't on the beach," Roslyn said, watching through the glass just as Dalton slammed his fist onto the desk in front of Dimitri.

"Where is Mia Roberts?" Dalton bellowed.

Dimitri looked unimpressed.

"I know who you could ask," Dimitri said, his swollen mouth stumbling over the words. "But I want something in return."

"You don't get to bargain here," Dalton hissed.

The bus driver sneered. "Shame. Cute little girl she was."

Dalton raged, but from the corner of my eye, I saw Roslyn's face change. Like an idea had popped into her head. She leaned over to knock on the glass.

Dalton reluctantly left the room. "Let me take him out back," Dalton fumed, slamming the door behind him. "Two minutes. That's all I want."

"No," Roslyn said. "I have a better idea." Grabbing his file, Roslyn swept into the interrogation room herself.

"Dimitri Ivanov," Roslyn breathed as she glided toward him. Dimitri's demeanor darkened, his swollen face twisting into a snarl. Roslyn flipped open the file. "Or are you back to going by 'Abram Lebedev' these days?"

She meandered lazily to the table.

"Ya ne sobirayus' tebe nichego rasskazyvat'. Chertovski pizda," Dimitri muttered under his breath. It sounded like Russian.

Roslyn sneered.

"Mozhet byt', tebe sleduyet, prezhde chem ya vyrvu tvoy yazyk iz tvoyey golovy i nakormu yego svoyey sobake," she said.

Dimitri's eyes widened in surprise.

"Do you know what she said?" I whispered to Dalton.

He snorted. "Do you?" he asked sarcastically.

From behind him, I caught Oliver typing something into Google Translate. His eyes widened, and he was quick to put his phone away before I could see the results.

"Each of these fraud charges is a couple of years in jail," Roslyn continued in English, probably for the benefit of the cops and agents listening on the other side of the glass. "But then you add the sex trafficking . . ." She pretended to be doing the math in her head, but I figured it was just for emphasis. ". . . That makes it sound more like a life sentence if you ask me. Then again, I'm sure that doesn't bother you too much. You've done time before. I bet you know your way around a prison."

Dimitri smirked.

"Which makes me wonder how you'll work around the pedophilia charges," Roslyn said, her words slapping the smug smile off Dimitri's face. "I hear that kind of reputation in prison tends to rub the other inmates the wrong way . . ."

Dimitri's purple face paled. "What?" he stuttered.

Roslyn regarded him indifferently as she took a seat. "The girl we found in your basement was sixteen, so while that doesn't technically count as pedophilia, she was still a minor . . . And you know rumors. Always mixing up the details. I wonder, how long do pedophiles typically last in gen pop? A day? Less?"

"I never touched her," Dimitri said.

Roslyn laughed darkly. "Come on, Ivanov. Do you expect anyone to believe that?"

"I never did! I was just—"

"Moving the merchandise?" Roslyn cut him off. "So, you didn't want to test the

product?" There was a momentary lapse in her composure as her face twisted into something sinister. "You know what the funny thing is?" she asked, leaning forward as if she were about to tackle him from across the table. "Whether you raped this particular girl or not won't matter to your little *friends*. Inmates don't fact-check before they shank someone."

Dimitri arched his body back, fighting to put as much distance as he could between himself and Roslyn. She stared at him for a long, agonizing moment, the rage in her eyes leaping for the chance to burn him alive as her lip twitched to reveal a flash of teeth. Then, just as quickly as the veil had been raised, it slammed shut. She leaned back in her chair, her face as flat and emotionless as ever.

Even from here, I could see Dimitri gulp.

"I want a deal," he said.

"I don't think you understand your situation," Roslyn said, getting up and beginning to circle him. "If you're not careful, the only thing you'll be getting is a knife in the back. Or perhaps, right through the carotid." She grazed a finger across his neck. He whirled, fear and rage in his bulbous eyes. "Ticklish, are we?" Roslyn purred, dancing out of reach as he strained against the cuffs to strike her.

"What do you want?" he asked. He sounded angry, but he looked scared.

"You know what I want," Roslyn said. "Tell me something I can use."

Dimitri glowered, his chest heaving. "They were fighting," he finally mumbled.

"Who?"

"Molly and her boyfriend," Dimitri said. His voice was low. Dangerous. "After school. I heard him on the bus ... He said he wanted Molly dead."

61

ROSLYN

"I was able to recover some of the pictures from Miles Elliot's SD card," Bonnie said. "They were all of Molly. Every single one."

"What kind of pictures?" I demanded.

"Normal ones. Some are a little suggestive, but mostly just nice, innocent shots."

"Why would he delete those?" Matilda asked. "That's not how you act when you lose someone you love."

"It's like he wanted to erase her," Dalton said. "Maybe he took that to the next level."

"Either way, he's hiding something," I said. "Dalton, you and I are going to his house."

Elle Wolfe started to get up from her seat.

"Nice try," I said. "You've had enough adventure for the day. You're staying here."

She looked like she wanted to argue but thought better of it.

It took far longer to navigate the windy roads of Cape August's residential area without her, and longer still for someone to open the door once we found the place.

"What do ya want?" a hard-looking man said through the crack of the worn door. From inside, I could hear children screaming. Something about who had the TV remote last.

"We need to talk with Miles Elliot," I said. "Is he home?"

The man grunted, before turning and yelling into the house. "MILES! DOOR! NOW!"

I could just make out the thin boy slinking down the stairs. When he saw us, he froze.

And then, he bolted.

"What the—"

"Miles!" I shouted, sprinting into the house and past the dumbfounded man. I leaped over a screaming toddler and two little girls fighting over broken Barbies. I smashed the back door open. The screen rattled in its frame.

I caught a glimpse of Miles Elliot taking off toward the nearby harbor.

"Miles! Stop!" Dalton shouted from behind me.

I took off. My feet flew over the dark pavement until I was sprinting down a gangplank. Miles turned his head and saw that I was gaining. He jerked one way, then another. He jumped onto the nearest boat, tripping on a rogue lobster trap as he scrambled off the other side.

"Loop around!" I shouted at Dalton as I followed Miles' path. I leaped onto the sailboat and rushed to the other side.

But Miles was just out of reach. Running. Desperate.

I could just make him out as he led us deeper into the fiberglass thicket. I pushed myself faster. Chest heaving. I ducked to avoid the sharp tip of a fishing pole. It grazed my cheek.

I lost sight of him for a second, but that was all it took. I whipped my head around, but Miles was gone. I looked around at the floating maze of docks, my fingertips tingling with adrenaline.

"Cover me," I muttered to Dalton, as I grabbed the gun at my hip. Moonlight bathed everything in a milky polish, illuminating the boats as their creaking frames swayed. The dock breathed underneath me. Slowly, I eased forward. Jasper moved phantom-like as he matched my gait. My ears strained against the blaring silence. I inched further, snaking my way through the night. The light overhead flickered as a cloud licked the edges of the moon. A breeze whispered in the air, hushed with its own sense of anticipation.

In front of us, a desperate-looking fishing boat rocked in place, its old latches creaking. *Cinderella* was painted in worn-out red on its rusted stern. I started to make my way around it before I heard a barely audible scuffle. It sounded like the tightening of a jacket. The slight rub of fabric.

I pointed my gun toward the back of the boat, my arms immediately tense. Jasper growled. Dalton stiffened in my peripheral vision.

"Miles Elliot," I called, my voice aggressive and dangerous. "Come out with your hands up."

The boat pitched slightly, revealing a figure huddled behind stacked, wooden crates. I swung my leg over the edge, stepping onto the rusted vessel.

"Come out, or I will have the dog drag you out," I threatened.

The boy didn't move.

"*Blaffen*," I commanded Jasper, who began to bark viciously. The sound ripped through the air, shattering the serenity of the marina. Behind the crates, I could see the boy's shadow begin to tremble.

"*Vooruit*," I instructed. Jasper stalked forward, shoulders hunched and ready to lunge. His fangs snapped. A savage beast.

"Stop!" Miles begged to be heard over the predatory growls. "Please. Call him off!"

"*Volgen. Stil*," I directed, halting and silencing Jasper. "Walk around the crates. Now."

Fingers trailing along the boat railing, Miles stayed in the perceived safety of the shadows, until the moonlight drew him out. His clothes were wrinkled and dirty with what looked like days of wear. The moon carved dramatic shadows onto his face, casting deep lines into his pale skin. His eyes appeared to have sunken deep within their sockets, just barely able to peek over the ridge of his cheekbones. He barely resembled a person, looking much more like a husk of something that was once human.

Once alive.

62

ELLE

Miles looked awful when Roslyn and Dalton brought him into the station. Much worse than the last time we'd seen him. His hair had become thin and patchy as if it had been falling out. His lips were so dry that it was hard to distinguish them from the rest of his gray face.

And he was sobbing hysterically in the interrogation room.

"Not me . . . N-not . . . Not . . ." he cried, gasping. It had been over thirty minutes, but those were the only words he could say.

"Miles—" Dalton tried, sitting across the table from him.

"NOT!" Miles screamed, ripping at himself. Writhing. It was manic. Terrifying. "NOT. NOT. NOT!"

"MILES!" Dalton yelled, but the boy couldn't hear him over his own cries. He clawed at his face, drawing blood.

"Restrain him," Roslyn ordered, rushing into the room to help.

"Looks like a psychotic break," Chief Ramos said next to me. A group of us watched from the other side of the one-way glass. "And no one can confirm his whereabouts for any of the murders. That, coupled with the fact that he had pictures of Molly on his camera—"

"*And* deleted them," someone called out.

Roslyn came back into the room.

"Miles Elliot has to be our guy," Ramos said.

"I'm not so sure. Something isn't right here," Roslyn said, raking a hand through her hair. "There's no way this kid did all of this. I mean, look at him. He's a mess. He wouldn't have been able to be so calculated, so brutal, so professional . . ."

"Maybe he snapped?" Jay offered. "After moving to another foster home, fighting with Molly . . ."

"And he's a smart kid. Always been advanced for his age," Ramos reasoned.

"This doesn't just speak to intelligence," Roslyn argued. "It speaks to experience."

"There was also no sign of the missing girl anywhere at Miles' house," Dalton added.

"Maybe he dumped her somewhere . . ." Ramos muttered, his eyes drifting toward the window.

"Search parties have come up short so far," Dalton said.

Roslyn pursed her lips in thought. "I don't think Miles is capable of doing any of this. Especially in such a manic state."

"Seriously?" Phil scoffed from behind us. "You got the guy, and that still isn't enough for you?"

"It doesn't add up," Harold agreed.

"Let us prove ourselves wrong," Roslyn said, looking imploringly at Ramos. The police chief studied her for a long while, his dark eyes searching her face.

"All right," he finally said. "We'll help you in any way we can."

"What?" Phil protested. "But sir—"

"Enough, Gregory," Ramos growled, his demeanor changing in an instant. Phil gave him a glare but said nothing.

"We'll make it quick," Roslyn promised, before looking at her team. "Where was Peter Edgars last seen?"

"Next town over," Bonnie said.

"I want him brought in. I don't care what reason you give him. Think of something," Roslyn said to Dalton and Matilda.

"Looks like he's been staying at a motel in the area," Bonnie said. "He must've moved out of Nelson's."

Roslyn nodded slowly.

"Then, I want police to sweep his room," she said, eyeing begrudging Cape August cops. "Bonnie, see if you can track his whereabouts yesterday when Mia Roberts was taken. Oliver, keep the media at bay." She turned to Harold last. "I need you to sit with Miles. See if you can get anything at all."

Roslyn turned to look at everyone. "I'm going to head back to Nelson Edgars' house. Take another look around. Maybe Peter Edgars left something behind."

"I can't believe you even suspect it's Peter after all this," Andrew piped up. "You're wrong."

"Do you know what we found in his sealed file?" Roslyn shot back. "He killed a classmate when he was fourteen. Beat him to death."

"Then, why was it sealed?" Andrew argued.

A muscle in Roslyn's face twitched. "He was a juvenile."

Andrew chuckled darkly. "And that's not good enough for you?"

"Not when he didn't own up to it when we questioned him," Roslyn said.

"Well, you're not going to find anything else at Nelson's house. We stripped the entire place."

"But you didn't check after Peter came back into town," Roslyn stated, taking a calming breath.

"There's nothing there," Andrew hissed.

"Well, then wouldn't you love the chance to prove *me* wrong?" Roslyn offered.

Andrew almost looked pleased by the prospect. "Fine," he said. "I'm coming." He went to grab his keys.

"You'll need some backup," Ramos said quickly. "I'll come with you."

Roslyn raised her eyebrows. "You wouldn't rather send—"

"I would prefer to accompany you there myself," Ramos said. "If you don't mind."

"Of course," Roslyn agreed.

"I just need to grab one thing," Ramos said, opening the door to his office. I heard the same song as before tinkling out of the room. The CD must have looped through all of the other sea shanties on the playlist.

Farewell and adieu, to you fair Spanish ladies . . .

When Andrew came back, our eyes connected for the first time in days. We hadn't spoken much since the night I went over to his house, and whenever we did it was limited to small talk and useless pleasantries. He cleared his throat and looked at Roslyn. "Elle gets to come too," Andrew stated, not even bothering to look at me again as he started toward the door. Roslyn pursed her lips, looking like she wanted to protest, but didn't.

The car was awkward and mostly silent, with even Ramos refraining from doing anything but muttering to himself. After the first few minutes, I gave up trying to find a neutral topic of conversation, hoping instead that Andrew could drive just a little bit faster to end all of our suffering. Finally, we pulled off the main road and onto the long dirt driveway of Nelson Edgars.

The dirt was cracked from baking in the summer sun, making the ride bumpy and slow. After a minute, we were at a fork in the driveway, one leading directly to the house, the other going deeper into the property where the barn was located.

"No one's home," Andrew noted.

"Makes sense. Nelson's at the shop," Ramos said. "Even so, leave me at this fork here. I'll radio in if anyone comes back."

"Good idea," Roslyn agreed. "If Peter's feeling cornered, he would likely return to what feels safe."

Andrew stopped the car to let Ramos out.

"Keep me updated with what you find," Ramos said, before turning toward a particularly gnarled tree. The same tune drifted from his lips as he walked away. The one from his office.

My gaze lingered on him as he leaned up against the bark until the car bumped further into the property. The trees twisted protectively around the driveway, blocking this deeper section from the street. Through their branches, I could just make out the backside of Nelson's house. Andrew parked off to the side of the large wooden barn.

"You want the house or the barn?" Andrew asked Roslyn bluntly, not ever taking his eyes off the road.

"Barn," Roslyn said. "If you finish with the house you can meet me there."

"Fine. Elle, let's go," Andrew muttered to me.

"No, Elle, you're staying in the car," Roslyn corrected.

"She can come in," Andrew said, shooting her a glare

"I'm not allowing that."

"You don't get to—"

"It's fine," I interrupted them both. "I'll just stay here. I don't mind."

"I'll leave Jasper with you," Roslyn said. The dog cocked his head at her as if asking her why he couldn't come.

"Won't you need him?" I asked, not wanting to separate the two.

Roslyn shook her head. "We won't be gone long."

"Okay," I said. I didn't want to argue. If she wasn't worried, I shouldn't be.

"Suit yourselves," Andrew growled at us both as he threw open the door.

Roslyn glanced over at me. "If you need me, call me."

"Don't worry," I said, patting Jasper. "I think we'll manage."

63

ROSLYN

I waded through the grass to get to the barn. The wood of the building was old and weathered. The door creaked in protest when I pulled it open. It was large inside, with neatly organized tools hanging on the walls and boxes stacked in even piles. The floors were well maintained, but the rafters were coated in a thick layer of dust. As I moved, specks of it floated down like artificial snow.

Off to the side was a ladder up to a loft. It looked old, but stable enough.

I climbed to the second floor. The atmosphere was warmer up there. More lived-in. The dark wood matched the red tones of an antique desk. A tall bookshelf was filled with first editions with faded pages and old covers. A thick, brown carpet covered the floor, with crochet pillows strewn about. Pictures of the full Edgars family lined the walls. Their faces looked genuinely happy.

Nothing stuck out.

I was about to head back down the ladder when I looked back at the desk. Or rather, underneath it. Purple flecks. Tiny. Barely visible. Like chipped nail polish. The same color Molly had on her nails when she was found.

Mixed in were eraser shavings. Lots of them too. Slightly yellow. I knelt down to pick up a few. They weren't hard with years of time. They still had some give to them.

But what had been erased, and from where? I looked around. There wasn't a single journal anywhere that Molly would have written in. No journal had been found with her.

My eyes landed on the bookshelf.

In a single stride, I was there, my fingers trailing over the spines. They were all old but well cared for. Cherished.

Except for one. Its cover was barely hanging onto the rest of it, and it was badly dented on one side. Like it had been thrown across the room.

And a singular purple shard was stuck on top of the spine. It was a book of Greek plays. I flipped through the pages, following the purple chips like breadcrumbs. The polish must've been picked at. There was nothing cheap enough to slough off like this.

I reached the story of Electra, and my blood ran cold. There, written in the margins, were Molly's last words, revealing *everything*. That was why the first murder had been so different. It was also why the killings in the Berkshires had seemed so eerily similar.

Molly had figured it out. It was the same killer.

And after everything, we had had him right in our fucking station.

I whipped out my phone, but there wasn't any service. I rushed to the ladder, taking the footholds three at a time. Backup. We needed more backup. I took off toward the police car and wrenched open the front door.

"Is everything ok?" I heard Elle's worried voice as I pulled the radio from its holster.

"This is Agent Roslyn Hunt with Dispatch 437 requesting backup at 29 Anchors Lane," I instructed, making sure each word was clear.

The radio gurgled for a moment, until: "Copy Agent Hunt. Standby. Backup is three minutes out."

"Roslyn, what's going on?" Elle pressed.

I could hear the panic in her voice. I tried to school my face. "Underneath the seat, there should be a bulletproof vest. Get it. Put it on," I directed. She did as she was told. I reached into the glove compartment and found two pairs of cuffs as Elle fumbled with the vest straps. I called Wells again, but again no service. I tried his radio and nothing. I hissed under my breath, weighing my options.

Waiting for backup wasn't going to happen.

I turned to Elle. "Stay here. No matter what you hear from inside, you will not leave this car. Your ass is glued to that seat. Do you understand?" I barked.

She blinked, confused. "Roslyn, I don't—"

"I need you to say you understand," I growled. Nineteen seconds. Nineteen seconds had gone by since I had called for backup. A lot could have happened in nineteen seconds.

"I do, but—"

I didn't listen to the rest of what she said. It didn't matter. If she was arguing now, then the moment she heard gunshots she could very well do something stupid.

"Give me your hand," I demanded. Shocked, she obeyed without thinking. I took a set of handcuffs and cuffed her to the back of the seat in front of her.

"What the hell are you—" she yelped, but I interrupted her.

"You have Jasper with you. He knows what to do if things go wrong." I saw all her emotions written clearly in her expression: fear, betrayal, shock. She looked from her cuffed hand to me and I felt a pang of guilt but pushed it away.

"I'll be right back," I promised.

"Wait! Ros—" The last of Elle's sentence was cut off as I slammed the door shut. I locked it as I flew toward the house.

I took long, noiseless strides, my feet barely skimming the ground as I reached the back. The window showed an empty, lifeless living room. I eased it open and I lifted myself through it, pausing as soon as my feet touched the oak floor. The house was almost completely silent, with only the eerie creek of the floorboards expanding in the midday heat.

I took out my gun and searched the house. I moved delicately. Each step deliberate. The first floor was empty.

Just then, a sound. It was quiet, like the pads of someone walking across a concrete floor. It came from below me. I inched toward the door of the basement, listening. There were murmurs of a man speaking.

I began to descend the stairs as quickly and as carefully as I could. As I pressed a foot to the next floorboard, I felt the telltale signs of a creak and adjusted my weight just so to keep it from groaning. My finger rested on the trigger of my gun. Ready.

The closer I crept, the easier it was to make out the murmurs into words.

"You're a good man, but I don't really have many options," the voice said. I heard a cough from someone else. It sounded thick with saliva or blood. It had to belong to Andrew Wells.

"Let's just think about this," Wells croaked. "*Nelson.* Please."

"I am truly sorry. I want you to know that I have the utmost respect for you. Please, don't take this personally," Edgars said.

There was the unmistakable click of the safety being pulled off a gun.

I pressed my back to the outside wall of the room and peeked around the side. Wells was in plain view. He was on the ground, bloodied and battered. A pillar was blocking my line of sight to the bookshop owner, Nelson Edgars. I couldn't get a clear shot without stepping into the room.

Making a quick decision, I whipped around the doorway, my gun raised.

"Put it down, Nelson," I commanded.

"Agent Hunt," Nelson Edgars greeted politely. His gun remained trained on Wells, his finger tight on the trigger. "How are you?" Despite his casual tone, Edgars' body was tense.

"Why don't you put down the gun and we can have a proper chat?" I took a calculated step toward him.

"You come any closer and I'll have to kill him," Nelson warned, his tone measured.

"I'll just have to shoot you right after, Nelson. You know that. I won't have a choice."

He sighed, pondering. "You're implying that I even care."

"I would like to think that you would want to explain everything. Help us understand," I reasoned calmly.

Edgars chuckled. "You want to understand someone like me?"

"If you put the gun down."

"You first, or I'll kill your friend," Nelson threatened. I looked at Wells. Watched the beads of blood slowly dripping down his terrified face as he looked at me for help.

Ironic.

My lips pursed, making a decision.

"Honestly, go ahead," I said, loosening my grip on the gun ever so slightly. "He's not my friend."

Wells shot me a horrified expression, shock and fear contorting his features beautifully.

"Really?" Edgars asked, curiosity making him hesitate.

"You'd be doing me a favor," I said apathetically. "He's useless, not to mention a prejudiced moron. He's a *defect* in the system." I looked at Wells, repeating the same word he had thrown so forcefully at me only weeks ago.

His eyes bugged out of his head.

"I would love nothing more than for him to be taken out by some nutcase," I went on. "God knows I can't do it myself. But you. . ." A wolfish, gleeful expression twisted my face as I glanced at Edgars. "*You* can do it. If you take him out, I can say that I did everything I could. I'll come out as the hero that risked her life to save this poor bastard, and I'll get to kill a true monster like you."

Edgars cocked an eyebrow at that in a silent question. I was all too eager to answer it.

"Do you think I want taxpayer dollars spent keeping you alive in some cushy cell?" I asked incredulously. "Let me be abundantly clear. I want you dead too, so please, give me an excuse. You and the loser can share one grave. Two birds, one stone. The world would be a better place . . . no offense."

I exhaled a savoring sigh.

"The media will sing my goddamn praises," I breathed. "After all, I'll be the hero that single-handedly killed the Berkshire Killer; murderer and child rapist."

Edgars froze, his face draining of color as his black eyes fastened on me.

"That would be you," I clarified, in case he didn't understand. "The madman who raped and killed his own daughter."

"No," Edgars hissed. "I never touched Molly. I would never hurt her."

"Except that you did," I responded calmly. "At least, that's what everyone will think after I tell *my* story. Much more exciting than the truth."

"You bitch," Edgars seethed. "No one will believe you." He shook the gun that was still pointed at Wells as if fighting the urge to point it at me.

"Why not?" I asked, feigning curiosity. "You will have killed a police officer at that point," I gave a carefree glance to Wells, "kidnapped a little girl, and murdered over a dozen people. Besides, the only witness left will be me, so I think people will believe whatever I choose to tell them."

A snarl twisted his face. "You can't—"

"I can," I interrupted. "Because what are you going to do about it if you're dead?"

I let my words hang in the space between us, letting Edgars absorb them. Slowly, without breaking eye contact with me, he lowered the gun to his side. I shot a glance at Wells, jerking my head to get him to move.

He scrambled behind me.

"Drop the weapon," I commanded Nelson. For a moment, I saw something flicker in the man's eyes. He looked to Wells, now shielded behind me: the woman who had claimed to want him dead. Nelson looked back at me. My expression of bloodlust was now replaced by a mask of cold hatred as I held my gun to his head.

A low chuckle started to rumble in his chest. He adjusted his glasses. "Well played. I'm not easily impressed, but I'm impressed . . ." he murmured, nodding his head.

"I said, 'drop the gun'," I repeated.

He continued to chuckle as he looked at the gun in his hand.

"Clever girl. You really had me going . . ." he murmured, a hint of something in his eye. I knew what he was going to do.

He was fast, but I was faster. Before he even got his gun up past his waist, I squeezed my trigger.

64

ELLE

A bang sliced through the cop car, echoing in my ears. The blood drained from my face as I lunged against the handcuff desperately. The edges cut into my wrist, but I couldn't feel it. Horrible images flashed across my mind as I thought about whoever was on the receiving end of that bang. That gunshot. Was it Roslyn? Was she lying in a pool of her own blood? Was she already dead? Was Andrew?

I needed to get out. To get to them. To help. To do something.

I fought against the restraint, putting all my body weight behind it. Blood dripped down my hand from where metal sliced skin. In my crazed state, all I could think was that maybe the blood could help my hand slip out. I pulled harder, like a chained animal trying to break free.

65

ROSLYN

Edgar yelled as the bullet smashed into his shoulder. He dropped his gun, clutching the wound and stumbling back. Before he could try anything else, I rushed forward, kicking the gun away and shoving him hard to the ground.

"Where's Mia Roberts?" I growled. When he didn't answer, I dug my fingers into his bleeding shoulder. Edgars let out a grunt of pain but said nothing.

"Don't make this harder on yourself," I hissed. "Do you really want to keep hurting another girl? Didn't you hurt your daughter enough?"

"Don't fucking talk about her," Edgars snapped. "You don't know anything—"

"I know she was scared," I cut him off. "Just like Mia is scared now. Don't abandon her like you did your own daughter."

"I never abandoned Molly," Edgars said thickly. "Not ever."

"Prove it. Where's Mia?" My voice almost shook as the adrenaline threatened to make my body tremble.

Edgars panted as he looked at me, his eyes glistening with loathing. He finally broke his eyes away from my face and looked at the old piano behind me. *Jesus*. Even a child as small as Mia couldn't squeeze into a piano . . . Unless she was in pieces.

"Wells. Piano," I barked, as I pulled the handcuffs from my pocket and secured them tightly around Edgars' wrists. I heard Wells scramble from his spot on the floor and rush to the piano.

"Nothing," Wells called, looking inside the lifted lid.

My lips pulled back into a fearsome expression. "If this is a fucking trick—

"Key," Edgars murmured.

Wells and I switched places. I thrust my hand into the instrument, pawing around the sides. Finally, my fingers felt something odd and angular. "What does it unlock?" I snapped at the cuffed man.

"There's a chest. Upstairs."

I took off up the stairs at full speed, leaving Wells to watch Edgars. I tore through the house, looking for a chest. I ripped every room apart on the first floor. Nothing.

I took the stairs three at a time to get to the next floor. Edgars' room was first. I careened into it, my eyes scanning the room for anything child-sized. In the corner of the room was a large cooler. I gasped, lunging forward. A lock kept the lid closed. There were holes drilled into the top. I shoved the key into the lock and wrenched open the top.

A small, strangled sob lodged in my throat as I looked in.

"Are we done now? Did I win?" Mia asked, popping her head up.

I took a shaky breath as I looked at her. She had been laying at the bottom of the cooler but looked unharmed. Her curly hair stuck up at odd angles from how she had been positioned, making it look like she had a terrible case of bedhead.

"How long have you been in there?" I croaked.

The girl shrugged. "I dunno. Bookman Nelson said he had to go somewhere, so I should hide. Like hide and seek! He promised to read me a story after."

I let out a long breath through my nose. It was a small town. Of course, she knew him. It looked like that had worked out for the better.

"Who are you?" Mia asked, cocking her head to one side. Her big eyes shined with curiosity.

"My name is Roslyn," I whispered, trying to keep my voice calm. Soothing.

"Oooh that's pretty." Mia smiled. "It sounds like roses. I like roses."

"Me too," I said, forcing back the tears. "Are you okay? Are you hurt?"

Mia shook her head, the smile never leaving her face.

"Are you playing hide and seek too?" Mia asked, her grin showing her missing tooth.

"Yup," I said. I smiled too. "And I found you."

66

ROSLYN

Ramos sprinted down the dirt driveway, almost doubling over by the end.

"H-hunt. I— You didn't wait for backup," he gasped. Sweat poured down his face and made his gray stubble glisten.

"There wasn't time," I explained. The police chief looked like he wanted to argue, but as his chest heaved, he seemed to realize I was right. He looked at Mia smiling in my arms and gave me a jerky nod.

"Edgars must have seen me," Ramos muttered, clutching a stitch in his side. "Must've parked in the brush there and taken a trail around the back." He shook his head, running a hand down his face to brush off some of the sweat. "God, I'm getting old."

The sound of sirens made us all pause as three police cruisers sped toward the house.

Three minutes, my ass.

"Woah," Mia praised as she hugged my neck.

"I can take her," Ramos offered, a relieved smile cracking through his flushed face. "I can at least do that much." He bent down slightly to look at the girl full in the face. "Want to go find your parents, darlin'?"

"Yeah!" Mia smiled, before looking at me. "Are you coming?"

"I'll be there in a bit," I said. Mia waved over Ramos' shoulder as he carried her to the closest police cruiser.

Cops rushed around me to sweep the property. They would find Wells and Edgars in the basement. I thought about going back in just to make sure everything went smoothly, but I fought the urge. I could let them handle a simple arrest.

I looked around the property. The sun was shining, but it seemed less harsh than any other day we had been there. I turned my face upwards, enjoying the moment of warmth. The millisecond of peace.

Approaching footsteps shattered it.

"Hey."

I didn't need to look in order to know who it was.

"Wells," I greeted with a weary sigh. I didn't bother to turn or open my eyes for that matter. "I trust that our friend has been secured?"

"Yup," Wells said. "I had them take him out through the side of the house. I didn't want him to run into Mia on the way." *So, Wells has a brain after all. Who knew.*

"He's on his way to the station right now," he continued. "The boys are searching through the house now, but we can head back to question him."

'We,' huh? Interesting.

Wells and I stood in silence, and I could sense that he wanted to say something by the way he kept fidgeting in place. Someone else might have asked him what it was to put him out of his misery, but I figured he could handle being a little uncomfortable.

"How did you . . .?" Wells started to ask. His voice was unsure, careful, but to his credit, he persevered. "How did you know that that would work? Saying all that to him?"

"I didn't," I admitted. "I just figured it was our best chance."

"It paid off," Wells chuckled softly. "You almost had *me* going for a second."

Amazing how nice someone is after you save their life.

"That was the idea," I muttered. I thought back to the look of terror on his face when he thought, for just a second, that I might actually want him dead.

"How did you decide that approach?" Wells asked.

I opened my eyes to shoot him a look. "What is this? An interrogation?"

"No," Wells rushed. "I just . . . wanted to know . . . for next time." He almost sounded humble.

"You really think there's going to be a next time?" I scoffed. Wells looked sheepish and I sighed.

"Edgars thought he was in the power position," I explained dryly. "By telling him to kill you, I took away the advantage he thought he had. But he still didn't seem to care about walking away alive. That would have been a problem because not only would he have killed you, but he would have forced me to kill him too, taking away the one person who knew where Mia Roberts was.

"By bringing up his daughter, I created a need for him to stay alive. The grief he felt for Molly was real. No matter what he is, he is also a parent. I knew that by accusing him of something as horrible and vile as raping and killing his own child, he would feel the need to set the record straight, for both himself and for the memory of his daughter."

"So, he didn't kill Molly?"

I shook my head, the sun suddenly feeling numb on my skin.

"She killed herself," I muttered.

I didn't look to see if Wells was surprised by my words. It didn't matter.

"Wh-what?" he whispered. "Are you sure?"

"I'm sure."

"How do you know?" he asked. I jerked my head in the direction of the barn.

"Over there you'll find a book of Greek tragedies. The suicide note is on page 312."

"Why?" Wells asked.

"312 has a nice ring to it," I said sarcastically.

"You know that's not what I meant . . ." Wells said.

I paused, taking a moment to look back at the barn. "She realized she was alone," I murmured, my throat constricting on the words more than I anticipated. "She learned the truth about her father, realized her uncle had known all along, and betrayed her, and then Miles dumped her. She was all alone when she needed support most."

"How did she even find out about her dad?" Wells asked.

"She and Miles found pictures . . ." I started. The explanation had been in Molly's letter. The real truth. "They were looking around the basement when Miles started spending more time here. They found some old film. Miles took it and developed it in Rita Tumbler's darkroom. Nelson had taken the pictures as trophies from his murders in the Berkshires."

"In the Berkshires . . . So . . ."

"He was the real Berkshire Killer," I said unceremoniously.

"B-but they caught that guy," Wells argued.

"Wrong guy."

For a moment, Wells fell silent.

"So, Molly made it look like she was murdered . . ."

". . . to protect her dad," I finished for him. "Miles threatened to go to the police when he saw the pictures. That's what he fought about with Molly on the bus. Dimitri misheard or lied to us. Molly would have truly lost everything then. Even if he was a monster, Nelson was still her father and she still loved him. She wanted to protect him. She timed it so that Nelson couldn't be a suspect. His alibi was solid and his grief was real."

Wells nodded at my words, taking them in. I half expected Wells to drill me further, but he seemed to wise up. "Well . . . Good work," he said. I didn't bother acknowledging the compliment.

I didn't need kudos from Andrew Wells.

I turned back to look at Nelson Edgars' house. I wondered if Molly's mother had really known the father of her child. Did she realize who she was leaving to raise her daughter? Had she suspected?

It didn't matter. Not really. Not anymore.

67

ELLE

At the sound of sirens, I whipped my head back. Cop cars rushed toward the house, but I couldn't see them once they took the turn at the fork. I was left staring uselessly at the back of the building.

I pulled harder.

"Come on!" I yelled, yanking against the chain. How the hell was the seat not even breaking?

Jasper barked. I followed his gaze out the window and saw Roslyn and Andrew. Alive. A sob struggled to claw out of my throat. They were alive.

All I wanted was to sprint out of the car and wrap my arms around the two of them, but as I sat, helplessly chained in place, my relief started to mix with a festering fury. It began to boil in the pit of my stomach. Growing hotter. Angrier.

Until it was all I could do not to scream.

68

ROSLYN

Heading toward the car, I tried not to dread my next interaction with the shackled journalist. I figured she didn't appreciate how I left her. One glance in Elle's direction confirmed my theory. As she strained to look out the window closest to us, her panic was soon replaced by outrage.

It was highly ironic that I was suddenly relieved to have Andrew Wells with me. At least I wouldn't be alone with the woman I had just chained to a car.

Wells raised his eyebrows when he saw Elle handcuffed to the back of the seat. I braced myself for the scathing words of criticism, but they never came. I guessed it was a peace offering. Or maybe he even agreed with that decision. He knew her well after all.

Opening the back door, I stretched forward to unlock the cuffs. My eyes froze when I saw where the metal had cut into her wrist. It didn't look too deep, but it was bleeding. I swallowed the guilt, schooling my face. If Elle had been fighting against the restraint, it only proved my point. She would have run into the house after me if she hadn't been safely secured.

She didn't say a word as I unlocked the cuffs, but I could feel her gaze. It was harsher than I thought she was capable of.

"Make sure to disinfect that when we get back," I said, glancing at her face. She nodded mutely. Jasper let out a low woof as if to agree on her behalf.

On the road again, I expected Elle to get over herself and launch into a volley of questions. She asked only one. In one word.

"Nelson?" Her voice was low and scratchy.

"Yeah," Wells said when it became clear I wouldn't. Silence fell over the car all the way back to the station. I got out of the car fast, Wells having barely put the cruiser in park. I dared to shoot a quick glance at Elle, but she refused to look in my direction as she stalked toward the station. That was just as well.

Harold rushed from the back room, his face flushed with relief.

"You got him," Harold said, something close to pride shining in his eyes as he looked at me. He glanced over my shoulder. "Is she okay?"

Turning to follow his gaze, I saw that he was looking at Elle. She had chosen a chair in the far corner of the station. Her shoulders curled in on themselves and her face was sullen.

"She's fine," I answered curtly, only to receive a questioning look from Harold.

I sighed. "She might be a little pissed."

"What'd you do?" Harold asked, clearly suppressing a smile. I couldn't help but feel the corners of my mouth twitch too.

"I may have cuffed her to the cruiser," I admitted. Harold let out a rumble of a chuckle as he glanced back at Elle. She was focused on glaring at a fly buzzing in the air waves of the window fan.

"Oh, yeah. She's pissed all right," Harold said.

"She'll get over it," I said, but I caught a tightness in my voice that I hadn't allowed.

Harold chuckled. "Good luck with that," he said. "Looks like you'll need it."

69

ELLE

Stupid fly, I growled to myself as I watched the creature buzz annoyingly right overhead. It was like everything else today. A problem that was just out of reach. A problem I could see, but that I was helpless in fixing. So close, but impossibly far.

Stupid fly. Stupid cuffs. Stupid Roslyn. Stupid Andrew . . .

I shot a look at Andrew as I thought about how irritated I should really be at him. He was the one who had given Roslyn such a hard time for even wanting to go to Nelson's place at all. Taking one look at him though, all of my anger disappeared. He looked delicate as he moved to his desk.

"Are you okay?" I asked Andrew, my eyes softening at the dried blood matted in his hair.

"Yeah," he mumbled. "One of the EMTs looked me over at Nelson's."

I nodded at the words, but I couldn't get past the haunted look in his eyes. "But are you really okay?" I asked again, my voice softer with a new meaning to the words.

Andrew scoffed. "I almost got Mia and myself killed because I was being such an asshole."

"What happened in there anyway?" I asked.

Andrew shook his head warily.

"I was looking through the basement when Nelson came home. He was with me as I searched down there, but I didn't think anything of it. I was about to leave when I saw some pink sequins in a crack in the concrete." Andrew closed his eyes for a moment as if remembering that moment all too vividly. "They were the same ones Mia's mother had described her having on her shoes. It clicked. But then Nelson saw them too. Before I could do anything, he grabbed the shovel next to him and hit me over the head before I could even touch my gun. If Hunt hadn't come when she did . . ." Andrew trailed off.

My heart pounded with his words. Without thinking, I wrapped my arms around him, burying my face in his chest. All of my anger and frustration evaporated in that instant. I felt his arms wrap around me, holding me close. We stayed like that for a while. I breathed in his warmth. His familiarity.

The sound of people entering the station broke us apart. I looked toward the entrance and saw Matilda, Dalton, and Benjie.

Dalton stalked toward the interrogation room. "Is he in there?" He was clearly chomping at the bit to get at Edgars.

Roslyn stepped in his path. "Yes, but before we question him, I want tangible evidence. I'll be damned if he goes free on a technicality," Roslyn said. "I want you to go back to the house and help look through everything."

Roslyn turned her attention to the others, giving instructions as she walked into the back room. I followed and no one stopped me. The agents and cops trickled out, talking quickly, and rustling through papers. Everyone had their assigned task, and they scattered to fulfill them.

Soon, Roslyn and I were the only ones left. She moved through the room, walking past me to collect papers and pictures, ignoring my presence all the while. I watched, trembling from the pent-up emotions of the last hour. She sat at a desk on the far edge of the room, furiously writing notes. The scratching of the pen echoed round the room. It was incessant, the sound grating on my already frayed nerves.

I snapped.

"You cuffed me to the fucking seat!" I screamed all the fear and anger I had forced down exploding into one mass of hysteria.

She looked up at me, her expression devoid of all emotion.

And said *nothing*.

"What if something had happened to you?" I yelped when she refused to respond. "What if Nelson had killed you? Killed Andrew?"

"Then there would have been nothing you could have done to prevent it," Roslyn stated. She was calm. Too calm.

"What if he had come out? I was chained to the fucking car!" I threw my hands up in frustration. "I was a sitting duck!"

Roslyn stared me down, her expression cold and calloused. "I made a calculated decision that would keep you alive," Roslyn said, her voice so low it came out as a hiss. "Edgars wouldn't have had the time to deal with Wells and me, find you, kill the police dog with you, and get away before the police showed up. And trust me, killing a *journalist* wouldn't have been his priority."

"You didn't even trust me to stay in the car!" I screamed at her, tears beginning to prickle behind my eyes. I fought them back, refusing to show weakness in front of this woman.

Especially in front of this woman.

She glanced at the raw wound around my wrist as if it was evidence enough. My face burned with either anger, embarrassment, or both.

"I had no idea what you were going to do," Roslyn said. Her cheeks tinted with sudden emotion. "So, I took that variable out of the equation. Want to be mad at me? That's fine. At least you're alive."

Before I could retort, she snatched the notebook from the desk and swept from the room with Jasper.

"You're just going to walk away? Just like that?" I screamed after her as she closed the door hard in my face. Fury gave way to frustration as I raked my fingers through my hair.

"Fuck!" I turned my back on the door and began pacing the room. I knew that I was being irrational, but part of me also felt like I had a right to be. Roslyn had run into the home of a man who had killed over a dozen people. She had had no backup (as Andrew was a little busy), and she hadn't even taken her dog! Wait . . . she hadn't taken Jasper because . . .

It hit me. That was because of me. Roslyn hadn't taken the dog with her because I had been there. She had left him behind to protect me, leaving her more vulnerable than she should have been. Hell, she gave me her bulletproof vest too. Guilt threatened to drown me as I sank into the nearest chair.

"Are you okay?"

I jumped at the voice and whipped around to see big eyes blinking at me from inside the room.

"Jesus, you scared me," I gasped. "I didn't hear you come in."

"I'm sorry," Matilda said, taking a seat next to me. "I just wanted to check on you. I was close to the door and thought I heard yelling."

Fuck these old wooden walls.

"I'm fine," I brushed off. I rubbed my forehead in frustration, mostly just to distract myself to keep from breaking down.

"No, you're not." Matilda didn't say it like an accusation. She just stated it like a simple fact. I laughed breathlessly, on the verge of tears.

"Okay," I admitted. It was hard to suppress feelings around her. "I'm not."

"And you're mad at Roslyn."

"Yeah. I am."

"Well, you shouldn't be," Matilda murmured. "She was just trying to protect you."

"She shouldn't have had to!" I yelled, but it came out sounding more like a squeak. Tears leaked out of my eyes and I angrily wiped them away. "She put herself in more danger because of me, and because no one here had believed her. They would have sent more backup from the start if they had just listened to her. Instead, you all had to spread out. If Edgars killed her, that would have been our fault . . . my . . . my fault."

I began to fully sob, feeling the full force of my part in everything. Matilda wrapped me into a hug and I let her. She smelled of sage. It was oddly soothing.

"It wouldn't have been your fault," she murmured, holding me tight. "And everything worked out all right." I nodded against her shoulder.

She pulled back to look at me. She took both of her small hands and grasped my face, using her short thumbs to wipe away the tears streaming down.

"She cares about you, you know," Matilda whispered knowingly.

"What do you mean?"

"Roslyn. She cares about you," Matilda explained.

I blushed, ducking my head.

Matilda smiled. "And you care about her too."

I just nodded. There was no point in arguing.

70

ELLE

After a few minutes of composing myself, I entered the interrogation observation room.

"Who do you want to go in there?" Harold asked Roslyn, jerking his chin at the bookshop owner. I looked at Nelson. He sat calm and composed. Peaceful almost. It made goosebumps rise up all over my body.

"I'll go," Roslyn said. Her tone was quiet but final. She let herself into the interrogation room.

"Agent Hunt." Nelson acknowledged her with a polite nod.

Roslyn didn't respond right away, sitting delicately across the table.

"We have cops going through every part of your house and bookstore," Roslyn said. "And an agent is about to question your brother." Roslyn slid a notepad over to him with a pen. "So, there's no reason not to give us a full confession."

There was a long moment where Nelson just looked at her. A second where it looked like his pupils dilated, turning his eyes black with hunger. There was a visceral, animalistic glint that made it seem like he was about to lunge across the table. But in a breath, it was gone. Nelson sighed, taking the pad.

Roslyn watched him write until he handed it back. Her eyes

scanned the page. "This'll do," she muttered, before getting up and sweeping toward the door.

Nelson gaped. "You're leaving?" he asked, surprise and irritation flirting with his features.

"I have what I need," Roslyn said, putting her hand on the door handle.

"Wait," Nelson called, desperation leaking into his tone. "Aren't you going to ask why?"

Roslyn stopped but didn't turn.

"I don't care," she said, her cold voice sending a shiver through me. "You killed sixteen innocent people. The reason changes nothing."

And with that, she swept from the room without another word.

71

ELLE

It was another twenty minutes before Oliver and Dalton got Roslyn's permission to continue questioning Nelson.

But she didn't stay to watch.

"I knew someone would be back," Nelson breathed when the two men came in. "Although I am disappointed that it's not my friend Agent Hunt."

"She let us come," Oliver said before he had seemed to have really thought about his words. Dalton shot him a look.

"*Let* you?" Nelson repeated before chuckling. "Woah. She really is all-powerful, isn't she?"

"Why'd you do it?" Dalton asked roughly.

"Ah . . . So, you do care?" Nelson smiled. "You might wish you didn't, but people always do."

"We care from a clinical perspective," Oliver squeaked. "It helps us catch people like you."

"Uh-huh," Nelson hummed, leaning closer. "It couldn't possibly be that you're just *curious*."

"Either tell us or don't," Dalton snapped.

Nelson crossed his arms over his sweatered chest. It was seventy degrees, but he wasn't even breaking a sweat in the thick wool. "It's interesting," he breathed. "People keep comparing this to *Jaws*, and yet, no one has ever questioned why the shark killed. The shark killed because it was a killer. The killing is part of what makes it what it is. So, couldn't my reasons be just as simple?"

"Is that why you killed the women in the Berkshires?" Dalton asked.

Nelson glanced at him, moving his head this way and that. Sizing him up. "I never used to understand emotion," Nelson started. "I didn't understand pain you couldn't see or the feeling of happiness. I learned how to replicate it, but I couldn't conjure it up on my own.

"Killing helped me feel," he said, his eyes fluttering as if savoring it. "Women especially. When they felt my hands on their throats, emotion oozed from them. The way they trembled. The emotion was raw. Tangible. I could believe it. Sense it. I could capture some of it for myself, just through the contact. It was leech-like I'll admit, but once I started, I was hooked. Hooked to feeling something other than nothing. I took pictures, but never needed to actually develop them. Just having that film was enough. Knowing that I had it. I could hold it in my hands and remember that feeling."

Nelson paused.

"When Molly was born . . . something changed. Holding this little ball of flesh in my arms . . . Seeing that natural light in her eyes . . . It flipped a switch. Suddenly, I became someone who cried at sappy dog movies. Someone who could coach the elementary school soccer team and sympathize with the kid who skinned their knee. Someone who found joy in singing Christmas carols. I could feel for the first time on my own. I didn't need to be a parasite off of others. I didn't need to feed off their emotion. For the first time in my life, I could create it for myself."

A small smile pulled at Nelson's lips, and for a second he was the innocent bookstore owner I grew up around. For a second, the darkness slipped out of the room and I could fool myself into thinking it had all been a terrible mistake.

"I forgot about the person I was before," Nelson went on, "probably because for all intents and purposes that man didn't exist anymore. When Molly's mother died, I brought us here. Buried my old life for good."

A dangerous shadow crossed over his face. The gentleness vanished, replaced by something cold. Inhuman.

"Losing Molly taught me something else," Nelson breathed. "It taught me what it meant to hate. To feel anger. An urge to destroy." He looked down at his hands. The hands that had snuffed the light out of sixteen people.

"The need to feel emotion wasn't why I killed this time," he murmured. "This time, I killed to try and dull the pain. To distract myself. To destroy something else." He sighed, interlocking his fingers to put his chin on his knuckles.

"That little girl got in the way," he murmured. "Mia. She saw me on the beach on the fourth of July. I should have killed her. Rationally. But I couldn't. She reminded me too much of Molly. But the rest of them." He chuckled darkly, flashing his white teeth in a way that made my skin crawl. "Well, they were in the wrong place at the wrong time."

"You killed for sport," Dalton spat, disgusted.

Nelson shrugged. "If that's what you got from all of that, then you really need to work on your interpretation skills."

72

ROSLYN

"He's my older brother," Peter started, his voice cracking. "When we were growing up, I was always picked on. Nelson defended me. Every time. Even if he only did it because he thought he should . . ." Peter took a deep breath, his shoulders hunching.

"About the sealed file . . ." He swallowed hard, breaking open the scab on the back of his hand. It didn't stop him from scratching. "Nelson was home from college in the summer of ninety-seven. I was almost seventeen. Nerdy. Awkward. This kid, Jimmy, hated me for breathing. Nelson and I were hanging out in this park and Jimmy jumped me. Maybe he was just playing a prank, I don't know. Either way, Nelson hit him. Hard."

A shiver rocked through Peter's body. He looked up at me, his eyes wide behind his spectacles. I remember seeing Nelson's face when he saw the blood," he whispered. "I'd never seen that look on him before. He watched the blood slip through his fingers, and his face just . . . darkened."

Peter's breath turned shallow, almost like he was running uphill. He scratched harder. I could hear his nails tearing at his skin. I could hear them rip through it.

"You know what he talked about? After Jimmy was dead?" he rasped. "The mess. Kept going on and on about it. How unnecessary it was." Tears ran down his face. "I thought that was his way of being remorseful. You know? Nelson was always a little off. So, I just thought, maybe he was processing his grief differently." Peter shivered.

"I was still a minor, so I took the fall. It was self-defense, so they sealed the file," he explained. "Nelson went back to college and everything seemed okay . . . Until the girls started showing up dead. I saw it on the news and just. . . knew." Peter bit his bottom lip so hard that it turned white. He kept scratching, blood pooling under his fingernails.

"I went and confronted him, but when he denied it, I chose to believe him. I had to. It was another few months before I saw it. I was staying with him for the week, and one night he didn't show up for dinner. I went looking and remembered he'd shown me this spot in the woods once. I went there and . . ." Peter trailed off, tears streaming faster down his face. "Well, he had a girl. I saw what he did to her. How he just killed her just like that. I told him I was going to turn him in, but he threatened me. He said if I did that, he would say it was me. After all, I was the one that 'killed Jimmy Roth' in cold blood. I was the one that was always awkward around women. I would be the obvious choice." He began to rock back and forth in the hard, wooden chair.

"Why would you ever choose to go back to the Berkshires?" I asked. "You could have chosen anywhere to go to college. Anywhere to teach."

"I thought . . . I don't know. Maybe I thought that I had to be there. To somehow make up for it."

"Make up for all the people your brother killed?" I asked, my voice cold and bitter.

"I'm not trying to say it makes sense," Peter mumbled.

"So, then what? You go to Italy, and you get a call from Molly . . ."

"She and that boyfriend of hers. He found pictures," he went on. "Nelson used to take them after his kills. Keepsakes. Never wanted to print them. Only wanted the film. I don't know why. I guess Miles developed some of it. What kid knows how to develop film nowadays? Anyway, when he confronted Molly about it, she was frantic. She called me as if I would have some sort of explanation. I panicked." Peter raked his bloody fingers through his hair. "She realized it was true. Before I could say anything, she hung up. I was terrified that she would confront Nelson, or that Miles would do something. So, I booked a flight back from Italy that night . . . But by the time I got back . . ." He trailed off, his mouth open, but unable to say the words.

"Molly was dead," I continued for him.

"She sent me a letter," he whispered. "To my house. Explaining what she was going to do." He hung his head and started crying harder. "When the killings started here, I knew that it was Nelson. And I knew I should turn him in. But how do you betray your own brother like that?" He leaned forward, his eyes glistening as he waited for me to answer. When I remained silent, his lips began to tremble.

"Do you have any siblings?" he asked.

The question caught me off guard. I froze, my fingernails digging into my palm. I planned on lying. And yet, sitting there, with him looking at me with eyes so full of pain, I couldn't. Instead, all I could do was say nothing.

I used to, I thought in my head. I fought the urge to touch my bracelet. To run my finger under the hidden underside that pressed into my skin. To feel the inscription. *Because plastic medical bracelets aren't your style. ~T.* My brother had given it to me a week after I had been diagnosed. It had needed to be resized once but was otherwise unchanged since the day he handed it to me with that lopsided bow on top made out of a broken guitar string.

My nails dug deeper into my flesh, forcing me back to reality. I couldn't think about my brother. Not now. I looked back at Peter, who was watching me.

My silence said so much more than words ever could.

"So, maybe you do understand, then," he whispered. "Wanting to protect them."

I bit the inside of my cheek so hard that I suddenly tasted blood.

"What am I supposed to do now?" Peter asked. "I'm alone. Completely alone."

My chest tightened, but my face felt like it had turned to stone.

"Everyone's alone," I heard my voice say. Cold. Harsh. I swept toward the door. "Live with it."

73

ELLE

"Where were you when they were checking the house?" Zoey asked.

I had gone to her place after driving Andrew to the hospital. He had a concussion but was otherwise fine.

"I was cuffed to the back of the cruiser," I sighed.

"What?" Zoey yelped.

"Roslyn put me in a handcuff so that I wouldn't follow her in," I muttered.

"Ohhh that's kinda hot," Zoey said.

I looked at her in disbelief. "Seriously? That's what you got from all this?" I shook my head, getting up from the couch to put some physical distance between us. "Nelson Edgars is a psychopathic serial killer, and all you can focus on is some far-fetched kinky detail?"

Zoey's face grew grave. It aged her features.

"I can't think about Nelson," she whispered. "Because if I do, then I'll think about the fact that I sold him a painting a month and a half ago. Which . . . would have been around the same time Jamie Kane was killed . . . and . . . I-I can't go there." She looked fragile. "And, as my best friend, you shouldn't make me. So, yeah, I'm going to focus on your love life instead. Because I can't handle the rest of it." Her hands trembled and she grasped them together. I immediately felt guilty. I knew that everyone dealt with grief differently, so after years of being friends with Zoey, I should have realized that her way would be a little unconventional.

I sank into the couch next to her.

"I'm sorry," I breathed.

She waved off the apology before she leaned against me, letting a shaky sigh run its course through her body. I rested my head on top of hers, holding my friend close.

We sat in silence, taking comfort in each other's presence.

". . . They weren't furry handcuffs . . . were they?" she hiccupped.

I laughed, a few tears escaping from the corners of my eyes. "I wish." I held out my battle-wounded wrist.

"No way," Zoey chuckled. "That's just as good as a sex injury, you know."

"Oh yeah," I said sarcastically. "Just without the sex."

"Still. This chick is badass."

I chuckled, thinking about how horrified Roslyn would be by this conversation.

"A total badass."

74

ROSLYN

Walking into the hotel room, I had to physically stop myself from making a beeline for the bed. I knew that if I even sat on it, I wouldn't get back up. The long days of this case were finally starting to hit me.

I shook my head, trying to ward off the fatigue for a little longer. I had an obligation to take part in at least one 'celebratory' drink with my team at the town bonfire. That was part of the deal as the boss. I had to show up. Team bonding, or whatever the fuck. It was important for morale.

Still . . . that bed looked awfully tempting . . .

No, I told myself, tearing my eyes away from it.

It was a conscious effort just to take off my heels, exhaustion making even the simplest of tasks an ordeal. I had just started unbuttoning my shirt when I heard a knock. I suppressed a groan as I redid the buttons and looked through the keyhole. I had half a mind to ignore the visitor, especially when I saw who it was.

"This is a surprise," I said, my voice rather lackluster as I opened the door to Lieutenant Wells. To my satisfaction, I heard a low growl from Jasper when he caught a whiff of the man.

"Sorry. I didn't plan on coming," Wells said.

He took a cautious look at the dog. I snapped my fingers and Jasper quieted.

"Well, don't be offended if I don't invite you in," I muttered, regarding him. Wells was still wearing his beat-up uniform. That bloodstain was never going to come out of that shirt.

"You don't need to," he assured me. He opened his mouth to say more, but nothing came out.

I cocked an eyebrow at him. "Did you need something then?"

"No," Wells stuttered. "I just . . . I wanted to say . . ." He struggled, trying to find the words. I waited a few seconds, crossing my arms over my chest as I leaned against the doorway.

"Any day now," I sighed.

"I'm working on it," he grumbled, looking anywhere but at me.

"Don't strain yourself," I said, mostly under my breath.

"Jesus, you're not making this any easier," he said, exasperated.

"If you came to confess your undying love for me, you can save your breath," I said wickedly.

He rolled his eyes. "Not exactly."

"Good. Because you aren't my type."

"Glad we established that," he snorted. Finally, he met my gaze.

"I . . . just wanted to thank you," he admitted. I schooled my face, hiding my surprise.

"You know . . . for saving my life," he clarified.

I pursed my lips, fighting a smirk. "Oh," I feigned a moan as I closed my eyes. "Say it again. Slower." I was going to savor this moment.

"You're an ass," he said.

"Correct. But I'm not the only one," I said, snapping my eyes open to look at him. I expected some fiery insult to be thrown back at me. Instead, I saw his shoulders slump a little.

"I know . . . and . . . I'm sorry," Wells muttered, hanging his head.

This time I was truly shocked. A thank you and an apology in the same thirty seconds? Maybe Edgars hit him harder than I thought.

"I was out of line," Wells continued. "I should never have said any of those things to you. I made everything personal."

"Yes. You did," I agreed.

"My feelings . . . they had nothing to do with you. I was just . . . pissed off," he admitted, his eyes becoming very interested in a spot on the floor. He actually seemed genuine. *Huh.*

"Because the FBI rejected you," I continued for him when he seemed unable to. There was no reason to beat around the bush about it.

His eyes blinked, surprised.

"I read your file," I clarified casually.

"Oh," he murmured. "I guess I should have figured." He shifted his weight as he stood. "I was still a little raw from all that. Not that it's an excuse at all. I had no right to take any of that out on you. Or your team."

His eyes looked directly into my own. "I truly apologize," he said.

We stood there for a long moment until it was too unbearable.

"Well. That's it," he said. "That's all I got." Wells shrugged. "I didn't mean to intrude. So . . . erm . . . Thanks again. For your help." He gave me a small, careful smile before starting back down the hallway.

I looked at the dog at my feet, raising my eyebrows at him as if to make sure he had heard the same thing I had. Jasper gave a low whine as his tail began to thump against the carpet. I sighed, making a split-second decision.

"Lieutenant."

Wells was a couple of strides down the hall. He turned back, his expression both confused and nervous. I pushed off the doorway, rolling my shoulders back as I strode toward him. I tried not to enjoy how skittish he looked.

Shoving down any last remnants of bitterness, I extended my hand to him. His eyes widened, as if not believing what was happening. With a visible surge of courage, he firmly clasped his fingers around mine in a strong shake. I fought a smile as I felt it. This was a real handshake. The one you give to equals, as opposed to one that resembles a limp noodle. Wells grinned at me stupidly. It was endearing in its way. I released first, spinning on my heels to head back to my room when a thought struck me.

"Why didn't you apply again?" I asked, looking over my shoulder.

He seemed taken aback. "What?"

"Why didn't you apply again to the FBI?" I repeated, knowing he had heard me the first time.

"I figured it wasn't worth it. They have my record on file so . . ." He rubbed the back of his neck.

"If you really care, you should keep applying until you get it," I said. "Your old file doesn't account for the experience you've gained. It's out of date."

He nodded at my words, a hopeful smile pulling at his lips. "That's true. Thanks," he said, then looked at me questioningly. "Why are you helping me?"

"I'm not," I muttered in irritation. "Anyone with half a brain would have been able to figure that one out for themselves."

He smirked. "No. That was your way of helping me. Even after I was a jerk," he pointed out.

Jesus, he's annoying.

"You think you're the first jerk I've had to work with?" I asked. "The difference between you and the rest of them is that you owned up to it."

He smiled, puffing out his chest with pride.

I offered him a conservative smile back. Yes, Andrew Wells had been a royal pain in my ass, but it took humility and courage to admit fault. It warranted respect.

"Besides," I continued, "as we have just discussed, I've saved your life now. It would be nice to have someone in the bureau who owes me a favor or two."

He barked a laugh. It was a rough sound, but not unpleasant. "So, this is really for your personal gain?"

"You're learning, Lieutenant," I said as I walked back to my door. "You're finally learning."

75

ELLE

I fiddled with the pin digging into my side as I watched the bonfire flames. Running out of clean clothes, I had borrowed an emerald-green wrap shirt from Zoey. Her bust was bigger than mine which had proved to be a problem when I bent down and almost flashed Travis. He quickly clapped a hand to his face, shielding himself from the nudity. Zoey had muttered something along the lines of 'wasting a free pass when the universe presents him with one.'

She helped me fix it with a giant bobby pin. No one would be the wiser.

Except that the way it rubbed was driving me crazy . . .

"Look who it is," a voice drawled from behind me. I grinned before I even turned, knowing exactly who it was. Sure enough, Dalton walked toward me with long, confident strides. His white teeth flashed even at a distance.

"You came," I called, patting a patch of sand next to me. I couldn't help but look to see if other members of the team were behind him, not that I could see past the flow of people as they clambered onto the beach.

"I never say no to free booze," Dalton said, holding up a beer he had already snagged from one of the many coolers scattered along the beach. "Even if it's warm."

"They ran out of ice."

"I noticed," Dalton said, taking a long swig before offering it to me.

I took it and smiled, taking a sip as my eyes scanned the faces around the fire. With the sun slowly sinking in the sky, the bonfire was in full swing. Around the roaring flames, people from all over town had decided to make an appearance: shop owners, tourists, the Cape August cops. As the minutes passed, the relief felt more tangible with every laugh, clink of glass, and smile. The stress of the last month was easing away, at least for the moment.

"You're going to have to visit Boston, you know," Dalton said, forcing my attention back on him.

"Is that so?"

"Yup. We're friends now."

I laughed. "I don't believe I ever agreed to that."

Dalton rolled his eyes. "We just swapped backwash. If that doesn't settle it, I don't know what could."

I grimaced as he chuckled.

"Did the rest of the team come too?" I asked casually, trying not to let myself hope.

"Most of them." Dalton pointed his beer toward the crowd behind a smoky haze. "Somewhere in there."

I was about to ask who *most* meant, but before I had to, Dalton gave a whoop.

"Speaking of—" he chuckled.

I followed his eyes, and my breath caught. There, on the edge of the bonfire, was Roslyn. She seemed hell-bent on keeping as far away from everyone as possible, while still allowing herself to be considered in attendance. She was wearing fitted white pants and a navy-blue tank top with her hair styled in a loose, tactfully messy bun. While simple, she looked as elegant as ever with a delicate silver necklace and matching earrings gleaming in the light of the bonfire. As if feeling my gaze, her eyes turned and fastened onto mine, the fire making them gleam.

"Look who finally decided to drop by," Dalton called as Roslyn began to weave through the sea of people toward us. Jasper loped at her side. "I thought for sure you were going to skip it."

"I considered that," Roslyn admitted, recoiling slightly as a group of teenagers almost bumped into her. "Crowds have never been my thing."

"Let's grab you a warm beer and you'll be fine," Dalton promised, getting up. Roslyn frowned at the prospect.

Before Dalton could lead the way, Benjie rushed forward from out of nowhere.

"I'll take her!" Benjie all but bellowed, grabbing Roslyn's arm before anyone could say otherwise and yanking her toward one of the coolers.

Dalton was about to sit back down when he looked over my shoulder. The smile slipped off his face.

"I'll give you a minute," he said to me, clearing his throat and backing away. Confused, I turned as Andrew took a careful step in my direction.

He smiled shyly. "Hey." He was dressed in khaki shorts and an obnoxiously yellow polo that strained against his broad chest.

"Hey yourself," I greeted. "Nice shirt."

"If that's supposed to be sarcastic, fuck you," Andrew teased, his tone still careful. Guarded almost. "It pops."

I couldn't help but chuckle. "Since when did you care about popping?"

"Since it seemed like there was something to celebrate. The end of the worst month on Cape August history." He sat next to me, leaving almost two feet of space between us. A buffer.

"So," he started, his voice sounding nervous. "When are you heading back to Providence?"

"In a few days," I said.

"Well, would you want to get dinner tomorrow night then?" he offered, before adding quickly, "No funny business. I promise."

I looked at his face and there was a softness that I hadn't seen in a while. It was the face I could recognize.

"I would really like that," I said. "I really missed my friend."

He grinned, light shining from his crystal-blue eyes. It was the smile of the man I had once loved. The man who would always have a part of my heart.

"Me too, Nancy Drew," he said. "Me too."

76

ELLE

Benjie was still trying to 'chivalrously' open a beer for Roslyn. His face flushed as he struggled, shaking it as if that would help. Roslyn looked like she was fighting every impulse not to rip the thing out of his hand and do it herself. He was sheepish once he finally got it. The bottle was frothing and Roslyn took it with the tips of her fingers. She wrinkled her nose.

I remembered with a smirk that she didn't even like beer.

"So," Benjie started, puffing out his cheeks before words tumbled out of his mouth. "Ithinkyourreallyprettyandamazingandwaswonderingifyouywouldwanttogooutsometime?"

Roslyn raised her eyebrows. "I don't think I caught that."

Benjie took a deep breath, clearly steeling his nerves before trying again. But he was interrupted before he had a chance to speak.

"Benjie! Come over here and tell the boys about the time you almost blew the head off a chipmunk!" Andrew called.

Benjie whipped around, his face turning purple. "It was a squirrel and it was huge! I thought someone was sneaking up behind me!"

"It was a fucking chipmunk. I saw it with my own eyes," Andrew challenged. Jay was almost doubled over with laughter.

Benjie steamed, yelping back a retort in such a high voice that I couldn't understand a word.

"Maybe we should let them figure it out," I whispered to Roslyn. "This could take a while."

She nodded and we retreated a couple of steps away from the fire as Benjie made a series of hand gestures to defend himself. Roslyn looked concerned underneath mild amusement.

"Did he actually almost blow a chipmunk away?" she whispered to me. "If so, he really should not be allowed to handle a firearm . . ."

"That was in training, I think," I said, trying to reassure her. "He's gotten a lot better since then."

"Hmm," she hummed, looking unconvinced. She continued walking down the beach with Jasper in tow, putting more distance between herself and the big group. I found myself walking with her, casting careful looks in her direction whenever I thought she wouldn't notice. Nerves boiled in the pit of my stomach as I searched for something to say.

She beat me to it.

"So, how did things go with Loverboy?" she asked bluntly. "Did you two kiss and make up?"

I snapped my head so fast, it was a small miracle that it didn't fly off. "What?" I choked, desperate to recover. "Andrew and I are just—"

"*Friends*, I know," Roslyn chuckled. "Relax. I was teasing."

"Yeah, well. . . What about you and Benjie?" I asked, throwing it back. "Does Emily have some competition?"

She paused, opening her mouth, but not saying anything. It was like she was deciding whether or not to get into the discussion at all.

"Oh," I said, interpreting the silence for myself. "Over?"

She sighed. "Honestly, it would have actually needed to be something in order for it to be over."

"Ouch," I winced sympathetically on Emily's behalf. I didn't have to like her to feel for her.

Roslyn shrugged. "You asked."

"Since when do you actually *answer* questions?"

Another shrug. "Maybe you forcing them down my throat for the past month has something to do with it."

"Ah-ha!" I cheered. "Wore you down."

"In some respects," Roslyn said. "Maybe you should quit while you're ahead."

"You know I'm not capable of that."

"You're right," she said, nodding slowly. She sighed. "Which means I should probably come clean about something. I'd want you to hear it from me." Her voice was suddenly low and serious.

I looked at her, instantly worried. "Of course," I said. "Anything."

Concern darkened her eyes as she came to a stop in the sand. Her mouth was pressed into a thin line. "You can't tell anyone," she muttered. Barely above a whisper. She almost sounded scared.

It was terrifying. Wrong.

"I won't. I promise," I vowed. My heart began to beat faster. Roslyn looked behind us as if to make sure we were out of earshot. With a dune blocking the bonfire from view, we were completely hidden. My nerves balled into a knot in my stomach as Roslyn leaned toward me.

"I've never seen that movie," she breathed, barely audible. "Or read the book."

Huh?

"What are you talking about?" I asked. "What movie?"

Her face was fraught with guilt until the last second.

Then, her composure faltered entirely as humor danced in her eyes. "*Jaws,*" she admitted. "Never seen it. Not once."

My mouth hung open. "Are you joking?"

She laughed. "I'm afraid not."

"That's so much worse than anything else you could have said," I groaned dramatically, sinking into the sand.

She chuckled, sitting next to me. "I had to come clean. It's all anyone can talk about here."

"I feel so betrayed," I moaned. "All this time, and you haven't seen one of the best cinematic experiences in history."

Roslyn rolled her eyes. "It's a movie about a shark looking for revenge. How good can it be?"

My eyes bulged. "Good enough to be considered a classic."

"Sounds like a rip-off of *Moby Dick* if you ask me."

"Don't make me hurt you."

"Easy," Roslyn laughed, holding up her hands. "But you have to admit it's a regurgitation of the same theme."

"You can say that about any story," I said. "All the greats borrow from something. They just make their own tweaks."

"Uh-huh. So, what tweaks would you make to *Jaws*?" she asked.

I scoffed. "*Jaws* is perfect."

"What about an adaptation?" she challenged.

"A waste of time."

"Maybe you just lack artistic vision," she mused.

My mouth dropped. "I do not!"

"Prove it," Roslyn baited, her eyes twinkling. "How would you finish this story, if it was one of your beloved mystery novels?"

I paused, my mouth suddenly very dry. She said it so casually, and yet there was something in her tone . . . Maybe it was how close I realized we were. Our hands were almost touching in the sand.

"Y-you mean the story here?" I clarified, my tone rising in pitch. "About this investigation?"

She nodded once, her gaze never leaving mine. My heart beat so fast that it almost hurt. Her face was so close. I felt chills run over my body. I had to be imagining the implications. There was no way she—

Unless. . .

"It might not be your kind of ending," I breathed, my eyes searching her face for something. Permission, maybe.

"You might be surprised," she murmured, so softly that if I hadn't been but inches away, I wouldn't have heard. Her head was cocked to the side as she looked at me. A knowing smile pulled at her lips. "Try me."

It was the perfect opportunity.

Before I could overthink it, I reached out to tuck a stray strand of hair back behind her ear. Testing her. My fingers brushed the side of her face and I let them linger, giving her the opportunity to reject the touch. She leaned into it instead. I could feel her breath on my face and it sent shivers down my entire body. Her eyes were trained on mine, looking at me with a rare tenderness that gave me a moment of bravery. Without another second of hesitation, I closed those few centimeters and captured her lips with my own.

The moment we connected, I felt a rush of electricity. I gasped when I felt her kiss me back. Her lips were soft and gentle. We sat in suspension. It was as if nothing else mattered. As if—

"HEY!"

Roslyn pulled away so fast that I fell forward from the loss of support. I caught myself before landing right into her lap and whipped my head around. My heart felt like it was about to jump out of my mouth and take off down the beach in an act of self-preservation. If Andrew saw . . . *Oh my God.*

A giant blur of a giant man in only his boxers sprinted down the beach, bypassing us entirely on his way toward the water. He was soon followed by an equally less-clothed Benjie.

"YOU GOT A HEAD START!" Benjie bellowed again, hurling himself toward the man who I could now see was Jay. "EVERYONE KNOWS YOU WAIT FOR GO! NOT THREE!" Even from here I could hear Jay laugh as he continued running toward the water.

God, he was fast.

"Better hurry up or I'll lap you around the buoy!" he called over his shoulder as he continued at full speed down the beach. Benjie sprinted after him, his white briefs glowing in the fading light.

I looked at Roslyn. She looked pale, and her eyes bugged out of her head. I opened my mouth to say something until she started to laugh.

It was quiet at first but seemed to grow until she was laughing so hard, she was almost doubled over in the sand. I had never seen her laugh like that, so carefree. So open.

It was contagious and soon I was laughing too. It wasn't until Roslyn was fully out of breath and I had a cramp in my side that we seemed to come back to our senses.

"Jesus Christ," she said breathlessly, leaning against me for support.

"They always make an entrance," I chuckled.

"Mmm," Roslyn murmured.

I felt the warmth of her body and fought the urge to wrap my arms around her. I settled for resting my head on the corner of her shoulder.

A good way down the beach, three men from the bonfire stumbled on the wet sand, laughing. One of them began belting a song, sloshing a beer high into the air. It wasn't in tune, and the words were a little slurred, but it carried nonetheless:

Show me the way to go home,
I'm tired and I wanna go to bed.

I glanced down, suddenly realizing that in the panicked moment, Roslyn had grabbed my hand and hadn't let go. She smiled gently, giving my fingers a little squeeze. I ran a thumb over her knuckles, memorizing the softness of her skin.

Drifting in the wind, the voices of the two other men joined in with their friend's song:

I had a little drink about an hour ago,
And it's gone right to my head.

Roslyn's eyes eased toward the water as the sun sank below the waves. I watched as she looked at nothing in particular. But somehow, I could sense that even if her gaze were elsewhere, her mind was still with me. Present.

Wherever I may roam,
On land or sea or foam,

The wind was gentle as it kissed my cheeks. The sky dimmed as the last of the daylight slipped away. And through it all, there was something about this moment, this one, uninterrupted second, that was perfect. Pure. Right. A moment of belonging.

You can always hear me singing this song.
Show me the way to go home.

THE END.

Made in United States
North Haven, CT
15 August 2022